VEFA ALEXIADOU

GREEK CUISINE

ATHENS 2007

2007 Twelveth Edition
© 1989 Vefa Alexiadou
Nevrokopiou 16, Thessaloniki 546 36, Greece
Tel.: +30210 2848086, Fax: +30210 2849689
No part of this book may be reprodused, photocopied
recorded or otherwise transmitted in any form or by any
means without the permission in writing from the publisher.

ISBN 960-85018-6-5
REGISTRATION NO TX 3 395 529

Editor and Publisher: Vefa Alexiadou, Athens
Cover Photographer: G. Depolas, Athens
Art Director: K. Kolios - M. Mourtika, Athens
Editional Supervision: Diana Farr Louis, Athens
Typesetting: COM•AD, Athens
Photography: Z. K. Anastassiadis, Ch. D. Nikoleri, Thessaloniki
and G. Drakopoulos, Athens
Color Seperation: ADAM Hellenic Reproduction ABEE, Athens
Printing-Book Binding: Pergamos SAIC, Athens

Vefa Alexiadou, a gifted cook from Volos, Greece, is the leading culinary authority in Greece today. With a degree in chemistry she combined her culinary talents with scientific principles to modernize Greek cooking without sacrificing the authentic character and flavor of traditional cuisine. During her frequent trips and extended studies abroad, she furthered her knowledge of culinary arts, food styling, table decoration, nutrition and dietetics.

In 1980 Ms. Alexiadou self- published Invitation to Dinner, fulfilling a life-long dream of creating a "user-friendly" cookbook. An immediate success, it firmly established Vefa Alexiadou Editions in the competitive world of cookbook publishing. After three more cookbooks in the "Invitation" series, she revitalized her interest in traditional Greek cookery for a whole new generation of urban cooks with her two-volume premier work, Greek Cuisine and Greek Pastries and Desserts, published in 1989-91 in Greek, English and German. To date, she has published a total of 13 cookbooks, of which four are available in English. In 2004, in conjunction with the Olympic Games, she issued a new volume. The Best of Greek Cuisine, a luxury edition containing 93 selected recipes in seven languages.

From 1990 to 2003 Vefa appeared daily on Greek Antenna TV's most popular "morning coffee" show. Since September 2003 she has been presenting her own one-hour cooking show, "Vefa's Secrets," weekdays on Mega TV. Viewed via satellite round the world, she has passed Greek food traditions to hundreds of thousands of households, thus becoming the First Lady of Greek Cuisine. In 1994 she conceived the idea of Vefa's House franchise, to which twenty shops throughout Greece now belong.

In 1995, her recipes began appearing in Greece's top-circulating family magazine, "7 Days TV." With its publisher, Liberis Publications, she and her daughter Alexia wrote and edited a series of 20-recipe booklets, "20 Best Recipes for...", which won the 1998 Diplome d' Honneur at the Perigueux World Cookbook Fair as the most successful commercial cookbook series.

Ms. Alexiadou served on the Board of Archestratos, the Center for the Preservation & Advancement of Traditional Greek Gastronomy.

She attended both the 1997 and 1999 Tasting Australia events, invited by the Australian government as a special guest, and is an active member of the International Association of Culinary Professionals (I.A.C.P.). Also a member of the Greek Publishers Association, she is a regular participant in Greek and international book fairs.

Her articles and recipes appear frequently in Greek and international magazines and she travels frequently within Greece and abroad to lecture and give demonstrations on Greek gastronomical traditions. At the 2000 World Cookbook Awards of the "Salon International Livre Gourmand of Perigueux", Vefa Alexiadou won the award for the "best Mediterranean cookbook in Greek" and the special prize for "best Culinary Business Professional".

In October 2001 the National Book Center honored her work as a writer in the field of gastronomy, ranking her among Greece's greatest authors. She was a finalist in the I.A.C.P.'s "Lifetime Achievement" Award of Excellence 2002 and in 2003 she won the Nova Leaders of the Year Award as "Business Woman of the Year."

She is married to Constantine Alexiades, Professor of Chemistry, Aristotle University of Thessaloniki. They have two married daughters, Angela and Alexia, and two granddaughters.

Introduction

Sit down at my table, enjoy my Greek food, and no matter where you come from, you will feel that you've come home. When it is good, Greek food always has that effect on people. Our cuisine is simple – but that doesn't mean it's either plain or bland. Greek food at its best does not need a lot of spices. The flavor comes from the purity and freshness of the ingredients. When I make fasolakia *with green beans from my garden, or moussaka with eggplant I've just picked, their flavor and texture are at their peak.*

When I'm cooking in my kitchen, looking out over the Mediterranean, I feel as though I've been cooking ever since I was born. Like my grandmother, a gifted cook from Constantinople, and my mother, a gifted cook who came to her Greek homeland from Constantinople when she was 12 years old, I continue our traditions. I have never felt the need to go out searching for recipes because I inherited enough to carry me through life. The dishes we prepared always brought a never-ending parade of fascinating guests to our tables, and those wonderful shared meals led to many life-long friendships. Being a good cook has its rewards. Now, through my cookbooks I can "invite" many more new friends to dine with us.

It pains me to hear foreigners speak of Greek food disparagingly. "Greasy" and "too sweet" they complain. But that is only because they haven't tasted good Greek cooking. How can you judge a cuisine when you've never been exposed to it lovingly prepared in somebody's home? To judge from restaurant cooking, especially uninspired restaurant cooking, is unjust.

That is why I want you to use my recipes. They are the next best thing to welcoming you to my table. If you select your ingredients with care and follow these life-tested recipes, you will understand why, no matter where I travel, I always return to Greece with the utmost joy.

I have seen many food fads come and go, but people never tire of good Greek cooking. It has an appeal that is somehow at the same time Greek, Mediterranean, and very universal: it is contemporary and timeless all at once. Isn't that always true of the best of human endeavors?

My goal in this volume is to share with you these traditional Greek recipes, together with a few of the most important Greek customs, which I inherited from my grandmother and my mother and which I aspire to pass on to my children and grandchildren and to generations to come.

Vefa Alexiadou

Greek cuisine, whether frugal or bountiful, has evolved with and been molded by the customs and traditions of the Greek people. We Greeks tend to celebrate our joys, sweeten our sorrows, and find fuel for our struggles by eating and drinking in the company of family and friends.

Some customs have to do with ceremonial foods, such as the koufeta *(sugared almonds)* distributed at baptisms and weddings, or kolliva *(boiled wheat)*, the very ancient dish given to mourners at memorial services. During the year, each important religious feast, such as Christmas, the Annunciation, Easter, and the Assumption of the Virgin, has its own specialties. There is also a whole range of dishes associated with the numerous fasting periods and days scattered throughout the year, which may vary depending on the season.

In Carnival, preparations begin for Lent, the most important fasting period. They involve the gradual abstention from animal products. Meat is still allowed during the first week, which is referred to as "Kreatinis", and during the second week, called "Tirinis" or Cheese Week, milk products are eaten with gusto for the last time before Easter. A sweet smell of cheese and custard pies permeates the air of the homes of Greek housewives who prepare them according to time-honored family recipes. While fish may be eaten on Annunciation Day (March 25th) and Palm Sunday, which fall during Lent, there are no restrictions on the consumption of seafood, since it contains no blood. In keeping with tradition, housewives all over Greece serve fried salt cod and garlic sauce on these days.

On Holy Thursday the custom is to dye Easter eggs and bake tsoureki, the brioche-like Easter bread. The pungent aroma of vinegar, mixed with the dye to help it set, tempers the irresistible scent from the oven. A few red eggs are used to decorate the Easter bread. The others are placed in glass bowls or in baskets on the living-room table, filling the house with the spirit of Easter. On Good Friday, however, it is customary not to cook at all. The meal, prepared the day before, is austere – usually plain boiled lentils with vinegar but no olive oil, served with olives, scallions, and halva, archetypal fasting foods. It seems that olive oil is prohibited on certain solemn days because long ago it was kept in sacks made from animal skins, and so its vegetable nature was contaminated. This is of course no longer the case, but the tradition remains.

Easter in Greece is a uniquely joyful and colorful event, perhaps unmatched anywhere else in the world. It seems to capture the essence of spring, renewal, and rebirth. What can compare with the sense of ceremony and drama leading up to the moment of Resurrection! Congregations throng darkened churches, spilling outside them as they wait for the priest to emerge at the stroke of midnight and announce "Christos Anesti" (Christ is Risen). His candle starts a river of flickering flames as everyone – from toddlers to the very old – lights their own white candles from their neighbor's and exchanges kisses of peace and love. Church bells peal, firecrackers explode, drowning out the magnificent Easter hymn, and all but the most pious wend their way home to break the fast. Saturday night's fare – red eggs, mageiritsa

(Easter soup), tsoureki, *and a little feta – prepares the stomach for the feast to come. The meal is simple – meat, meat, meat – lamb, usually grilled outdoors over charcoal,* kokoretsi *(lamb innards also grilled on the spit) – with plenty of wine plus a few salads and dips to stave off hunger pangs until the animal is finally ready, and thick creamy yogurt for dessert. The festive atmosphere lingers well into the evening and almost always ends with dancing, a very Greek way of celebrating. Easter is the holiday that, more than any other, makes Greeks abroad think longingly of home.*

On August 6th, Transfiguration Day, worshippers in the countryside still carry baskets overflowing with grapes to be blessed in the village church. Later, they are distributed among the congregation. No one is supposed to have tasted the sweet fruit before then. In September, when the grapes are crushed and the must starts to ferment, many housewives rush to make moustokouloura, *must-flavored biscuits, and* moustalevria, *a pudding made with flour and the fermenting grape juice.*

On December 4th, the feast of St. Barbara, it is still customary in some areas to share the Varvara, *a pudding-like cream made from wheat, sprinkled with walnuts and cinnamon, with one's neighbors.*

Christmas is the most important holiday in the Church Calendar after Easter. For centuries Christmas has been linked with special treats. Mountains of kourabiedes, *crushed almond and butter cookies, and* melomakarona, *cookies filled with chopped walnuts and spices, decorate pastry shop windows all over the country. A delectable aroma wafts through home kitchens where women are making paper-thin pastries like* kataifi, baklava, diples, Christopsomo *or Christmas bread, traditional roast lamb with potatoes and turkey stuffed with chestnuts and pine nuts.*

No sooner is Christmas over than preparations begin for New Year's Eve. One of the few customs which is just as alive today as it was centuries ago is the cutting of the Vassilopita *(New Year's Cake) in all Greek homes. In the past, despite the fact that people were poorer, the coin in the* Vassilopita *was always gold. Today the gold coin is often replaced by a small, common metal coin or favor. Nevertheless, who does not believe that the coin will bring good fortune if it happens to be in our slice of cake? On New Year's Eve, before retiring, housewives traditionally set the table with delicacies – kaloudia – such as Greek pastries, fresh and dried fruits, and a variety of nuts. They are intended for St Basil (our Santa Claus) who will pass by, taste, and bless the food when he leaves his gifts. His blessings will help keep the kitchen cupboards well stocked throughout the year.*

These and other traditions – such as the sharing of the Artoklassia, *the five loaves of bread that worshippers bring to church to be blessed on their name day); the* Fanouropita, *the cake dedicated to St Fanourios, the Greek St Anthony, whenever someone loses something; baptismal and wedding dishes; and a host of customs particular to each Greek region – prove how indelible are the ties between our traditions and our cuisine.*

Vefa Alexiadou

Cuisine and Greek Tradition

Appetizers

50 selected appetizers or mezedes – Greece's famous precursors to a meal – which can constitute anything from nibbles with ouzo, wine or beer to the meal itself. Made from a rich variety of seafood, cheeses, meats, stuffed and wrapped vegetables, innards, tiny pies, and dips, they awaken the appetite, delight the eye, and please the taste buds.

Salads

22 wonderful Greek salads with garden vegetables, raw or lightly steamed, and flavored with fresh, aromatic herbs – a complement to any main dish.

Soups and Sauces

17 hearty, warming soups for cold winter days and light, nourishing, healthful dishes made with vegetables, pulses, chicken, fish or seafood. The perfect start to a midday meal or a simple supper. Also, 15 of Greece's best known sauces.

Pies and Pastas

30 tasty, attractive pies from the traditional Greek repertoire, filled with vegetables, greens, cheese, eggs, milk or meat, seasoned with fragrant herbs, and wrapped in feather-light sheets of crackling pastry. Plus a selection of choice delicacies to offer with a cup of tea or coffee.

Contents

Vegetables

39 recipes for the most characteristic of Greek dishes, made with pulses, grains, fresh vegetables, herbs, and olive oil – ingredients that form the basis of the Mediterranean diet. Health-giving, filling, and delicious, they can easily constitute the main meal of the day.

Meats

63 meat recipes chosen from Greece's centuries-old gastronomical tradition, perfected and easy to execute. Besides barbecued and roasted cuts, there are dozens of wonderful stews combining lamb, especially, with vegetables, pulses, rice or pasta, as well as dishes that illustrate the Greek talent for using ground beef in original yet economical ways. Special preparations for parties and buffets are also included.

Fish and Seafood

40 of Greece's finest recipes for fish and seafood – a constellation of dishes from the simplest grilled catch of the day to sophisticated concoctions with the most luxurious ingredients.

Poultry and Game

15 recipes for poultry of all kinds that are delicious, easy and quick; plus 12 incomparable recipes for game, to present as a family treat or as the star of a formal dinner party.

Appetizers
(Mezedes)

The number and variety of appetizers (Mezedes) in the Greek repertory is astonishing. Almost any savory dish can be considered a meze, as long as it is served on a small plate. It can range from something as simple as a few olives, sticks of crisp cucumber sprinkled with coarse salt, a sliced tomato, and a slab of chalk-white feta cheese to dishes that require as much preparation as a main course and which indeed are substantial enough to constitute one. Even leftovers can be dressed up and given a new role as an accompaniment to the classic Greek aperitifs, ouzo, wine, and raki.

A meze can be either raw or cooked. Among the more famous uncooked starters are tzatziki, cucumber and yogurt dip; taramosalata, made of fish roe, crumbled bread or potato, olive oil, and lemon juice; and ktipiti, feta mashed with chili pepper. Cooked appetizers range from mint-flavored meatballs, tiny fried cheese pies, stuffed vine leaves, snails smothered in onions, and the spicy meat stew known as Bekri Meze or Drunkard's Delight, because it goes so perfectly with wine.

Mezedes can be so appealing that one can make a whole meal of them. There are even restaurants, known as ouzeris or mezedopoleia, where the menu consists of nothing but appetizers. After ten or fifteen such dishes, only the greediest could even contemplate a roast, a steak, or a rich casserole.

Food, for Greeks, is not just a biological need, but rather a celebration, a source of amusement and joy. The habit of picking at appetizers and slowly sipping a glass of chilled ouzo or retsina wine while making small talk, teasing, and laughing with friends around a table in the open air is something that a Greek would not trade for any other entertainment in the world. It is a habit to which visitors to Greece quickly become addicted.

In this chapter you will find a wide selection of appetizers which delight the eye, tempt the appetite, and please the palate, so that you can recreate this unique Greek experience in your own home.

General Instructions

The number of servings suggested in each recipe in this chapter is purely symbolic. You will find that everything depends on the amount and variety of appetizers served and the mood and appetite of the particular moment. You may wish to serve a dish as a single first-course in the Western manner or you may include it along with six or seven other appetizers for a larger number of guests at a buffet or cocktail party.

Apart from those appetizers that require some time to prepare, a whole series of delicious ready-made treats can be offered with equal success. For example, Greeks are very fond of the various kinds of dry, salted and smoked fish (mackerel, tuna, trout, sardines, eel), pickled vegetables, olives, and sliced cured sausages. It is useful to have some of these on hand for an emergency.

Octopus in Vinegar
(Ktapodi Xidato)

Serves 4-6
Preparation time 15 minutes
Cooking time 12 hours and 30 minutes

4 lbs octopus
1 cup vinegar
2 celery stalks
2 small carrots, scrubbed
1 medium onion, peeled
10 peppercorns
salt

the marinade
1/2 cup olive oil
1/3 cup vinegar
10 peppercorns
a pinch of salt

To clean the octopus, turn the head inside out, remove and discard the viscera. Wash octopus thoroughly. Greek fishermen tenderize octopus by beating them against rocks repeatedly. If your octopus is fresh and has not been tenderized, you can achieve the same effect by freezing it for several days. Thaw out, place in a pot, add the vinegar and enough water to cover octopus. Bring to a boil, reduce the heat, and simmer, covered, for about 1 hour and 30 minutes. Drain and rinse in cold water. Peel off the skin. Return to the pot, add celery, carrots, onion, peppercorns, salt, and water to cover. Simmer, covered, for about 1 hour, or until tender. Drain, cool slightly, and cut into bite-sized pieces and place in a bowl. Mix the marinade

ingredients and pour the liquid over the warm octopus. Refrigerate for at least 24 hours. Garnish with chopped pimientos and parsley. Moisten with some of the sauce and serve. Delicious with ouzo.
Note: For greater effect at a buffet, you can leave the octopus whole and then cut it into bite-sized pieces after everyone has admired it.

Charcoal-Grilled Octopus
(Ktapodi sta Karvouna)

Serves 4
Preparation time 10 minutes
Cooking time 1 hour and 30 minutes

2-3 lbs octopus
1 cup vinegar

the marinade
1/2 cup olive oil
1/2 cup white wine
1 teaspoon oregano
2 bay leaves
10 peppercorns
salt to taste

Wash octopus and prepare according to the preceding recipe for Octopus in Vinegar. After you remove the skin, put the octopus into a bowl. Mix and shake all the marinade ingredients and pour them over the octopus. Marinate octopus up to 24 hours, in the refrigerator, turning occasionally. Just before serving, charcoal grill octopus on both sides, basting with the marinade. Serve sprinkled with olive oil and oregano and garnished with lemon wedges. Delicious with ouzo.

Steamed Mussels
(Midia Achnista)

Serves 4
Preparation time 45 minutes
Cooking time 5 minutes

4 lbs live mussels
1/2 cup olive oil
3 tablespoons finely chopped parsley
1 long hot green pepper, cut into rings
salt and pepper to taste
1/4 cup lemon juice

Scrub the mussels, under running water, with a stiff brush to remove seaweed and barnacles. Discard any open shells. Place mussels in a pot of clean, salted water. They will stay alive for several hours and expel any sand or grit they contain. Change the water once or twice. Pull off the hair-like strands (beard). To open, steam them in a little water for about 2-3 minutes and shell, reserving the liquid. Set aside. In a heavy-bottomed saucepan combine the oil, 1/2 cup of the reserved liquid, parsley, pepper rings, salt, and pepper. Bring to a rolling boil, add the mussels, and boil for 5 minutes. Remove from the heat, and stir in the lemon juice gently. Pour into a soup tureen and serve immediately. Delicious with ouzo.

Fried Squid
(Kalamarakia Tiganita)

Serves 4
Preparation time 1 hour
Frying time 15 minutes

2 lbs small squid
salt
Batter for Frying (page 51) or
flour for dredging
oil for frying
salt and pepper to taste
1 lemon

Clean the squid. Detach the head from the body. Using a sharp knife, sever the tentacles from the rest of head, cutting just above the eyes. (They should not separate.) Squeeze out the beak at the base of the tentacles. Discard the head with viscera and ink sac. Pull the quill-shaped pen out of body and discard. Keep the tentacles. Wash under running water and peel the translucent purplish membrane off the body. Rinse well inside and out. If the squid are very small leave whole; if large cut into rings. Rub the squid with a lit-

tle salt and place in a colander to drain. Dredge with flour and shake off excess or dip in batter. Deep-fry until golden brown in very hot oil. Remove with a wire scoop to a platter. Garnish with lemon wedges and serve hot with Tzatziki, Eggplant Salad, or Taramosalata (pages 14 and 29).

Fried Picarel
(Marides Tiganites)

Serves 4
Preparation time 1 hour
Frying time 5-7 minutes

2 lbs picarel or any small fish such as whitebait, fresh
anchovies, etc.
flour for dredging
salt and pepper
cayenne pepper (optional)
oil for frying

Wash and clean the fish well; they will not need scaling or gutting. If they are very small, do not remove the heads. Drain well in a colander and pat them dry with paper towels. In a plastic bag put a cup of flour, salt, pepper, and cayenne. Add the fish, and shake well to coat evenly. Transfer to a sieve and toss gently to shake off any surplus flour. Deep fry or pan fry in very hot oil, until the fish are lightly browned. Remove with a slotted spoon, drain on paper towels, and arrrange on a platter. Garnish with lemon slices and serve immediately, accompanied by a green salad or Tomato and Onion Salad.

Grilled Shrimp
(Garides sti Skara)

Serves 4
Preparation time 30 minutes
Cooking time 8 minutes

2 lbs large shrimp
2 tablespoons lemon juice
4 tablespoons olive oil
1 small garlic clove, finely chopped
1 teaspoon prepared mustard
1 tablespoon finely chopped parsley
salt and pepper to taste

Peel and devein the shrimp, leaving tail fins intact. Wash and drain. Mix all the other ingredients together, pour the mixture over the shrimp, and toss well. Marinate for at least 1 hour. Arrange the shrimp on a grill pan and broil, under the grill, for about 4 minutes on each side. Serve immediately, accompanied by a salad.

Fried Mixed Seafood
(Thalassina Tiganita)

Serves 4
Preparation time 1 hour
Cooking time 30 minutes

2 lbs large shrimp
1 lb sole fillets
1 cup flour
2 teaspoons salt
3/4 teaspoon white pepper
1 teaspoon seafood seasoning (optional)
2 egg whites
2 tablespoons olive oil
fine bread crumbs
oil for frying
lettuce leaves, to garnish

Peel the shrimp, leaving the tail fins attached to the flesh. Devein and slit the undersection of each shrimp to prevent excessive curling. Wash and dry them thoroughly. Cut the sole fillets in narrow, finger-size strips. In a plastic bag, combine the flour, salt, pepper, and the seafood seasoning, if using. Dredge the shrimp, then the fish, by shaking them, a handful at a time, in the bag. Transfer to a sieve or colander, and shake gently to remove the excess flour. Lightly beat the egg whites with the oil. Dip the seafood, one piece at a time in the egg-white mixture, then roll in the bread crumbs. Arrange the coated seafood on a sheet of wax paper and refrigerate for an hour. (At this point you may freeze the seafood, if desired, in plastic containers. Layer each row with wax paper. Store shrimp and sole in separate air-tight containers. When ready to cook, there is no need to defrost beforehand.) Deep fry the seafood in very hot oil. When browned, remove with a wire scoop, drain on paper towels, and transfer to a platter lined with lettuce leaves. Serve immediately, accompanied by cocktail, tartar, or other seafood sauce.
Alternate: Dip the flour-coated seafood into a batter (page 51) instead of beaten egg whites and bread crumbs.

Fried Mussels (Midia Tiganita)

Serves 4
Preparation time 30 minutes
Frying time 15 minutes

2 lbs shelled large mussels, fresh or frozen
Batter for Frying (page 51) or
flour for dredging
oil for frying
salt and pepper to taste
1 lemon

Dip mussels one at a time in batter or dredge with flour according to the recipe for Fried Picarel (page 11). Be sure to shake off excess flour before frying. Heat the oil in a deep-fryer until very hot and fry the mussels, a handful at a time, until golden brown. Remove with a wire scoop, drain on paper towels, and place on a heated platter. Season with salt and freshly ground pepper. Garnish with lemon wedges and serve immediately with Tzatziki, Eggplant Salad, or Taramosalata.
Alternate: If using fresh mussels, prepare according to the recipe for Steamed Mussels (page 11). Drain the shelled mussels well before dipping into the batter or dredging with flour.

Braised Cuttlefish
(Soupies Aspres)

Serves 4
Preparation time 30 minutes
Cooking time 1 hour

2 lbs small cuttlefish or squid
2/3 cup olive oil
2-3 garlic cloves, sliced
salt and pepper to taste
1/3 cup dry white wine
1 tablespoon lemon juice

Wash cuttlefish thoroughly in cold water. Slip out the cuttlebone and scoop out and discard the viscera and ink sac. Pull out the beak and eyes and discard. Wash under running water inside and out and peel off the translucent skin. Alternatively, ask your fish dealer to clean the cuttlefish for you. Place in a colander and drain well. Push the head and tentacles of each cuttlefish into the body. Heat the oil in a heavy-bottomed saucepan, add garlic, and sauté briefly over high heat. Add the cuttlefish, cover, and boil gently until the liquid evaporates. Pour in the wine and lemon juice, and season to taste. Cover and simmer, for 5-10 minutes. Remove from the heat and sprinkle with freshly ground pepper. Hot or cold, this is delicious with ouzo.

Steamed Mussels with Wine
(Midia Achnista me Krasi)

Serves 4
Preparation time 30 minutes
Cooking time 15 minutes

2 lbs live mussels
1/2 cup butter or olive oil
1 medium onion, chopped
1 garlic clove, sliced
salt and pepper
1 cup dry white wine
1/2 tablespoon oregano or
2 tablespoons chopped parsley
2 tablespoons lemon juice

Prepare the mussels according to the first half of the recipe for Steamed Mussels (page 11). Debeard and wash the mussels and drain in a colander. Heat the butter or oil in a large heavy-bottomed saucepan, and sauté the onion and garlic, until golden. Add the mussels, wine, oregano or parsley, and seasonings. Cover and boil rapidly over high heat, 3-5 minutes, until the mussels open. Shake the pan 2-3 times, during cooking, to redistribute the mussels. Remove from the heat, sprinkle with lemon juice, and serve at once in soup plates with some of the cooking juices.

Salted Cod Fritters
(Tiganites Bakaliarou)

Yields 40-50 fritters
Preparation time 12 hours
Frying time 10 minutes

2 lbs salt cod fillets
1 cup all-purpose flour
1 tablespoon olive oil
1 teaspoon oregano (optional)
black pepper to taste
1 cup beer
1/2 cup finely chopped dill
1/2 cup finely chopped parsley
1/2 cup finely chopped spring onions
2 tablespoons lemon juice
oil for frying

Soak the cod fillets as described in the recipe for Fried Salted Cod (page 131). Lift out the fish, squeeze out excess water, and cut up the fish into small pieces. Using an electric mixer, beat the flour with the oil, oregano (if using), pepper, and beer – the fish should provide enough salt – until you have a smooth, thick batter. Add the chopped fish along with the rest of the ingredients and mix well. Just before you are ready to eat, heat about 1 inch of oil in a large, heavy-bottomed frying pan. When it starts to smoke, drop in spoonfuls of the fish mixture, a few at a time, browning them on both sides. Lift them out with a slotted spoon and drain them on paper towels. Serve the fritters hot, accompanied by Garlic Sauce *(skordalia)* and Beet Salad.

Russian Salad (Rossiki Salata)

Serves 4
Preparation time 30 minutes
Cooking time 30 minutes

1/4 cup small dried white beans
1 medium potato
1 large carrot
1/4 fresh shelled peas
2 tablespoons capers (optional)
2 tablespoons chopped pickle
2 tablespoons chopped pimiento
2 hard boiled eggs, chopped
1 tablespoon lemon juice
1 cup mayonnaise
salt and pepper to taste

Soak the beans in water overnight. Drain, cover with cold water, and boil until tender. Rinse and drain well. Peel the potato and carrot and cut into small cubes. Put in a saucepan along with the peas, add a little water, and boil for about 15 minutes. Do not over-cook. Drain and cool. Put all ingredients except the mayonnaise in a large bowl and mix well. Add the mayonnaise and toss lightly. Mound on a platter and garnish with rosettes made of carrots and sliced pickles. Serve with crackers and ouzo. Delicious with meatballs or cod patties.
Alternate: Canned or frozen vegetables may be used instead of fresh. Do not cook the canned vegetables.

Fish Roe Dip (Taramosalata)

Serves 6-8
Preparation time 15-40 minutes
In a processor 5-10 minutes

6 thick slices dry bread, crusts removed (8 oz)
8 oz tarama paste (salted fish roe)
2 tablespoons minced onion
1 cup olive oil
1/4 cup lemon juice
2 spring onions, chopped
black olives to garnish

Soak the bread in a little water for 5 minutes, squeeze gently, and crumble. Pound the fish roe to a thick paste with a large mortar and pestle, if you have one. Add the onion, a few drops of the oil, and continue pounding or beating, adding a little bread along with a little oil. Continue until the bread and other ingredients are combined. Add the remaining oil little by little and then lemon juice to taste. Add it slowly to prevent curdling. Continue beating until thick and pale pink. Transfer to a serving dish, cover, and chill. Garnish with chopped green onions sprinkled on top, or with black olives. Serve with fresh country bread and ouzo.
Note: This dip can be prepared in a food processor. Put the fish roe, onion, and about a third of the oil in the machine and process for a few seconds, until the red centers of the roe have been broken down and the mixture is smooth. Add the crumbled wet bread, little by little. Trickle in the remaining oil. Add the lemon juice slowly to prevent curdling and process for a few seconds until the mixture is thick and pale pink.
Alternate: Substitute 8 oz cooked potatoes for the bread. Add 2/3 cup blanched ground almonds, peanuts, or hazelnuts. If the taramosalata is too thick, add a little soda water and beat until light and soft.

Pastry-Wrapped Olives
(Bourekakia me Elies)

Yields about 30 pieces
Preparation time 20 minutes
Baking time 20 minutes

1¼ cups all-purpose flour
1 cup grated kefalotiri or Romano cheese
1/2 cup olive oil
3 tablespoons ice water
1 teaspoon paprika
30 pimiento-stuffed green olives
sesame seeds

Combine the first 5 ingredients in a bowl, mix, and knead lightly. Pinch off small pieces of dough and flatten. Wrap each piece around an olive, rolling into small balls, between your palms. Roll the balls in sesame seeds. (At this stage you may freeze them. When ready to bake, let them thaw out first.) Place on a greased baking sheet, preheat oven to 400°F, and bake for 15-20 minutes. Serve hot.

Piquant Cheese Dip
(Ktipiti me Piperia)

Serves 8-10
Preparation time 20 minutes

2 long hot green peppers
1 lb soft feta cheese
1/4 cup olive oil
2-3 teaspoons vinegar to taste
1/4 teaspoon freshly ground pepper

If the cheese is very salty, soak it in cold water for a few hours, until it is soft and lightly salted. Grill the peppers or fry them in a little hot oil. Seed and peel them. Mash the peppers and the feta with a fork, gradually adding a tablespoon of olive oil at a time, until the oil is incorporated and the mixture is smooth and soft. Add freshly ground pepper and vinegar to taste. If the mixture is stiff, add a little milk to make it creamy. If hot peppers are not available, use 2 mild peppers for the aroma and 10-15 drops of Tabasco for the bite. Serve with crackers, raw vegetables, or fresh bread.
Note: Ktipiti also can be prepared in a food processor or blender.

Shredded Wheat Pastry
and Cheese Rolls (Kataifi me Tiria)

Yields 30-40 pieces
Preparation time 1 hour
Baking time 40 minutes

6 eggs
freshly ground pepper
2 cups feta cheese, crumbled
1/2 cup Roquefort cheese, crumbled
1½ cup various cheeses, crumbled
1 lb store-bought kataifi pastry (shredded wheat)
1/3 cup butter
1/3 cup corn oil
1 cup milk
1 cup heavy cream

Lightly beat 3 eggs in a bowl. Add the pepper and mix in cheeses. Separate the kataifi dough into 30-40 pieces. Cover with a damp cloth to keep them moist. Take one piece of kataifi dough and pat it gently between your palms. Place a tablespoon of the cheese filling on top and fold it in to make a ball. Continue until all the pieces are filled. Place them in a buttered baking pan, close together. Melt the butter and corn oil together and pour a tablespoon over each roll. (At this point you may wrap and freeze the rolls. They will keep in the refrigerator for 24 hours.) One hour before baking, lightly beat together the milk, cream, and

remaining eggs. Pour the mixture over the rolls. When the liquid has been absorbed, preheat the oven to 350°F, and bake for 35-40 minutes, or until golden brown. Serve hot.
Alternate: Substitute 1 cup of finely chopped ham or chopped bacon for 1 cup of the cheese mixture.

Grilled or Fried Peppers
(Piperies Psites i Tiganites)

Serves 4
Preparation time 10 minutes
Cooking time 10 minutes

1 lb long green peppers
1 long green chili pepper (optional)
salt to taste
Oil-Vinegar Dressing (page 47)

Wash the peppers, and carefully remove the stems and seeds, taking care not to tear the peppers. Grill on charcoal or fry in a small amount of olive oil, turning them to brown all over. Arrange the peppers in a deep plate and while still hot, sprinkle them with salt and oil-vinegar dressing to taste. If you fry the peppers, do not add dressing. Spoon over 2-3 tablespoons of the frying oil, add salt and vinegar to taste. The chili pepper will give the dish a slightly hot flavor. More chilis can be used, if a hotter flavor is desired. Peppers served the second day are more tasty. Delicious with ouzo or retsina.

flour and mix in enough water to make a smooth light batter. Allow the batter to stand for at least 30 minutes at room temperature. Dip zucchini and eggplant slices, one at a time, into the batter and deep fry in hot oil. Remove with a slotted spoon and drain on paper towels. Delicious hot with Tzatziki or Garlic Sauce.
Alternate: Dip the vegetables into a plain batter (page 51) instead of the yeast batter. Or fry the eggplant without batter for a softer texture. Dip the zucchini in flour, shake off the excess, and arrange slices on a piece of wax paper, side by side, until frying time. Deep fry in deep hot oil until light brown. Remove with a slotted spoon and drain on paper towels. Serve immediately.

Fried Cheese (Tiri Saganaki)

Serves 6
Preparation time 5 minutes
Frying time 5-7 minutes

2/3 lb kefalotiri or Romano cheese
oil for frying
1 lemon
flour
1/4 teaspoon pepper

Cut the cheese into 4 slices, each about 1/3 inch thick. Mix a few spoonfuls of flour and the pepper in a dish and coat the cheese slices with the mixture. Pour enough olive oil into a frying pan to cover the bottom and heat until smoking. Fry the cheese, turning once, until crisp and brown on both sides. Transfer to a platter, sprinkle with lemon juice, and serve immediately. Wonderful with ouzo.

Scrambled Eggs Greek Style
(Strapatsada)

Serves 4-5
Preparation time 10 minutes
Frying time 10 minutes

3-4 tablespoons butter or margarine
8 eggs
1 cup crumbled feta cheese
1 tablespoon finely chopped parsley
1/2 cup Red Pepper Sauce (page 50)
salt and freshly ground pepper

Heat the butter in a deep frying pan until it stops bubbling. Meanwhile, beat the eggs lightly in a bowl and stir in the cheese, parsley, and the pepper sauce. Pour the mixture into the frying pan and stir over medium heat until the eggs are done to your taste. Transfer to a platter and sprinkle with salt and freshly ground pepper. Serve immediately.
Alternate: The Tomato Sauce on page 53 or your own favorite recipe, with a little green pepper and a pinch of chili pepper, may be used in place of the Pepper Sauce suggested here.

Fried Eggplant and Zucchini
(Melitzanes ke Kolokithia Tiganita)

Serves 4
Preparation time 30 minutes
Frying time 30 minutes

2 lbs eggplant
2 lbs zucchini
1 teaspoon dry yeast
2 cups all-purpose flour
oil for frying
salt

Wash, trim, and cut the eggplant and zucchini in 1/3 inch rounds or slices. Sprinkle generously with salt and let stand separately in two colanders, for about 2 hours. Rinse the eggplant well and squeeze out the water with your hands. Drain the zucchini and pat dry with paper towels. Dissolve the yeast in a little warm water, add the

Zucchini Flowers
Stuffed with Cheese
(Kolokithoanthi me Tiri)

Serves 4
Preparation time 30 minutes
Frying time 8-10 minutes

20 zucchini flowers
1 cup crumbled feta cheese
1 cup grated kefalograviera or other hard cheese
2 tablespoons self-raising flour
1 large egg, lightly beaten
3 tablespoons finely chopped mint
freshly ground pepper
flour for dredging
oil for frying

Wash the zucchini flowers in plenty of running water, trim the stems, and remove the pistils and stamens. Drain. Beat the cheeses with the flour and stir in the beaten egg. Add the mint, pepper, and a little salt, if needed. (Taste it first, the cheeses should provide enough.) Mix lightly. In the center of each zucchini flower place a heaping spoonful of the cheese mixture and close by pressing the tips of the flower together. Dredge the stuffed flowers in flour and deep fry them over medium heat until golden. Wonderful with ouzo.

Stewed Snails
(Salingaria Yiachni)

Serves 6
Preparation time 30 minutes
Cooking time 2 hours

2 lbs snails, live or cleansed and dormant
1 cup flour
1 cup olive oil
2 lbs onions, sliced
6 cloves garlic, sliced
2 lbs ripe tomatoes, finely chopped
2-3 bay leaves
6 allspice berries
salt, pepper
1/4 cup dry red wine

If you gather your own snails from the fields, place them in a bucket covered with wire mesh for 8 to 10 days, and shake a handful of flour over them every 2-3 days. Eating the flour will purge their intestines of any undesirable substances they may have fed on in the wild. If you don't cook them immediately, store them in a loosely-woven cloth bag. Dormant like this, they will keep for a long time, ready for cooking whenever you want. Many shops and markets in Greece stock purged snails; if you live abroad, you may have to resort to canned snails.

To cook the snails, wash their shells well in plenty of water, remove the membrane covering the opening, and let them sit in cold water until they wake up. Test any that do not poke their antennae out by pricking them with a thick needle. Discard the ones that don't react. Drain the snails, sprinkle with salt, and let stand 5 minutes. Rinse again with lots of water. With a sharp knife, cut off the point on the curved part of the shell. This will allow the sauce to seep into the shell, making the snails tastier, but it will also make it easier to coax out the meat.

Place the snails in a pot with salted water to cover and bring to the boil. Skim off the foam that rises to the top and boil slowly until the meat becomes softer, but not completely cooked. Fill a cup with clear broth from the surface and discard the rest. Heat the oil in a large pan and lightly sauté the onion and garlic. Add the snails, tomato, bay leaves, allspice, pepper, and broth. Cover the pan and simmer until the snails are very tender and have absorbed most of the liquid. Pour in the wine and simmer for a few minutes more. Serve the snails at room temperature. They will be even more delicious the next day.

Lamb's Liver Phyllo Rolls
(Tziyerobourekakia)

Yields 30-40 pieces
Preparation time 2 hours
Baking time 40 minutes

1 lb packed phyllo or
1 recipe, Homemade Phyllo Dough (page 56)

the filling
organ meats (heart, liver, spleen, sweetbreads) from 1
spring lamb (1½ lb)
3 tablespoons olive oil
8 spring onions, finely chopped
1/2 cup finely chopped parsley
1/4 cup finely chopped dill
salt and pepper to taste
1 egg, lightly beaten
3 tablespoons cream
1/2 cup olive oil or butter, melted
1/2 cup sesame seeds

If preparing homemade phyllo, divide the dough into 12 small balls. Cover with a damp cloth and set aside for 1 hour. Blanch the meats and chop. Set aside. Heat 3 tablespoons olive oil in a saucepan, add the onions, and sauté lightly. Add the chopped meat, season to taste, cover, and simmer until all juices have evaporated. Remove from the heat, add parsley and dill, and fold in the egg, lightly beaten with the cream. Roll out the dough balls into fine sheets, according to the recipe on page 56. Butter two phyllo sheets at a time and cut into strips. Place 1 tablespoon of the filling at the bottom of each double strip and fold into triangles or small rolls. Arrange the pastries on a buttered baking sheet, brush with oil, and sprinkle with sesame seeds. Preheat oven to 350°F and bake for 35-40 minutes. Serve hot.

Alternate: Use only lamb's liver and heart, if the other organs are not available. Lamb's liver also can be successfully replaced with calf's liver.

FRIED TRIANGLES, PAGE 19 • BAKED CHEESE TRIANGLES, PAGE 20 • PHYLLO ROLLS WITH PASTRAMI, PAGE 21

Baked Meat Triangles
(Kreatopitakia)

Yields 3-4 dozen
Preparation time 1 hour
Baking time 30 minutes

2/3 cup butter or extra virgin olive oil
1/2 lb ground lean meat (beef or veal)
1 small onion, finely chopped
1/2 cup grated Swiss cheese
pepper and salt (if needed)
2 eggs, lightly beaten
1/2 cup heavy cream
1 lb packaged phyllo
1 egg yolk
sesame seeds

Heat 3 tablespoons butter in a saucepan. Add the ground meat and the onion. Sauté lightly. Remove from the heat and allow to cool. Add the cheese, salt, pepper, eggs, and the cream. Mix well. Melt the remaining butter. Lay the phyllo sheets on a flat surface and cut in strips, lengthwise, about 2¹/₂ inches wide. Brush a strip with melted butter and put another on top. Butter the surface, put 1 teaspoon of the meat filling in the bottom left corner and fold the right corner over it, to form a triangle. Then fold the triangle over and over up the pastry strip until you reach the end. Continue with the remaining pastry and filling until both are used up. (At this stage you may wrap the pies and freeze them. Let them thaw out, before baking.) Arrange the triangles on a buttered baking sheet, prick the tops with the prongs of a fork. Beat the egg yolk with 1 teaspoon water. Brush the meat pastries with beaten egg yolk and sprinkle with sesame seeds. Preheat oven to 400°F and bake for about 30 minutes, or until golden brown. Serve hot.

2 tablespoons melted butter
1 cup crumbled feta cheese
1 cup grated Swiss cheese
salt and pepper

the meat filling
1/2 lb ground beef or veal
2 spring onions, chopped fine
1 small garlic clove, crushed
1 tablespoon finely chopped dill
1 tablespoon finely chopped parsley
1 tablespoon olive oil
2-3 tablespoons milk or water

Prepare the Cheese Filling: In a saucepan heat the milk with the cream of wheat, stirring constantly, and boil for a few minutes, until smooth and creamy. Remove from the heat, add the remaining ingredients, and mix well. The filling should not be runny. If it is, add more feta.

Prepare the Meat Filling: Mix all the ingredients in a small bowl. Add just enough milk or water, as needed, to make the filling moist and malleable. Carefully unfold the phyllo sheets on a flat surface. With a sharp knife cut lengthwise into strips 2 inches wide. To prevent from drying out and becoming brittle, cover the phyllo strips with a damp cloth. Place two strips one on top of the other and brush with melted butter. Put 1 teaspoon of cheese filling or meat filling in the bottom left corner and fold the right corner over it, to form a triangle. Fold the triangle over and over up the pastry strip until you reach the end. Continue with the remaining pastry and fillings until all are used up. (At this point you may freeze the triangles in plastic containers. Layer each row with wax paper. Store cheese and meat bourekakia in separate containers.) When ready to cook, deep-fry the triangles, whether frozen or freshly made, in very hot oil. Serve hot.

Fried Triangles
(Bourekakia Tiganita)

Yields 50-60 pieces
Preparation time 2 hours
Frying time 15-30 minutes

1 package ready-made phyllo
olive or vegetable oil for frying

the cheese filling
1 cup milk
3 tablespoons cream of wheat or fine semolina
1 whole egg and 1 egg yolk, lightly beaten

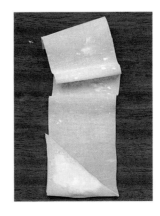

Baked Cheese Triangles (Tiropitakia)

Yields 3-4 dozen
Preparation time 1 hour
Baking time 30 minutes

> 2 eggs plus 1 egg yolk
> 1/4 cup heavy cream
> 1 lb feta cheese, crumbled
> white pepper
> nutmeg (optional)
> 1/2 cup butter
> 1/2 cup margarine
> 1 lb packaged phyllo
> 1 egg yolk, beaten with a little water
> sesame seeds

Lightly beat the eggs with the cream in a bowl. Add cheese, pepper, and a few gratings of nutmeg. Mix well until the mixture is very thick. If necessary, add more cheese. Melt butter and margarine in a small saucepan. Lay the phyllo sheets on a flat surface and cut into strips, lengthwise, about 2^1/$_2$ inches wide. Brush a strip with melted butter and put another on top. Butter the surface, put 1 teaspoon of the cheese filling in the bottom left corner and fold the right corner over it, to form a triangle. Then fold the triangle over and over up the pastry strip until you reach the end. Continue with the remaining pastry and filling until both are used up. Arrange the triangles on a buttered baking tray, prick the tops with the prongs of a fork. (At this stage you may wrap the pies and and freeze them. Always let them thaw out before baking.) Brush with beaten egg yolk and sprinkle with

sesame seeds. Preheat oven to 400°F and bake for about 30 minutes, or until golden brown.

Meatballs (Keftedakia)

Serves 4
Preparation time 10 minutes
Cooking time 20 minutes

> 2 thick slices day-old bread (crusts removed)
> 1 cup finely chopped onion
> 1 lb ground lean meat (beef or veal)
> 1/4 cup olive oil
> 1-2 eggs
> 1/4 cup chopped parsley, dill, or mint
> 1 tablespoon vinegar
> 1 tablespoon oregano
> 1/4 teaspoon baking soda
> salt and pepper
> flour for dredging
> oil for frying

Soak the bread in water and squeeze out the excess with your hands. Crumble the bread and mix it with all the other ingredients in a bowl. The mixture should be moist. Add a little water or beer, if necessary. Chill the mixture, covered, for 2 hours.
Fried Keftedakia: Pinch off small pieces of the meat mixture and roll into walnut-sized balls. Dredge with flour and fry in hot olive oil until brown and crisp. Serve hot.
Grilled Keftedakia: Shape the meat mixture into large patties and flatten slightly. Brush with oil and grill over charcoal, turning frequently, for about 15 minutes or until the meat is done to your taste. Serve hot with Garlic Sauce and Pepper Sauce (pages 50 and 51).
Keftedakia with Sauce: Prepare the fried meatballs and put them in Tomato Sauce (page 53). Cover and simmer 5-7 minutes. Serve them hot with french fried potatoes or rice.

Meat Rolls with Garlic (Soutzoukakia)

Serves 4
Preparation time 15 minutes
Cooking time 20 minutes

> 1 lb ground meat (beef or veal)
> 2 medium onions, finely chopped
> 2 garlic cloves, crushed
> 1 teaspoon oregano
> 1/4 cup dried bread crumbs
> 1 tablespoon vinegar
> 1/4 cup olive oil
> salt, pepper

Mix all ingredients in a bowl and knead for 2 minutes. Cover and chill for 1-2 hours. Roll the meat mixture into 20 sausage-shaped rolls and brush with oil. Grill under the broiler or over charcoal, turning frequently, until browned all over. Serve with Eggplant Salad, Tzatziki, or Pepper Sauce.

Phyllo Rolls with Pastrami
(Floyeres me Pastourma)

Serves 8-10
Preparation time 30 minutes
Baking time 30 minutes

20 slices pastrami
4 eggs, beaten
8 spring onions, finely chopped
1 cup olive oil
1 cup grated kefalotiri or Romano cheese
20 thin slices Swiss cheese
1/2 lb packaged phyllo
1/4 cup sesame seeds

Soak the pastrami slices in the beaten eggs for at least 1 hour. In a small saucepan sauté the onions lightly in about 3 tablespoons of the oil and set aside. Warm the remaining oil. Brush half of each phyllo sheet, width-wise, with oil; fold the other half over it. Place one slice Swiss cheese 1 inch from the bottom at the center of the phyllo sheet. Put a slice of pastrami on top and sprinkle with some sautéed onion and grated cheese. Fold the two sides of phyllo on top of the filling. Brush again with oil, and roll it up. Repeat until you have used up all the pastrami and cheese slices. Arrange the rolls on a greased baking sheet and brush them with the remaining oil and the beaten eggs. Sprinkle with sesame seeds. Preheat oven to 400°F and bake until golden brown. Serve immediately.

Lamb Liver Tidbits
(Frigadelia)

Serves 4
Preparation time 30 minutes
Frying time 15 minutes

1 lamb liver, cut into bite-sized pieces
1-2 lamb cauls
oil for frying
salt and freshly ground pepper
oregano
lemon juice

Wash the caul well and cut it into small round or square pieces. Wrap the liver pieces in them. Cover the bottom of a frying pan with oil and heat until it reaches the smoking point. Add a handful of liver morsels at a time and fry, turning frequently, until crisp and brown. Transfer to a platter, sprinkle with salt, pepper, oregano, and a little lemon juice, and serve at once.
Note: Lamb's heart or kidney can be also used.

Shrimp in Tomato-Cheese Sauce
(Garides Saganaki me Feta)

Serves 2
Preparation time 15 minutes
Cooking time 15 minutes

8 large shrimps
1/4 cup olive oil
1/4 cup finely chopped onion
2 cloves garlic, slivered
1/4 cup dry white wine
1 cup chopped fresh or canned tomatoes
1/2 cup cubed feta cheese
1/2 teaspoon oregano
2 tablespoons finely chopped parsley

Peel the shrimp, leaving heads and tails intact. Heat the oil in a frying pan – in Greece, there is a special pan called a *saganaki* – and sauté the onion and garlic until translucent. Add the shrimp and fry them on both sides until they turn red. Pour in the wine and tomato and boil the shrimp, uncovered, for a few minutes, until the sauce starts to thicken. Add the cheese and oregano and stir over the heat until the cheese begins to melt into the sauce. Remove from the heat, sprinkle parsley on top, and serve immediately with plenty of country-style bread.

juice and salt. Remove the stems and arrange the mushroom caps in a buttered broiling pan. Finely chop the stems. In a small pan heat the butter and olive oil and lightly saut'e both kinds of onions. Add the chopped mushroom stems, the wine, salt, and pepper, and simmer until the juices evaporate. Remove from the heat, add the dill, cream, and cheeses, stir well. Fill the mushroom caps, sprinkle with a little grated Parmesan, and broil for about 10 minutes. Serve immediately.

Breaded Stuffed Eggplant
(Melitzanobourekakia)

Serves 8-10
Preparation time 1 hour 30 minutes
Frying time 20 minutes

2 lbs long, thin eggplant or
2 lbs zucchini or
1 lb long green peppers
1/2 lb haloumi or kefalograviera cheese, diced
flour for dredging
oil for frying

for the breading
2 eggs, lightly beaten with
2 tablespoons olive oil
1 cup dry bread crumbs

Cut the eggplant or zucchini into very thin slices. Sprinkle them with salt and let stand 1 hour in a colander to drain and soften. Rinse and dry them. If using peppers, preheat the oven to 350°F and roast them for 10 minutes. Remove and cover them with plastic wrap so that their skin peels off more easily. Cut each one into 2-3 long strips. Wrap each slice of eggplant, zucchini, or pepper around a piece of cheese and secure with a toothpick. Dredge the rolls in a plastic bag with a cup or so of flour and shake gently in a colander or sieve to remove excess. Dip the rolls one by one in the beaten egg and then in the bread crumbs. Place them on a platter and refrigerate for 1 hour to let the coating set. Deep fry the rolls, a handful at a time, over medium heat until they are browned on all sides. Serve hot, accompanied by Yogurt Sauce with Garlic and Tomato Salad. Perfect with ouzo.
Alternative: Fry the eggplant and zucchini strips before you wrap them around the cheese pieces. Arrange the rolls in an ovenproof dish along with the pepper and spread a little Tomato Sauce (page 53) on top. Sprinkle with crumbled feta cheese and a dash of oregano. Bake in a preheated oven at 400°F for about 30 minutes or until the cheese is lightly browned.

Stuffed Mushrooms
(Manitaria Yemista)

Serves 4
Preparation time 30 minutes
Broiling time 10 minutes

30 large fresh mushrooms
3 tablespoons lemon juice
1 tablespoon olive oil
1 tablespoon butter
2 tablespoons finely chopped green onions
2 tablespoons grated onion
2 tablespoons white wine
salt and pepper
fresh dill, finely chopped
2 tablespoons heavy cream
1 cup soft grated cheeses (kasseri, Swiss, or other)
grated Parmesan cheese

Trim mushroom stems. Wipe clean with a damp cloth. Blanch the mushrooms in boiling water with lemon

Cheese-Stuffed Peppers
(Piperies Yemistes me Feta)

Serves 4-8
Preparation time 20 minutes
Cooking time 15 minutes

8 long green peppers
2 tablespoons olive oil
2 tablespoons grated onion
2 tablespoons chopped tomato
1 tablespoon ketchup
pepper
oregano
cayenne
1 tablespoon chopped parsley
1/2 lb feta cheese, crumbled
olive oil

Wash the peppers, remove the stems and seeds, taking care not to split the skin. Blanch the peppers in boiling water for about 5 minutes. Drain and allow to cool. In a saucepan heat the oil and lightly sauté the onion. Add the tomato, ketchup, and seasonings. Stir for a few minutes and remove from the heat. Allow to cool slightly. Mix in the feta and parsley. Fill the peppers with the mixture, place on a broiler tray, and brush them with olive oil. Broil for about 15 minutes, turning frequently. Serve hot or cold. Delicious with ouzo, these peppers can also be fried.

Easy Cheese Appetizer
(Tiromezes)

Serves 4
Preparation time 5 minutes
Cooking time 6-8 minutes

4 large, thick slices feta cheese
1 large tomato
1 long green chili pepper
a little olive oil
freshly ground pepper
oregano

Place the cheese slices next to each other in a shallow oven-proof dish. Cut the tomato into thin slices and cover the cheese with them. Cut the pepper into thin rounds and scatter them on top of the tomatoes. Sprinkle a little oil, pepper, and oregano over the dish and bake in a microwave oven or broil under a grill until the tomato and peppers have browned slightly. Serve immediately. Delicious with ouzo.

Drunkard's Delight
(Bekri Mezes)

Serves 4
Preparation time 10 minutes
Cooking time 20 minutes

1 1/2 lbs pork filet or boneless pork, in bite-sized cubes
1 tablespoon prepared mustard
1/4 cup olive oil
2 garlic cloves, finely chopped
1 cup dry red wine
1 cup tomato juice
20 drops Tabasco
pinch of oregano
5-6 allspice berries
salt and pepper

Put the meat in a bowl, add the mustard, and toss together until all the pieces are streaked with mustard. Heat the oil in a heavy-bottomed frying pan and lightly sauté the garlic. Brown the meat and add the wine in three doses, stirring gently over high heat, until the wine has evaporated. When the wine is finished, add the tomato juice, tabasco, and other seasonings and simmer for about 15 minutes or until the sauce thickens. Serve immediately. A wonderful accompaniment to wine.

Fried Liver with Wine Sauce
(Sikotakia Tiganita ke Krassata)

Serves 4
Preparation time 10 minutes
Frying time 20 minutes

> *2 lbs calves' liver, sliced*
> *salt, pepper, and oregano*
> *flour for dredging*
> *olive oil*
>
> *the wine sauce*
> *1 tablespoon lemon juice*
> *1/3 cup dry red wine*
> *1 teaspoon dry mustard*
> *chopped red pepper and parsley to garnish*

Season the liver slices with a mixture of salt, pepper, and oregano. Allow to stand for about 5 minutes, dip liver in flour and shake off the excess. In a heavy-bottomed 12-inch skillet, heat the oil and fry the liver slices, for about 4 minutes per side. When browned, transfer them from the skillet to a platter with a spatula. Sprinkle 2-3 tablespoons of the frying oil on top and serve with lemon wedges.
Alternate: To serve the dish with wine sauce, strain the oil into a clean frying pan and reheat. Place the fried liver in the pan. Shake the lemon juice, wine, and mustard in a jar to blend, pour the liquid over the meat, and boil rapidly for 2-3 minutes, until the wine evaporates. Transfer to a serving platter. Garnish with red pepper and parsley. Serve at once.

Eggs with Anchovies
(Avga me Antsouyes)

Serves 6
Preparation time 20 minutes

> *6 hard-boiled eggs*
> *3-4 tablespoons mayonnaise*
> *1/4 teaspoon freshly ground pepper*
> *2 mashed anchovies or*
> *1 teaspoon anchovy paste*
> *1 tablespoon lemon juice*
> *finely chopped parsley*

Peel the eggs and slice them in half lengthwise. Remove the yolks and mash them in a bowl. Add the remaining ingredients and mix well to blend. Put the mixture in a pastry bag and fill the egg whites. Sprinkle with chopped parsley and garnish with a rolled anchovy.

LAMB ENTRAIL ROLLS, PAGE 25 • FRIED LIVER WITH WINE SAUCE, PAGE 24

Lamb Entrail Rolls (Tziyerosarmades)

Serves 4-5
Preparation time 1 hour
Baking time 20 minutes

1 spring lamb organ meats (heart, liver,
spleen, sweetbreads)
3 tablespoons olive oil or margarine
8 fresh spring onions, chopped fine
salt and pepper
1/2 cup finely chopped dill
1/2 cup finely chopped parsley
3 tablespoons short grain-rice
1/4 cup tomato juice (optional) or water
2-3 large lamb cauls

Drop the meats in boiling water, boil for 5-8 minutes, and drain. When they are cool, chop coarsely. Heat the oil in a saucepan, add the onion and one cup water. Cover and simmer, until most of the water evaporates. Stir in the chopped meats, and simmer, covered, over medium heat, until the juices are reduced. Remove from the heat, add dill, parsley, rice, and the tomato juice or water. Mix well, and set aside. Wash the caul in cold water and a little vinegar. Rinse well under running water and drain. On a cutting board stretch out the caul and cut in 5-inch circles or squares. Place 1 tablespoon of the filling on each piece of caul and wrap tightly into rolls. Arrange the rolls in a baking pan, folded side down, close together. (At this point you may freeze them.) Or bake in a preheated oven at 400°F for about 20 minutes, until golden brown. Remove with a slotted spoon or a spatula and transfer to a platter. Garnish with tender lettuce leaves and carrots. Serve at once with tossed green salad.
Note: If caul is not available, veal or pig sausage casings may be used.

Baked or Fried Lamb Innards
(Entosthia Psita i Tiganita)

Serves 4-5
Preparation time 10 minutes
Cooking time 30 minutes

1 spring lamb organ meats (heart, liver,
kidneys and sweetbreads)
1/2 cup olive oil
1/3 cup lemon juice
salt, pepper, and oregano to taste
1/2 cup white wine (optional) or water

Wash the meats well and cut into small pieces.
For Baking: Put the meats in a bowl, pour the oil, lemon juice, and wine on top. Add the seasonings and mix well. Cover and let stand at room temperature for 3

hours or in the refrigerator for 6 hours, turning the pieces in the marinade from time to time. Transfer to a baking pan, preheat the oven to 350°F, and bake for about 30 minutes, turning over once, until the meats are tender and all juices have evaporated.
For Frying: Place the marinated meats in a frying pan, cover, and simmer, over medium heat, until all the liquid has evaporated. Take the lid off and fry, stirring, to brown all over. Garnish with lemon wedges and serve at once.

Meatballs Wrapped in Caul (Seftalies)

Serves 6
Preparation time 30 minutes
Cooking time 15-20 minutes

2 lbs ground pork
1 cup grated onion
1 garlic clove, crushed (optional)
1/2 cup finely chopped parsley
2 tablespoons fine bread crumbs
1 teaspoon oregano
1/2 teaspoon ground allspice or dried mint
salt and freshly ground pepper
2 large lamb cauls
2 long green peppers, cut in pieces

In a mixing bowl, combine the meat with the onion, garlic, parsley, eggs, bread crumbs, and seasonings. Knead for 2 minutes. The mixture should be moist. Add a little water if necessary. Wash the cauls in cold water and a little vinegar. Stretch out on a board and cut into 4-inch squares. Shape the meat into slightly smaller sausages and wrap each sausage in a piece of caul. (At this stage you can refrigerate overnight or freeze them, if you like.) Using metal or wooden skewers, thread three rolls on each with a piece of green pepper between them. Grill over charcoal, turning frequently, for about 15-20 minutes, until the meat is done to your taste. Serve hot with Tzatziki (page 29).
Note: If cauls are not available, use sausage casings.

Egg Salad (Avga Salata)

Serves 4
Preparation time 15 minutes

6 hard-boiled eggs
Oil-Lemon Dressing (page 47)
freshly ground pepper

Peel the eggs, cut in quarters, and arrange them on a serving plate. Pour oil-lemon dressing over them and, just before serving, sprinkle with freshly ground pepper.

Skewered Lamb Innards
(Kokoretsi)

Serves 6-8
Preparation time 1 hour and 30 minutes
Grilling time 1 hour and 30 minutes

> *organ meats (4 kidneys, 2 livers, 2 hearts, 4 lungs, and*
> *sweetbreads) from 2 spring lambs*
> *3 large lamb cauls*
> *3 lbs intestines from a spring lamb*
> *salt, pepper, and oregano*
> *3 long skewers*
> *olive oil*

> *the garnish*
> *lettuce leaves, radishes, spring onions*

Cut the meat into medium-sized pieces. Remove any tubes and membranes and wash well. Sprinkle with salt, pepper, and oregano, and set aside. Wash the intestines according to the recipe for Greek Easter Soup (page 48). Take care not to cut the intestines while washing. Thread the organ meats onto three long skewers, and wrap the cauls around them. Tie them securely to the skewer by winding the intestines up and around, so that they cover the whole skewer. Brush with olive oil and refrigerate until ready to cook. (You may also wrap and freeze them. When ready to grill, let them thaw out first.) Brush with olive oil and grill, preferably over charcoal, basting and turning frequently until browned all over and no pink juices flow when pricked with a fork. Place in a platter on a bed of lettuce and garnish with radishes and spring onions. Kokoretsi is an Easter specialty. It is roasted on a spit along with the spring lamb and served as a meze before the lamb is ready.
Alternate: Bake kokoretsi in a preheated oven at 400°F for about 1 hour and then brown both sides under the broiler.

Stuffed Spleen (Splina Yemisti)

Serves 4-6
Preparation time 40 minutes
Cooking time 40 minutes

1 cup olive oil
2 calf spleens or
6 lamb spleens
1 1/2 cup grated onion
2 spring onions, chopped
1 cup finely chopped parsley
6 garlic cloves, finely chopped
1 lb ripe tomatoes, puréed
1/2 cup white wine
salt and pepper

Heat half the oil in a saucepan. Add the onions and garlic and sauté, until transparent. Add the tomato purée, parsley, and seasonings, and simmer until the sauce is very thick. In the meantime, wash the spleens well and drain. Pushing a sharp knife into the spleen through the top end, make a horizontal cut in each spleen. Shape a pocket and be careful not to puncture the sides and the outer membrane. Strain the sauce through a fine sieve, reserving the liquid. Fill the spleens with the sauce that has remained in the strainer and sew them shut. Heat the rest of the oil in a large skillet and sauté the stuffed spleens on both sides. Pour the reserved liquid and the wine over the spleens, add salt and pepper to taste. Cover and simmer for 30-40 minutes, adding a little water if necessary, until the spleens are tender and very little liquid is left. Exceptional with retsina.

Stuffed Intestines

(Splinandero)

Serves 6
Preparation time 2 hours
Cooking time 30 minutes

6 large thick pieces lamb or
goat intestines or sausage casings
vinegar
6 lamb spleens
3 lamb hearts
2 lamb livers
salt, pepper, and oregano to taste
some olive oil

Wash the intestines thoroughly inside and out. Sprinkle them with vinegar and set aside for about 15 minutes. Rinse well. Wash the spleens and cut them with kitchen scissors, into 6 long circular strips. Wash the hearts and cut them in half. Cut each half into a long circular strip. Following the same procedure, cut the liver first horizontally, into 3 slices and then into 2 circular strips. You should have 6 strips of each organ meat. Sprinkle them with salt, pepper, and oregano. Take one intestine, tie one of its two ends in a knot. Take three strips together (one of each organ meat) and holding them next to the knot, push them into the intestine. While pushing them, slip the rest of the intestine on top, reversing it and totally enclosing the strips of meat. Tie the loose end well. Thread the 6 stuffed intestines onto skewers, forming a braid from left to the right. Mix some oil with a little oregano and brush the skewered meats. Grill, preferably over charcoal, basting regularly with the oil-oregano sauce, and turning frequently until the meat is done to your taste. Serve hot accompanied by ouzo or retsina.

Baked Innard Bundles

(Gardoumbakia)

Serves 4-6
Preparation time 1 hour
Cooking time 1 hour

1 spring lamb organ meats (heart, liver, lungs, spleen)
a few lamb kidneys
salt, pepper, and oregano to taste
2 lbs lamb intestines
1/2 cup olive oil
8 fresh green onions, chopped
3 tablespoons finely chopped dill
2 tablespoons lemon juice
1 cup water, meat broth, or tomato juice

Wash the meats very well and cut them into long narrow strips. Sprinkle with salt, pepper, and oregano. Wash the intestines, turning them inside out according to the recipe for Easter Soup (page 48). Blanch them to make them easier to work with. Wrap a length of intestine around 3 strips of meat at a time to form small bundles. Heat the oil in a saucepan, and lightly sauté the onions. Add the dill, lemon juice, and the water, tomato juice, or broth. Arrange the bundles in a shallow baking dish and pour the sauce over them. Preheat the oven to 350⁰F and bake for about 1 hour. Serve hot. *Alternate a:* Wrap the meat strips in pieces of caul before binding them with the intestine. Brush them with oil and grill over charcoal. While grilling, baste frequently with oil.
b: Prepare the dish using intestines only. Braid them loosely in long thick braids and place in a baking pan, just large enough to hold them. Moisten with olive oil and sprinkle with salt, pepper, and oregano. Preheat the oven to 350⁰F and bake for about 40 minutes, turning several times to brown evenly. When done, cut the braids into smaller pieces, adjust the seasonings, and sprinkle with a little lemon juice just before serving. Serve at once.

sieve and add to the sautéed onion. Add the sugar and seasonings to taste. Remove from the heat and stir in the parsley. Pour the sauce over the beans, and arrange the sliced tomatoes on top. Sprinkle with salt, pepper, oregano, and a little olive oil. Preheat the oven to 350°F and bake for about 1 hour until all the liquid has evaporated and the beans are tender. Add water if necessary while baking. Excellent hot or at room temperature.

Rice-Stuffed Vine Leaves
(Dolmadakia Yialantzi)

Serves 8
Preparation time 2 hours
Cooking time 30 minutes

1 lb fresh or preserved vine leaves
2 cups finely chopped spring onion
2 cups grated onions
1lb short-grain rice
1 cup chopped parsley
1 cup chopped fresh dill
2 cups olive oil
salt and pepper
1/4 cup pine nuts (optional)
1/4 cup currants (optional)
1/3 cup lemon juice

Wash the vine leaves and trim the stems. Blanch them, a few at a time, in boiling water. Drain and let cool. Blanch preserved vine leaves the same way. Put the onions in a strainer, sprinkle with a little salt, and rub with your fingertips. Rinse with a little water. Squeeze out the water with your hands. Mix the rice with the onions, herbs, half the oil, seasonings to taste, pine nuts, and currants (if used). Lay the vine leaves one by one on a flat surface, shiny side down. Put about one tablespoon of the rice mixture in the lower center of a leaf, fold the sides over, and roll it up into a neat parcel. Continue stuffing the vine leaves in this way, until all the filling is used. Save any torn or damaged leaves and line the base of a large heavy-bottomed pan or flameproof casserole with them. Arrange the stuffed vine leaves on top, packing them in, seam side down, in more than one layer if necessary. (At this stage the dish can be frozen. Defrost before cooking.) Pour in the remaining oil, 2½ cups boiling water, and lemon juice. Put a heavy plate upside down on top of the stuffed vine leaves, to keep them from opening. Cover the pan and bring to a boil. Reduce the heat and simmer until all the water is absorbed, about 35-40 minutes. Let them cool in the pan and place a thick piece of paper towel or a clean dish cloth between the pan and the lid to absorb the steam. Transfer to a platter. Serve with Tzatziki or plain yogurt. Equally good served at room temperature the next day.

Baked Lima or Giant Beans
(Yigantes Plaki)

Serves 4-6
Preparation time 1 hour
Cooking time 1 hour

1 lb dried lima beans or butter beans
2 celery stalks
1 carrot, scraped
a few peppercorns
1 cup grated onion
5-6 garlic cloves, slivered
1 cup olive oil
salt and pepper
1 teaspoon sugar
1/2 cup finely chopped parsley
2 lbs fresh or canned tomatoes
2 large tomatoes, sliced

Soak the beans in plenty of water for at least 24 hours. Drain, put in a large pan, and cover with cold water. Add the celery, carrot, and peppercorns, and bring to a boil. Reduce the heat and simmer until tender. Drain and put in a baking pan or a flameproof dish. Heat the olive oil in a saucepan, add onion and garlic, and sauté until transparent. Force the ripe tomatoes through a

Eggplant Salad
(Melitzanosalata)

Serves 4-6
Preparation time 30 minutes

2 lbs eggplant
1/4 teaspoon salt
2-3 garlic cloves, crushed
1/2 cup olive oil
1/4 cup vinegar
2 tablespoons chopped parsley (optional)
1 green pepper, seeded and chopped
1 tomato, seeded and chopped

Wash, wipe, and tightly wrap each eggplant in aluminum foil. Put them on or under a grill and turn frequently to cook on all sides, for about 20 minutes, until soft. Alternatively, grill the eggplant unwrapped, over charcoal, turning them frequently. The flavor is better if they are charcoal grilled. Pass each eggplant quickly under running water to cool slightly and peel them immediately, while they are still hot. Do not let eggplants cool unpeeled; their flesh will turn black. Chop the peeled flesh and season with the salt and garlic. Put in a bowl and, beating continuously with an electric beater on medium speed, add the oil in drops at first, then in a trickle, until all of it is used. Add vinegar a little at a time, still beating continuously. Fold in the parsley, transfer to a serving dish, cover, and chill. Garnish the eggplant salad with chopped green pepper and tomato. Sprinkle with a little salt and olive oil. Serve with crackers or fresh bread.
Alternate: Replace the garlic with 2 tablespoons grated or minced onion and use lemon juice instead of vinegar. Purée the grilled eggplant with salt and garlic, and fold in 1 cup mayonnaise. Add a few drops of Tabasco, if desired.

Fried Lima or Giant Beans
(Yigantes Tiganiti)

Serves 6-8
Preparation time 24 hours
Cooking time 1-2 hours

1/2 lb large dried lima or giant beans
salt, peppercorns
flour for dredging
olive oil for frying
1 cup mayonnaise combined with
2 tablespoons ketchup

Soak the beans in water overnight. Drain and put them in a pot with water to cover, salt, and a few peppercorns. Bring to a boil, reduce the heat, and simmer, covered, until tender. Drain well. Put a handful of beans at a time in a bag with flour and shake to coat thoroughly. Remove to a colander and shake off excess flour. Repeat until all the beans are coated with flour. Heat olive oil in a frying pan. Add the beans, a dozen or so at a time, and fry lightly. Remove from the pan with a slotted spoon and drain on paper towels. Put the beans on a platter, allow to cool slightly, and spread with the mayonnaise and ketchup mixture. Serve the dish warm or cold.

Cucumber and Yogurt Dip
(Tzatziki)

Serves 6
Preparation time 10 minutes

3 cups plain yogurt
1 cucumber, peeled, chopped, and squeezed to remove
excess liquid
3-4 garlic cloves, crushed
1/4 teaspoon salt
3-4 teaspoons olive oil
3 tablespoons finely chopped fresh dill
radish roses to garnish (optional)

Line a sieve with muslin or double-thick absorbent paper towels and place the yogurt in it. Allow to drain for about 2 hours. Transfer the drained yogurt to a bowl. Stir in the cucumber, garlic, and oil. Season to taste, cover, and chill. To serve, sprinkle with chopped dill, and garnish with radish roses, if desired.

Salads
(Salates)

Greek village salad has in recent years become as well known abroad as moussaka. Every summer legions of tourists make a full meal of what began as a farmer's snack. It may be merely a bowl of sun-ripened tomatoes, crunchy cucumbers, sweet onions, black olives, and capers, topped with a slab of feta cheese, sprinkled with a little oregano and drenched in fruity olive oil spiked with a splash of wine vinegar, but it can be a revelation. All that's required are garden-fresh ingredients of the very best quality. Don't even dream of making it with watery winter tomatoes or a seed oil.

Greeks classify both raw and cooked vegetables as salads, side dishes to accompany a main course of some kind. So this chapter includes recipes for some of the most typical, such as boiled cauliflower, greens, and beets. Whether raw or cooked, these salads share simple, straight-forward dressings – olive oil mixed with either lemon juice or vinegar, depending on personal preference and the type of vegetable. The secret to both is a minimum of handling and a good source: a farmers' market or your own garden.

General Instructions

Raw Salads: Almost all vegetables or greens can be eaten raw, which, of course, is healthier and more nutritious. Marvelous salads can be created not only with traditional vegetables such as tomatoes, cucumbers, lettuce, and cabbage, but also with spinach, escarole, cauliflower, and mushrooms. Mixed salads are also tasty and attractive to look at. Finely chopping vegetables makes them easier to digest. Chop them with a sharp knife and handle them with care so that they retain their juiciness and crispness.

Dressings, whether a vinaigrette or oil and lemon or other, should be mixed with the salad a few minutes before serving. The only exceptions to this rule are marinated salads, where the ingredients absorb the flavors of the marinade. A good salad has to be tossed well, whence the saying in Greek: "Ta'kanes salata" (You messed everything up). Toss green salads lightly to prevent bruising and wilting.

Cooked Salads: When making cooked salads, do not overcook the vegetables. Too much cooking destroys their flavor and color as well as their nutritious value. Some cooks prefer to steam vegetables in a wire or perforated basket over boiling water in a tightly covered pot. Most vegetables can be steamed, but it is preferable to boil delicate green vegetables. They should be plunged into lots of rapidly boiling water and removed the moment they are ready, tender but still crisp. Do not add salt to the water; it makes them lose their color.

Most of these vegetables can be boiled ahead of time and dressed with oil and lemon juice just before serving. Greeks prefer their boiled salads cold or at room temperature. But if you prefer your salad warm, you can reheat the vegetable in the microwave or plunge it for a few seconds into rapidly boiling water just before serving. Keep precooked vegetables well wrapped in the refrigerator. Pour the dressing on a few minutes before serving, unless otherwise specified.

31

Tomato and Onion Salad
(Domatosalata)

Serves 4
Preparation time 15 minutes

4 tomatoes, each cut into 8 wedges
1 medium onion, sliced
oregano to taste (optional)
Oil-Vinegar Dressing (page 47)

Mix the tomato wedges and the onion together in a bowl. Just before serving, mix in oil-vinegar dressing, adjust the seasonings, and serve with fried fish or seafood.

Greek Village Salad (Horiatiki Salata)

Serves 4-6
Preparation time 15 minutes

2 large tomatoes
1 cucumber
1 medium onion, sliced
10 black olives
1/4 lb feta cheese, cubed (optional)
2 hard-boiled eggs, sliced (optional)
Oil-Vinegar Dressing (page 47)
parsley or watercress

Wash, dry, and cut the tomatoes in 8 wedges each. Peel and slice the cucumber. Mix the tomato and cucumber in a large bowl with the rest of the ingredients. Toss well with the oil-vinegar dressing and serve, garnished with chopped parsley or watercress sprigs.

Hummous (Revithosalata)

Serves 4
Preparation time 12 hours
Cooking time 1-2 hours

1/2 lb dried chick-peas
1/2 teaspoon baking soda
1/4 cup tahini (sesame seed paste)
1-2 tablespoons lemon juice
1/4 cup olive oil
1-2 garlic cloves, crushed
salt and pepper
finely chopped parsley

Cover the chick-peas with water mixed with the baking soda, stir well, and soak overnight. Rinse the chick-peas. Place them in a saucepan with cold water to cover and boil until very soft. Drain and mash through a potato ricer or in a blender. Mix the mashed chick-peas with the garlic and seasonings. In a separate bowl beat the tahini with 1-2 tablespoons water. Stir the tahini, a little at a time, into the chick-pea mixture. Then slowly add the olive oil and lemon juice alternately, beating well with your fork after each addition, until you have a smooth paste. Cover and chill for several hours before serving. Serve sprinkled with finely chopped parsley.
Note : The salad also can be prepared in a food processor or blender. Tahini is an emulsion made from ground sesame seeds, and can be found at Greek and Middle Eastern groceries, health food stores, or in the foreign food sections of supermarkets.

Marinated Vegetables
(Lachanika Marinata)

Serves 6
Preparation time 24 hours

1/2 lb fresh green beans
1 large carrot, sliced in rounds
1 large red pepper, cut in julienne strips
1 cup cauliflower florets
2 small zucchini, sliced
6 large mushrooms, sliced

for the marinade
1/2 cup olive oil
1/4 cup vinegar
2 garlic cloves, mashed
3 tablespoons finely chopped parsley, dill, or mint

Prepare the marinade by beating all the ingredients together and set aside. Trim and string the beans and cut into halves or thirds. Parboil them together with the carrot in salted water and drain. Add them to a bowl with the remaining vegetables. Pour in the marinade and toss well. Cover with plastic wrap and refrigerate for at least 24 hours before serving.

Cucumber and Tomato Salad
(Angourodomata)

Serves 4
Preparation time 15 minutes

2 large tomatoes
1 cucumber
2 tablespoons finely chopped parsley
1 small green pepper (optional)
1 small garlic clove, crushed (optional)
Oil-Vinegar Dressing (page 47)

Wash the tomatoes and cut into 8 wedges. Peel and slice the cucumber. Mix the vegetables in a bowl with the chopped parsley, green pepper, and the garlic, if using. Toss lightly with oil-vinegar dressing just before serving.

Asparagus Salad (Sparangia Vrasta)

Serves 4
Preparation time 15 minutes
Cooking time 5-6 minutes

1 lb tender young asparagus
Oil-Lemon Dressing (page 47)

Break ends off asparagus, where they snap, and wash well. In a large shallow pan put enough water to cover the asparagus and bring to a boil. Add the asparagus, cover, and bring back to the boil. Remove the cover and boil gently for 5-8 minutes. Immediately lift out the asparagus, drain, and arrange on a platter. Pour the oil-lemon dressing over them, season to taste, and serve hot. Asparagus may be cooked in advance. When cool, wrap and refrigerate. Add the dressing just before serving.

Salad-Filled Tomato Cups
(Salata se Koupes Domatas)

Serves 4
Preparation time 45 minutes

4 large tomatoes
1 small cucumber, chopped
2 long green peppers, sliced in thin rings
4 spring onions, chopped
6 small radishes, thinly sliced
2 tablespoons chopped parsley

the dressing
2 tablespoons vinegar
5 tablespoons olive oil
salt to taste
1/2 teaspoon dry mustard

Wash and dry the tomatoes. Cut out the top of the core with a sharp knife. Place the tomatoes stem end down on a chopping block and slice each tomato into 8 wedges, taking care not to sever them all the way. The wedges will form a cup. Carefully nudge the wedges outward. Scoop some of the flesh from each wedge. Arrange on a platter and set aside. Chop the tomato flesh and mix it in a bowl with the cucumber, peppers, onions, radishes, and parsley. Fill the tomato cups with the mixture. Put the oil, vinegar, seasonings, and mustard in a jar with a tight lid and shake well. Just before serving pour the dressing over the filled tomatoes.

Arugula Salad with Tomatoes
(Roka me Domata)

Serves 4
Preparation time 10 minutes

2 bunches arugula (1 lb)
2 medium tomatoes, coarsely chopped
3 oz goat cheese
1/4 cup olive oil, beaten with
3 tablespoons best wine- or balsamic vinegar
salt, freshly ground pepper, and pine nuts (optional)

Trim, wash, and drain the arugula, taking care not to bruise it. Cut it with scissors into large pieces. Arrange them on a platter and place the chopped tomato in the center. Grate the cheese over the salad and sprinkle with the vinaigrette. Season with salt, pepper, and a handful of pine nuts. Serve immediately.

Beet Salad
(Pantzaria Vrasta Salata)

Serves 6
Preparation time 30 minutes
Cooking time 1 hour

2 lbs beets, greens included

the dressing
1/2 cup olive oil
1/4 cup vinegar
2 garlic cloves, crushed
salt to taste

Trim the beets, discarding stems and any withered leaves. Wash the roots and greens well. Place the roots in a large kettle with enough cold water to cover them and boil for about 20 minutes. Add the greens and continue boiling, until roots and greens are soft and tender. Do not overcook. Drain and separate the roots from the greens. Peel the skin from the roots and slice. Arrange the beet roots and greens attractively on a platter. Combine the dressing ingredients in a jar with a tight lid, shake well, and pour the dressing over the beets. Cover and let stand in the refrigerator for several hours before serving. Serve accompanied by Garlic Sauce made with bread or yogurt.

Boiled Zucchini
(Kolokithakia Vrasta Salata)

Serves 4-6
Preparation time 10 minutes
Cooking time 15-20 minutes

2 lbs small zucchini
Oil-Lemon Dressing (page 47)

Lop both ends off zucchini and wash. Drop into a large pan half filled with boiling water and boil 15-20 minutes, until tender. Do not overcook. Drain in a colander and pour a little cold water over them, to set the fresh green color and the texture. Drain well. Cover and refrigerate until ready to use. Before serving, drop them in boiling water for a minute and drain. Arrange on a platter whole or cut in rounds. Pour on the oil-lemon dressing just before serving.

BOILED ZUCCHINI, PAGE 34 • BEET SALAD, PAGE 34 • GREEN BEAN SALAD, PAGE 35

Curly Endive and
Wild Asparagus Salad
(Antidia kai Agriosparanga Salata)

Serves 6
Preparation time 15 minutes

1 lb tender curly endive
1/2 lb wild asparagus
1/2 cup olive oil
1 garlic clove, finely chopped
2 slices bread, cubed
1/4 cup coarsely chopped walnuts
2 tablespoons vinegar
salt and freshly ground pepper

Wash and trim the endive and asparagus. Discard any tough leaves and reserve the tender leaves at the heart of the endive, along with the tips and tender shoots of the asparagus. Cut these in 2-inch pieces and leave to drain in a colander. Meanwhile, brown the garlic in half of the oil, remove with a slotted spoon, and discard. Fry the bread cubes in the same oil and drain on paper towels. Arrange the vegetables on a platter with the croutons and walnuts in the middle. Shake the rest of the oil, vinegar, salt, and pepper together in a jar with a tight lid and dress the salad.

a minute and drain. Arrange on a platter, garnished with red pepper or pimiento. Put the dressing ingredients in a small jar with a tight lid, shake well, and pour the dressing over the beans just before serving. Equally good hot or cold.

Green Bean Salad
(Fasolakia Vrasta Salata)

Serves 4
Preparation time 20 minutes
Cooking time 15 minutes

1 lb green beans, fresh or frozen
2 large preserved pimientos or
2 large red peppers, parboiled and peeled

the dressing
1/4 cup olive oil
2 tablespoons vinegar
1/8 tablespoon sugar
1 small garlic clove, crushed
salt and pepper to taste

Trim the tips of the beans and string them. Wash in cold water and drain. Snap beans in half, slice lengthwise or leave whole. Drop them into a pot half filled with rapidly boiling water, and boil, uncovered, for 10-15 minutes. Drain and dip them quickly into a bowl of cold water, to set the fresh green color and the texture. Drain well and pat dry with paper towels. If not used immediately, refrigerate, covered, until ready to serve. Before serving, drop them into boiling water for

Cauliflower Salad
(Kounoupidi Vrasto Salata)

Serves 6
Preparation time 30 minutes
Cooking time 15 minutes

1 small cauliflower
1 tablespoon lemon juice
2 carrots, peeled and halved lengthwise
1 green bell pepper, sliced into rings
tender lettuce leaves
Oil-Lemon Dressing (page 47)

Cut off and discard cauliflower stalks and leaves. Wash well. Steam cauliflower in a little water with the lemon juice for 10-15 minutes, or until the cauliflower is done to your taste. Drain and separate the cauliflower into florets. Place in a bowl. Cover and refrigerate until ready to use. Before serving, pour oil-lemon dressing over the florets and marinate for 15 minutes, tossing them gently from time to time. Transfer the cauliflower to the center of a platter with a slotted spoon. Garnish with the carrot sticks, pepper rings, and lettuce leaves. Pour the dressing over all the vegetables and serve.

Constantinople-Style Salad
(Salata Politiki)

Serves 4
Preparation time 30 minutes

> 3 cups shredded cabbage
> 3 tablespoons chopped green pepper
> 3 tablespoons chopped red pepper
> 1/4 cup chopped celery
> 1 large carrot, grated
> Oil-Vinegar Dressing (page 47)

Combine the vegetables in a large bowl. Mix well, cover, and keep refrigerated for several hours, until used. Just before serving pour the dressing over the salad and toss well.
Alternate: Add 1 cup strained yogurt to the tossed salad and mix well. Refrigerate for a few hours before serving.

Carrot Salad
(Karotosalata)

Serves 4
Preparation time 15 minutes

> 4 large carrots
> Oil-Lemon Dressing (page 47)
> 1 teaspoon capers
> 4 radishes

Peel, wash, and grate the carrots. Place in a salad bowl and, just before serving, pour the dressing over the carrots and toss lightly. Garnish with the capers and the radishes.

Broccoli Salad
(Brokola Vrasta)

Serves 4
Preparation time 30 minutes
Cooking time 5-7 minutes

> 2 lbs broccoli
> Oil-Lemon Dressing (page 47)

Separate the broccoli florets from the lower stalks. Trim off any leaves, except for the very small and ten-der ones. Peel the stalks and cut in chunks. Wash the florets under running water. Half fill a large kettle with fresh water and bring to a rapid boil. Drop in the broccoli, cover, and bring back to the boil rapidly. Remove the cover, lower heat back to medium, and boil gently for 5-6 minutes. Do not overcook. Transfer the broccoli with a slotted spoon to a colander. Place in a bowl, season lightly, and pour on the dressing.
Note: To save time blanch broccoli in advance of when you want to use it. When cool, wrap and refrigerate. Plunge into boiling water just before serving.

Boiled Greens
(Horta Vrasta Salata)

Serves 4
Preparation time 15-20 minutes

> 2 lbs mixed greens (endives,
> dandelions, and spinach)
> Oil-Lemon Dressing (page 47)

Trim the greens, discarding the roots, thick stalks, and withered leaves. Wash in lots of cold water. Half fill a large kettle with water and bring to a rapid boil. Drop in the greens, cover, and bring back to the boil rapidly. Remove the cover and boil gently for 15-20 minutes, until the greens are tender. Strain well and place in a serving bowl. When ready to serve, pour oil-lemon dressing over the greens and toss lightly.

Cabbage Salad
(Lachanosalata)

Serves 4-6
Preparation time 15 minutes

> 3 cups shredded cabbage
> Oil-Vinegar or
> Oil-Lemon Dressing (page 47)

Place shredded cabbage in a salad bowl. Just before serving, pour on oil-vinegar or oil-lemon dressing and toss well. Shredded red cabbage may be used along with the green cabbage. Place red cabbage in the center of a salad platter and arrange the green cabbage around it. Attractive arrangement for a party.

BOILED GREENS, PAGE 36 • CONSTANTINOPLE-STYLE SALAD, PAGE 36 • CUCUMBER AND TOMATO SALAD, PAGE 33 • CARROT SALAD, PAGE 36

DRIED BEAN SALAD, PAGE 39 • LETTUCE AND DILL SALAD, PAGE 39

Dried Bean Salad
(Fasolia Salata)

Serves 4
Preparation time 30 minutes
Cooking time 1 hour

1/2 lb small dried white beans
1 small red or Bermuda onion, sliced
3 spring onions, chopped
1 small green pepper, chopped
2 tablespoons finely chopped parsley
3 tablespoons chopped dill pickle
black olives, pitted
Oil-Vinegar Dressing (page 47)

Wash and soak the beans in water overnight. Drain, place in a pan, cover with cold water, and boil for 30 minutes. Drain and return the beans to the pan. Pour enough cold water over the beans to cover and boil until tender. Drain and let cool. Place in a bowl and mix with the rest of the ingredients. Toss gently with the oil-vinegar dressing. Allow the salad to stand for a few hours before serving. Garnish with olives and serve accompanied by canned tuna fish, if desired.

Lettuce and Dill Salad
(Maroulosalata me Anitho)

Serves 4
Preparation time 20 minutes

1 lb romaine or other type lettuce
5 spring onions, chopped
2 tablespoons finely chopped fresh dill
Oil-Vinegar or Oil-Lemon Dressing (page 47)

Wash the lettuce carefully and drain well. With a sharp knife cut the lettuce leaves crosswise into strips 1/3 inch wide. Try not to bruise the lettuce. Combine with the rest of ingredients in a bowl. The salad may be kept covered in the refrigerator for several hours. Just before serving toss lightly with oil-vinegar or oil-lemon dressing. Garnish with radishes, a few whole lettuce leaves, and dill.

Potato Salad
(Patatosalata)

Serves 4
Preparation time 15 minutes
Cooking time 30 minutes

4 large potatoes
1 small onion, sliced in rings
3 spring onions, chopped
2 tablespoons chopped parsley, mint, or dill
1 carrot, cooked and sliced

the dressing
1/3 cup olive oil
1/4 cup lemon juice or vinegar
1/2 teaspoon dry mustard (optional)
salt and pepper to taste

Scrub and rinse the potatoes. Boil them in their skins until tender. Drain, peel, and cut into thick slices. Place in a salad bowl and add the rest of the ingredients. Put the dressing ingredients in a jar with a tight lid and shake vigorously. Toss the potatoes with the dressing, cover, and let the salad absorb the flavors for a few hours before serving.

Cretan Rusk Salad
(Dakos)

Serves 4-6
Preparation time 15 minutes

2-3 Cretan barley rusks
3-4 large firm, ripe tomatoes
10 oz Cretan sour mizythra or crumbled feta
salt, freshly ground pepper, oregano
1/2 cup olive oil

Moisten all surfaces of the rusks with running water and place on a small platter. Peel and deseed the tomatoes and chop into small pieces. Spoon the tomatoes and the cheese on top of the rusks. Sprinkle with salt, pepper, and oregano, to taste. Dribble olive oil over the tops.

Variation: Blend the olive oil with 1 minced garlic clove and 1 tablespoon balsamic vinegar. This simple Cretan dish is often served with *tsikoudia*, a grappa-like local spirit.

Soups and Sauces
(Soupes ke Saltses)

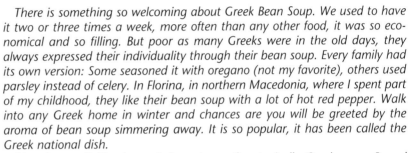

There is something so welcoming about Greek Bean Soup. We used to have it two or three times a week, more often than any other food, it was so economical and so filling. But poor as many Greeks were in the old days, they always expressed their individuality through their bean soup. Every family had its own version: Some seasoned it with oregano (not my favorite), others used parsley instead of celery. In Florina, in northern Macedonia, where I spent part of my childhood, they like their bean soup with a lot of hot red pepper. Walk into any Greek home in winter and chances are you will be greeted by the aroma of bean soup simmering away. It is so popular, it has been called the Greek national dish.

"Avgolemono" (Egg-Lemon) Soup is another typically Greek soup. Bound with egg, flavored with lemon, almost any broth can be turned into avgolemono, but it is especially good when made from chicken, lamb, ground meat, or fish. "Mayeritsa" (Easter Soup) is thick and soothing, intended to reinvigorate people who have been fasting during Lent. Its chief ingredient is lamb innards, and foreigners who are not used to eating such things are often somewhat hesitant about trying Mayeritsa. Nevertheless, when I manage to coax them into tasting it at my home, they always admit that it's delicious. "Kakavia," a traditional Fishermen's Soup made with a mixed catch of small fish, is also renowned in Greece for its rich flavor.

Soups made out of lentils, beans, chick-peas, chicken, fish, meat, and all sorts of other combinations can be a healthy, satisfying meal, whether served as a light lunch or as a first course for dinner. Steaming hot soup is a staple in many Greek home in winter, while fish soup and even lentils are favorites in summer, too. In Greece, soup is never eaten cold. The thickening agents used in Greek soups are mashed boiled potatoes in the case of fish and meat soups, rice in chicken and meat soups, or chopped or puréed vegetables in vegetable soups.

Sauces – the ultimate finishing touch to practically every dish – embellish and enliven poached and roasted meats, fish, pasta, salads, and vegetables. Besides being succulent, sauces can also be a feast for the eyes, stimulating the appetite with an attractive display of beauty and color. As if by magic, they transform the dish they grace into a visual banquet. Sauces are considered by some to be the magic tricks of cookery. But, just as illusion depends on a magician's dexterity, so the creation of a sauce depend more on the cook's expertise and experience than on superficial devices. The different kinds of sauces make up the cook's palette, which he or she will use discerningly to give each dish that personal touch.

Greek cuisine, like all other cuisines, has its own characteristic sauces. Among the most representative are Egg-Lemon Sauce, Olive Oil-Lemon Sauce, Olive Oil-Vinegar Sauce (Vinaigrette), Tomato Sauce, Yogurt Sauce, Red-Pepper Sauce, and Garlic Sauce. The thickening agents used for sauces are mainly flour, cornstarch, puréed vegetables and, less often, egg yolks or fresh cream.

DRIED BEAN SOUP, PAGE 42

2 small whole onions
5 whole garlic cloves
2 tablespoons vinegar
1/2 teaspoon sugar
salt and pepper to taste
2 bay leaves (optional)
1/2 teaspoon oregano (optional)

Wash and pick over the lentils. Put all the ingredients except the lentils in a large pot with 2 pints of water. Add all the ingredients except for the lentils. Bring to a boil. Add the lentils, cover, and simmer for about 30 minutes to 1 hour, depending on the quality of lentils, until they are tender and the soup is thick. Add some more water if necessary. Some people remove and discard the onions, garlic, and bay leaves before serving. Others find the first two delicious. Serve hot or cold, sprinkled with freshly ground pepper and accompanied by olives, pickled vegetables, or smoked trout.

Bean Soup
(Fasolada)

Serves 6
Preparation time 1-2 hours
Cooking time 1 hour

1 lb dried, small white beans
1 cup olive oil
1 large onion, finely chopped
1 lb fresh or canned tomatoes, peeled
1 tablespoon tomato paste
2 medium carrots, sliced
1 stalk celery, sliced
1 small green pepper, chopped
1 small hot pepper (optional)
salt and pepper

Wash the beans well, put them in a large pan, add enough cold water to cover, and bring to a boil. Reduce the heat and simmer, covered, until soft. Do not overcook. Drain in a colander. In a heavy pot heat the oil and sauté the onions until transparent. Purée the tomatoes in a food mill or blender and dilute the tomato paste in the purée. Add to the pot. Then add the carrots, celery, green pepper, drained beans, and seasonings. Pour in about 2 pints hot water and bring to a boil. Reduce the heat to low and simmer, covered, for 1-2 hours, or until the beans are cooked and the soup has thickened. Add more water as needed. Cooking time will depend on the freshness of the beans. Serve hot, accompanied by olives, pickled vegetables, and smoked fish.

Lentil Soup
(Faki Soupa)

Serves 6
Preparation time 15 minutes
Cooking time 30 minutes to 1 hour

1 lb lentils
1½ cups puréed fresh or canned tomatoes
1 cup oil

Meatball Soup with Egg-Lemon Sauce
(Yiouvarlakia Avgolemono)

Serves 4-6
Preparation time 30 minutes
Cooking time 30 minutes

1 lb ground meat
1 small onion, finely chopped
1/4 cup short-grain rice
3 tablespoons finely chopped parsley
2 tablespoons finely chopped dill or mint
2 tablespoons olive oil
salt and pepper
flour for dredging
5 cups beef stock or water
1/4 cup butter or olive oil
2 eggs
1/4 cup lemon juice

In a large bowl, combine the ground meat, chopped onion, rice, herbs, olive oil, and seasonings. Knead for a few minutes, shape the mixture into small balls, and roll them in flour. Set aside. Pour the beef stock or water into a large saucepan, add the butter, and bring to a boil. Gently lower in the meat balls, a handful at a time. Do not add them all at once or the temperature will drop. Reduce the heat and simmer, covered, for about 30 minutes, until the meat is cooked. Meanwhile, lightly beat the eggs in a bowl. Add the lemon juice a little at a time, beating continuously. Then, still beating, ladle in some of the hot broth from the saucepan. Stirring vigorously, add the warm egg-lemon mixture to the soup. Immediately remove the saucepan from the heat and serve.

Chick-Pea Soup
(Revithosoupa or Revithada)

Serves 6
Preparation time 12 hours
Cooking time 1 hour and 30 minutes

1 lb chick-peas
1 tablespoon salt
2/3 cup olive oil
2 small whole onions
salt and pepper to taste

Wash chick-peas and let soak overnight in warm water with the baking soda. Next day drain and rinse thoroughly. Place the peas in a large pot with cold water to cover. Slowly bring to a boil, removing the scum that rises to the top. Pour in the oil, add the onions, and simmer, covered, until the chick-peas are tender and the liquid has reduced to the desired consistency. Add a little hot water, if necessary. Remove the onions with a slotted spoon and discard or, if desired, mash one of them and return it to the soup, stirring well. Add salt to taste and cook for about 15 more minutes. Serve hot, sprinkled with freshly ground pepper and accompanied by olives and a selection of pickles.

Meat Stock (Zomos Kreatos)

Yields 8 cups broth
Preparation time 15 minutes
Cooking time 7 hours

2 lbs veal or beef knuckle bones
2 lbs meaty trimmings (neck, shank, or rib tips)
2 medium onions
4 large carrots
1 small celery root or 4 celery stalks
1 leek
4-5 parsley sprigs
1 whole garlic
2 cloves stuck in one of the onions
1 bay leaf
salt

Put the meat and bones in a large, heavy, nonstick pot. Add cold water (about 6 pints) to cover. Slowly bring to a boil over medium heat and skim off the scum that rises to the top. Keep skimming, occasionally adding more cold water to delay the boiling, until no more scum appears. Add all the other ingredients and continue to skim, until the boiling point is reached. Reduce the heat and simmer slowly for 5-7 hours, occasionally skimming any scum that may appear and spooning off any excess fat from the broth surface. Strain through a very fine sieve and discard the solids. Allow stock to cool and skim fat from the surface, or refrigerate the stock and remove the solidified fat when cold. Divide the jellied stock in 1- or 2-cup portions and place in heavy plastic bags or containers. Stock will keep up to 1 week in the refrigerator and 6 months in the freezer.

Chicken Stock (Zomos Kotas)

Follow the recipe for meat stock. Substitute chicken wings, backs, and necks for the meat bones and meat. For a variation, combine chicken and meat bones. After cutting up meat or chicken for cooking, the uncooked meat bones or chicken necks, wings, and backs can be saved and frozen. When enough have accumulated, cook up the stock and freeze.

Fish Stock (Fish Fumet)
(Zomos Psariou)

Yields 4 cups
Preparation time 30 minutes
Cooking time 45-50 minutes

1 lb sole or other flat fish bones (excluding fins and tails)
1 onion, sliced
1 celery stalk, chopped
1 carrot, thinly sliced
1 leek, sliced
1 garlic clove (optional)
1 cup white wine
1 tablespoon lemon juice
6 parsley springs
1 bay leaf
6 peppercorns

Wash fish bones well. Put in a pot with the onion, celery, carrot, leek, garlic, and seasonings. Add 2 pints of water and bring slowly to a boil. Remove the scum that rises to the surface. Keep skimming until the broth reaches the boiling point. Boil for a few minutes, add the remaining ingredients, cover, and simmer for about 40 minutes. Strain the stock through a fine sieve and allow to cool. Stock will keep up to 3 days in the refrigerator and 2 months in the freezer. To freeze, put in refrigerator to cool and gel. Divide into 4 parts, put in plastic bags or containers, and freeze. Each bag should have about 1 cup of fish stock ready for future use.

Chicken Soup with Egg-Lemon Sauce
(Kotosoupa Avgolemono)

Serves 4-5
Preparation time 15 minutes
Cooking time 1 hour

1 whole chicken
1/4 cup butter or margarine
1 small carrot (optional)
1 small onion (optional)
salt and pepper
1/2 cup short-grain rice
1 egg
1/3 cup lemon juice
freshly ground pepper

Take the skin off the chicken and discard. Wash the chicken inside and out under cold running water. Place in a large pot. Pour in enough water to cover the chicken. Slowly bring to a boil, skimming off the scum from the top. Add the butter, carrot, onion, salt, and pepper. Cover and simmer until the chicken is tender. Remove the chicken and vegetables and strain the broth into a clean pot. Bring the strained broth back to the boil, add rice, and stir well. Cover, reduce the heat, and simmer for about 20 minutes until the rice is tender. Lightly beat the egg in a bowl and add the lemon juice, a little at a time, beating continuously. Gradually pour 5-6 tablespoons of the hot soup into the egg mixture, beating all the time. Pour the egg-lemon sauce back into the soup, stirring constantly. Remove from the heat immediately to prevent curdling. Sprinkle the soup with freshly ground pepper and serve hot, accompanied by the chicken which may be either hot or cold. Serve the chicken with mayonnaise or tartar sauce.

Fish Soup with Egg-Lemon Sauce
(Psarosoupa Avgolemono)

Serves 6
Preparation time 30 minutes
Cooking time 50 minutes

1/2 cup olive oil
1 small whole onion, peeled
1 small whole carrot, scrubbed
2 celery stalks
10 peppercorns
salt
3 lbs fish (cod, sea bass, or grouper)
1/3 cup short-grain rice or
2 large potatoes, cubed
1-2 eggs
1/3 cup lemon juice
freshly ground pepper

Pour 6 cups of water and the oil in a large pan. Add the vegetables, peppercorns, and salt. Bring to a boil and simmer, covered, for 15 minutes. In the meantime clean and wash the fish. In the fish is large, cut in half and place it in the boiling broth. Bring back to the boil, reduce the heat and simmer for 15-20 minutes, or until the fish is done. Do not overcook. Remove the fish with a perforated spoon onto a platter. Strain the stock through a fine sieve into a clean pot. Bring to a boil, stir in the rice or potatoes, and simmer, covered, for about 20 minutes. If potatoes are used, when soft, remove them with a slotted spoon, mash, and return to the stock, stirring well. Lightly beat the eggs in a bowl, add the lemon juice, a little at a time, beating continuously. Gradually spoon in some of the hot soup, beating all the time. Pour the egg-lemon sauce into the soup, stirring constantly, and remove from the heat immediately to prevent curdling. Serve the soup hot, sprinkled with freshly ground pepper. Serve the fish either plain or covered with mayonnaise and garnished with capers and pickles. A dish of Boiled Greens would complete this menu.

Fish Soup (Psarosoupa)

Serves 6
Preparation time 1 hour
Cooking time 1 hour and 10 minutes

3 lbs fish (cod, grouper, or other soup fish)
6 large carrots
1 celery stalk
1 leek
1 small whole onion
1 large green bell pepper
3 small zucchini
4 large potatoes, quartered
2/3 cup olive oil
15 peppercorns
1/3 cup lemon juice
salt and freshly ground pepper

Trim and wash the vegetables. Place all the vegetables in a large pot, except for the potatoes. Add 2 pints of water together with the olive oil, peppercorns, and salt, and bring to a boil. Reduce the heat and simmer for 30 minutes. In the meantime, clean and wash the fish. Cut it in half, if too large for the pot. With a slotted spoon remove the vegetables, reserving the celery, zucchini, and carrots. Place the fish in the broth, bring to a boil, reduce the heat, and simmer for 10-15 minutes. Try not to overcook the fish. Remove the fish to a platter and strain the broth through a fine sieve into a clean pot. Bring back to the boil, add the potatoes and simmer until done, approximately 20 minutes. Mash one or two potatoes and stir into the broth to thicken it. Coarsely chop the carrots, celery, and zucchini and add them to the broth. When the soup returns to the boil, remove it from the heat, stir in the lemon juice, and sprinkle with freshly ground pepper. Serve hot, accompanied by the fish, either plain or garnished with mayonnaise, capers, and sliced pickles.

Meat Soup (Kreatosoupa)

Serves 6
Preparation time 1 hour
Cooking time 1 hour and 30 minutes

4 lbs beef shoulder or neck
1 large onion, halved and studded with
2 cloves
2 bay leaves
1/4 cup olive oil
1 small celery root, cubed
2 celery stalks, finely chopped
3 medium carrots, thickly sliced
3 medium potatoes, cubed
2 ripe tomatoes, chopped
1 cup tomato juice
salt and freshly ground pepper
1 red chili pepper, finely chopped (optional)
2 tablespoons lemon juice

Place the meat in a large pot with 8 cups of water, the clove-studded onion, and bay leaves and bring to the boil over medium heat. Skim off the foam that rises up, cover, and simmer, until the meat is tender. Remove the meat, drain, and debone. Strain the broth through a sieve into a clean pot and add the oil, vegetables, and tomato juice. Bring to the boil, cover, and simmer until the vegetables are half cooked. Add the meat, salt, and pepper and continue to simmer until the vegetables are tender. Pour in the lemon juice and remove from the heat. Serve in deep bowls, accompanied by croutons.

Garlic-Vinegar Sauce (Skordostubi)

Preparation time 5 minutes

2-3 garlic cloves
1/3 cup vinegar

Mash garlic, add vinegar and blend well.

Trahana Soup (Trahanosoupa)

Serves 6-8
Preparation time 5 minutes
Cooking time 20 minutes

8 cups Meat Stock (page 44) or
water
3 tablespoons butter
1 cup Sweet or
Sour Trahana (page 57)
feta cheese, crumbled
salt and freshly ground pepper
minced parsley

Pour the broth or water into a saucepan, and bring to a boil. Add the butter and trahana and cook for about 10 minutes, until slightly tender. Add crumbled feta to taste, and continue cooking for 10 minutes more, or until the trahana is soft and the broth has reduced to a thick consistency. Remove from the heat and check the seasoning, adding a little salt, if needed. Serve the soup sprinkled with parsley and freshly ground pepper.

Tripe Soup (Patsas)

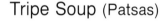

Serves 6
Preparation time 1 hour
Cooking time 2 hours

4 lbs lamb or
veal tripe and feet
1 medium onion, sliced
salt and pepper
Garlic-Vinegar Sauce or
Egg-Lemon Sauce (page 52)

Scrape and trim the tripe and feet well, wash several times. Place them in a large pot, pour in enough water to cover and bring to a boil. Strain and rinse well. Cut the tripe into small pieces, place in a large kettle, add the feet and enough water to cover. Add the onion, salt, and pepper, and cook slowly, until the tripe is tender and the meat falls off the bone. Strain the stock into another pot and reserve. Remove the meat from the bones. Discard the bones and the onion. Put the tripe and meat in the broth and cook for a while longer. Pour the garlic-vinegar sauce over the soup, and stir well. Or use egg-lemon sauce instead of the garlic-vinegar sauce. Both are delicious. Serve the soup hot.

Oil-Lemon Dressing (Ladolemono)

Preparation time 5 minutes

2 parts olive oil
1 part lemon juice
salt and pepper to taste
finely chopped parsley (optional)

Shake all the ingredients vigorously in a tightly-sealed jar until well blended. Use on boiled greens, vegetable salads, grilled fish, or seafood.

Oil-Vinegar Dressing (Ladoxido)

Preparation time 5 minutes

2 parts olive oil
1 part vinegar
salt and pepper to taste
oregano (optional)
mustard powder (optional)

Shake all the ingredients vigorously in a tightly-sealed jar until well blended. Use on any fresh vegetable salad. Add oregano or mustard powder, according to taste.

Greek Easter Soup (Mayeritsa)

Serves 12
Preparation time 1 hour and 30 minutes
Cooking time 40 minutes

1 lb lamb intestines or tripe
a little vinegar
1 lb lamb's heart
1¹/₂ lbs lamb's liver
6 pints lamb broth or water
1/2 cup butter or margarine
2 cups chopped spring onions
1/2 cup finely chopped dill
1/2 cup finely chopped parsley
1/2 cup short-grain rice
salt and pepper
2 eggs
1/2 cup lemon juice

Wash the intestines thoroughly under running water. To make this easier, cut them into pieces about 1 to 3 feet long. Turn them inside out, with the aid of a knitting nee-dle. Wash thoroughly. Put them in a bowl with a little vinegar, for a few minutes, rinse, and drain. If tripe is used, wash it the same way. Rinse the heart and liver. Place organ meats in a saucepan, cover with water, and bring to a boil. Boil for 10 minutes, drain, and let the meats cool. Cut them in tiny pieces, discarding all tubes and membranes. Pour the broth or water into a large pot, add the butter, and bring to a boil. Add the chopped meats, spring onions, and herbs. Simmer, covered, for 20 minutes. Add the rice, season to taste; recover the pot and simmer until the rice is cooked. Meanwhile, beat the eggs lightly in a bowl. Add the lemon juice a little at a time, beating continuously. Still beating, ladle in some of the hot broth from the pot. Stirring vigorously, pour the warm egg-lemon mixture back into the soup. Immediately remove the pot from the heat and serve.

Note: Usually this soup is made with the innards from the spring lamb to be roasted on Easter Sunday. The soup can be enriched by frying the blanched organ meats and chopped onions in butter, before adding them to the broth or water. You can make a simpler version of this soup with the organ meats alone, omitting the intestine.

Greek Fishermen's Soup
(Kakavia)

Serves 5-6
Preparation time 1 hour

3-4 lbs mixed small fish
1 lb onions, thinly sliced
1 lb tomatoes, peeled and thinly sliced
2-3 tablespoons parsley, finely chopped
salt and freshly ground pepper
1/2 cup olive oil

Clean and wash the fish. Place in a large pot and pour in enough water to cover the fish. Bring to a boil and simmer for about 20 minutes. Strain the stock and save. Bone the fish and add it to the strained stock with the remaining ingredients. Cook slowly for 2-3 hours, until you have a thick soup. Serve the soup hot, sprinkled with freshly ground pepper.
Note: This is how Greek fishermen prepare "kakavia" when they are away from home. After cleaning the fish, they place sliced onions on the bottom of a large pot. They place the tomatoes on top, sprinkled with the parsley, and cover them with the fish. They add salt, pepper, and olive oil and enough water to cover the fish. The soup simmers, covered, for 3-4 hours, until the vegetables and fish bones have disintegrated. Fishermen do not bother to strain the soup before eating it.

Vegetable Soup (Hortosoupa)

Serves 5-6
Preparation time 45 minutes
Cooking time 45 minutes

1/4 cup butter or olive oil
1 small onion, finely chopped
1 small leek, chopped
4 cups Meat or Chicken Stock (page 44)
1 cup tomato purée
2 carrots, cubed
1 celery stalk, chopped
1 green bell pepper, chopped
1 zucchini, cubed
2 medium potatoes, cubed
1/2 cup fresh peas, shelled
salt and pepper
1/2 cup orzo, little stars, or any small pasta
2-3 tablespoons lemon juice

Heat the butter in a large saucepan and gently sauté the onion and leek until soft but not brown. Add all ingredients, except for the pasta and lemon juice, and simmer covered for about 35 minutes, until the vegetables are half done. Add the pasta and continue cooking for 10 minutes more, until the pasta is soft. Remove from the heat, stir in the lemon juice, and serve the soup hot with toasted garlic bread.

Vegetable Broth
(Court Bouillon) (Zomos Lachanikon)

Yields 8-10 cups
Preparation time 15 minutes

1 large onion, sliced
1 large carrot, thinly sliced
1 leek, sliced
5 parsley sprigs
1 celery stalk, sliced
1 garlic clove (optional)
1 bay leaf (optional)
1 small green pepper (optional)
6 cups water
salt
1 1/2 cups white wine (optional)
10 peppercorns

Place all the above ingredients, except for the wine and the peppercorns, in a large pot; cover and simmer for 10-20 minutes. Add the wine and the peppercorns and simmer for 15 minutes longer. Strain into a bowl or another pot. Broth may be used immediately or stored in the refrigerator for 3-4 days.

Tomato Soup (Domatosoupa)

Serves 5-6
Preparation time 10 minutes
Cooking time 35 minutes

2 cups tomato juice
4 cups Meat or Chicken Stock (page 44)
salt and pepper
1 cup angel hair pasta, stars, or alphabets
1/4 cup butter
finely chopped parsley

Put the tomato juice and the stock in a pot. Add the seasoning, cover, and simmer for about 20 minutes. Add the pasta and cook slowly for about 15 minutes more, until the pasta is soft. Remove from the heat, and stir in the butter until well blended. Sprinkle the soup with freshly ground pepper and parsley and serve with toasted garlic bread.

Garlic Sauce with Potato, Island Style
(Aliada, Skordalia Nissiotiki)

Yields 2 cups
Preparation time 40 minutes

2 oz day-old bread, crusts removed
4-5 garlic cloves
3/4 teaspoon salt
2 small potatoes, cooked (10 oz)
1/4 cup white vinegar
1/2 cup olive oil

Soak the bread in 1/3 cup of water and squeeze out excess with your hands. Mash garlic and salt with a mortar and pestle. Add the potatoes, one by one, and pound well. Mix in the vinegar and bread, a little at a time. Add the oil in a slow trickle, pounding constantly, until all of it is absorbed and the mixture is thick and smooth. Serve the sauce with fried fish or fried or boiled vegetables.
Note: This recipe can also be prepared in a food processor. Add all the ingredients together and blend well for a few seconds.

Garlic Sauce with Bread
(Skordalia me Psomi)

Yields about 2 cups
Preparation time 30 minutes

6 slices day-old bread, crusts removed (8 oz)
5-6 garlic cloves, finely chopped
1/2 cup olive oil
1/4 cup vinegar or to taste
1/4 tablespoon salt
1/4 teaspoon white pepper

Soak the bread in water. Squeeze out as much water as you can with your hands. Mash the garlic and a small amount of salt in a large mortar with pestle. Add a few drops of oil, pounding continuously. Add a handful of crumbled bread and a little oil alternately, until the bread and oil are used up. Stir in the vinegar a little at a time. If the sauce curdles, reblend it by slowly adding a little warm water. Cover and chill. Serve with fried fish and fried or boiled vegetables.
Note: This sauce can also be prepared in a food processor. Add all the ingredients together and blend well for a few seconds.

Walnut-Garlic Sauce
(Skordalia me Karidia)

Yields 2 cups
Preparation time 15 minutes

4 garlic cloves
1/2 teaspoon salt
1$\frac{1}{2}$ cups finely ground walnuts
2 bread slices (crusts removed) (2 oz)
1/2 cup olive oil
1/4 cup vinegar

Crush garlic and salt with mortar and pestle until well blended. Add nuts gradually and blend well. Soak bread in water and squeeze it dry. Add bread, a little at a time, to the mixture and blend well. Slowly add the olive oil and the vinegar, alternately, beating well after each addition, until it resembles a smooth paste. If the mixture looks curdled, blend it slowly, adding a little warm water. Cover and chill. Serve with fried fish and vegetables.
Note: The recipe can also be prepared in a food processor or blender. Add all the ingredients together and blend well for a few seconds.

Red Pepper Sauce
(Saltsa me Kokkines Piperies)

Yields 4 cups
Preparation time 20 minutes
Cooking time 40-60 minutes

2 lbs long or round red peppers
4 lbs ripe tomatoes, peeled,
seeded, and chopped
1 cup olive oil
8 garlic cloves, chopped
2 tablespoons finely chopped parsley
salt and pepper
1/4 teaspoon cayenne

Roast the peppers, remove the stems, seeds, and skin. Chop coarsely. Put the tomatoes, oil, garlic, and parsley in a large saucepan. Simmer, stirring occasionally, until all the liquid evaporates. Add the peppers, seasonings, and cayenne, to taste. Boil slowly, stirring occasionally, until the sauce is reduced to a thick pulp. Remove from the heat and allow to cool. This sauce will keep in the refrigerator for several months. Serve the sauce as a dip, with sausages, hamburgers, and meatballs. It may also be used in Strapatsada (page 16), or Chicken in Red Pepper Sauce (page 145).

Batter for Frying
(Hilos yia Tiganisma)

Yields about 2 cups
Preparation time 1 hour

1 cup all-purpose flour
salt and pepper
1 tablespoon olive oil
1 cup beer or club soda (carbonated water)
2 egg whites

Sift flour with salt and pepper in a bowl. Make a well in the flour, add the oil and beer. Gradually stir them into the flour until you have a smooth, thin batter. Do not overmix. If a thicker batter is desired, add a little more flour. Allow to stand for about 1 hour. When ready to use, beat the egg whites until foamy, and fold them slowly into the batter.

Yogurt-Garlic Sauce
(Yiaourti Skordato)

Yields 1 cup
Preparation time 5 minutes

1 cup drained yogurt
2 garlic cloves, crushed
2 tablespoons olive oil
1/8 teaspoon salt
1/8 teaspoon white pepper

Mix all the ingredients in a bowl. Cover and chill. A delicious dip for raw or fried vegetables or seafood. Top with chopped parsley or dill.
Alternate: Replace yogurt with sour cream, or use half sour cream and half yogurt.

YOGURT-GARLIC SAUCE, PAGE 51 • EGG-LEMON CREAM SAUCE, PAGE 52 • POTATO-GARLIC SAUCE, PAGE 50 • RED PEPPER SAUCE, PAGE 50 • WALNUT-GARLIC SAUCE, PAGE 50

Marinade 1 (Marinata 1)

Preparation time 5 minutes

1 part olive oil
1 part wine or vinegar
garlic cloves
salt
peppercorns
bay leaves
other spices that strike your fancy

Mix all the ingredients well. May be used to marinate meat, game, fish, or vegetables.

Marinade 2 (Marinata 2)

Preparation time 40 minutes

1/2 cup olive oil
2 small carrots, sliced
2 small onions, whole
1 small celery stalk, chopped
2 garlic cloves, finely chopped
3 parsley sprigs
10 peppercorns
2 spring onions, chopped
2 bay leaves
2 cloves
3 cups white wine
1/2 cup vinegar

Heat the oil in a saucepan, add the vegetables and seasonings, and sauté, stirring, for about 10 minutes, until they are lightly browned. Pour in the wine and vinegar. Cover and simmer the marinade for 30 minutes. Allow to cool. Remove the onions, bay leaves, and cloves. This marinade is used primarily for game and other meats.

Egg-Lemon Sauce
(Saltsa Avgolemono)

Preparation time 5 minutes

1-2 eggs
juice from 1 or 2 lemons
broth or pan juices

Lightly beat the eggs in a bowl and add the lemon juice, a little at a time, beating continuously. Gradually add some of the broth to the egg-lemon mixture, beating all the time. Add the egg-lemon sauce to your soup or dish, stirring well or shaking the pot gently to distribute the sauce.

Egg-Lemon Cream Sauce
(Avgolemono Crema)

Yields 2 cups
Preparation time 10 minutes
Cooking time 10 minutes

3 egg yolks
1/4 cup lemon juice
1/4 cup water
1 tablespoon cornstarch
1 cup broth from the prepared dish
1/2 cup heavy cream (optional)

Beat the egg yolks with the lemon juice in a small, heavy-bottomed saucepan. In a small bowl blend the water with the cornstarch to make a smooth paste, and pour it into the egg and lemon mixture. Gradually add 1 cup broth from the recipe being prepared. Stir the mixture constantly over a low heat, until it is thick and creamy. To prevent curdling, do not let the sauce start to boil. Remove from the heat and stir in the cream. Pour the sauce over the prepared dish.

Béchamel (White Sauce)
(Aspri Saltsa)

Yields 1 cup
Preparation time 5 minutes
Cooking time 15 minutes

light sauce
1 cup milk
1 tablespoon all-purpose flour
1 tablespoon butter
salt and white pepper
nutmeg

thick sauce
1 cup milk
2 tablespoons all-purpose flour
2 tablespoons butter
salt and white pepper
nutmeg

Heat the milk in a small pot. Melt the butter in a heavy-bottomed saucepan. Stir in the flour and sauté 2-3 minutes. Off the heat, pour in the hot milk, stirring constantly with a wire whisk to blend the mixture. Return to the heat and simmer until thick. To remove any lumps, strain the sauce through a sieve placed over another pan. Return the strained sauce to the heat and simmer for about 15 minutes, whisking constantly to prevent the sauce from sticking to the bottom of the pan. Remove from the heat. Season with salt, white pepper, and a pinch of nutmeg.

Tomato Sauce
(Saltsa Domatas)

Yields 2 cups
Preparation time 15 minutes
Cooking time 20 minutes

1/3 cup olive oil
1 small onion, finely chopped
1-2 garlic cloves, finely chopped (optional)
2 lbs fresh or canned tomatoes, puréed
salt and pepper
1 tablespoon vinegar
1 teaspoon sugar
2 tablespoons finely chopped parsley

In a heavy-bottomed saucepan, gently sauté the onion and garlic in the oil, until soft but not brown. Add the tomatoes and the remaining ingredients, and simmer, covered, for 20 minutes, or until the sauce is thick. Adjust the seasonings and serve the sauce with pasta, rice, fried potatoes, or fried eggplants.
Note: Two tablespoons of ketchup may be used instead of the vinegar and sugar.

Meat Sauce
(Saltsa me Kima)

Yields 3 cups
Preparation time 15 minutes
Cooking time 1 hour

1/3 cup olive oil or butter
1 medium onion, grated
2 garlic cloves, finely chopped
1 lb ground beef or veal
salt and pepper
3 lbs fresh or canned tomatoes, puréed
2 tablespoons ketchup
3 tablespoons finely chopped parsley

Heat the oil in a saucepan. Gently sauté the onion and garlic in the hot oil until soft and brown. Add the ground meat and sauté for about 15 minutes. Add all the remaining ingredients and simmer, covered, for about 1 hour, or until the sauce is thick. The sauce may be served over pasta or rice and is also used in making Moussaka or Pastitsio.

Pies and Pasta (Pites)

The pie or pita is to Greek cooking what the pizza is to Italian. We usually make them with paper-thin phyllo dough and there is almost no limit to what they can be stuffed with. Perhaps the most common savory filling is cheese – feta, myzithra or kasseri – but white cheese, especially, is often combined with a vegetable, such as zucchini, mixed greens, spinach, leek, or eggplant. We also have pies containing chicken, meat, and even seafood, seasoned with onions, fresh herbs, spices, milk, or cream. Then there are the sweet pies, made with pumpkin, fruits, sweetened cheese, or custard. And they all come in an extraordinary variety of shapes, ranging from small triangles to a whole baking pan, baked or fried. The possibilities are endless. Pies are the most flexible of Greek specialties. You can turn them into main dishes, light meals, snacks, desserts. Easily portable, they fit nicely into a lunch box or picnic hamper. They can be eaten hot or cold, plain or drenched in syrup. Use your imagination and experiment once you have mastered the art of using phyllo.

In this chapter you will also find recipes for a Balkan rustic pasta called trahana, used in soups instead of rice, and homemade noodles. My mother used to make trahana and noodles every year, and in my mind's eye I can still see the linen cloth on our balconies spread with knobs of this pasta drying in the sun. Moreover, all our neighbors' balconies looked exactly the same. It was trahana that saved us during the German occupation; in those dark days we had little else to eat. I have given traditional recipes for trahana, using whole sheep's milk, but since even in Greece this is no longer available unless you live close to a sheep farm, you can substitute cow's milk.

General Instructions

If you do not have the experience or the time to roll out homemade phyllo dough, you can use store-bought packaged phyllo sheets with excellent results. It is stocked in most supermarkets under the name strudel leaves, if not phyllo. However, bear in mind that ready-made phyllo does not absorb as much melted butter or oil as homemade. There are a couple of things you should know before working with phyllo. First, always keep the sheets covered with a damp cloth while you're preparing the pie; they dry out and become brittle extremely quickly. And second, to counteract the paper-like texture of ready-made phyllo, either sprinkle the pie with soda water AFTER baking it for 15 minutes, OR make a light batter of water, oil, and 2 to 3 tablespoons of flour and spread it over the pie BEFORE baking. Otherwise, sprinkle the surface with a little water, to prevent it from curling.

Before baking, always score large pies into serving portions to let the steam escape. Bake in a medium to hot oven so that the pie bakes quickly, without drying out the filling. If the pie is frozen, thaw it before baking or the top and bottom will burn and the filling will remain uncooked. Greek pies should not be very thick, so the pan you use should be large, the size of the oven. Cut up the vegetables and prepare the filling just before you are ready to bake. The vegetables tend to lose their juices, making the filling thin and watery and the pastry soggy. To keep the phyllo crunchy until the last bite, leave the cooked pie uncovered. Any leftovers may be stored covered in the refrigerator. Reheat it in the oven, before serving, and the phyllo will be crisp again.

SPINACH AND CHEESE TARTS, PAGE 66 • LAMB'S LIVER PHYLLO ROLLS, PAGE 18 • SPINACH AND CHEESE PIE, PAGE 67

Home-made Puff Pastry
(Sfoliata Spitiki)

Yields about 1 lb
Preparation time 2 hours

1/2 lb all-purpose flour
1/2 lb cold butter or margarine
1/2 cup water

Sift the flour and salt into a bowl. Using two knives, or a pastry blender, cut the butter into the flour, until coarse crumbs are formed. Add enough water to hold the pastry together and work the dough with your fingers until it comes cleanly away from the sides of the bowl. Shape into a ball and wrap in cellophane wrap. Refrigerate for 45 minutes or place in the freezer for half that time. Place the dough on a cool, floured surface and flatten with a rolling pin. Roll the pastry into a rectangle 3 times wider than it is long. Fold the short sides so that they meet in the middle. Then fold the pastry in half where they meet to make four layers. Give the dough a quarter turn. Roll out the dough again, into a rectangle, as you did the first time. Repeat process. Wrap in cellophane and refrigerate for 30 minutes. Repeat the process one more time or more, if desired, always allowing the dough to rest for 30-minute intervals in the refrigerator. The dough will keep in the refrigerator for 2 or 3 days and up to 6 months in the freezer.

Home-made Phyllo Dough
(Zimi yia Phyllo)

Yields about 1 lb
Preparation time 30 minutes

1 lb all-purpose flour
2 tablespoons oil
1 tablespoon vinegar
2 teaspoons salt
2 teaspoons baking powder (optional)
1 cup lukewarm water

Sift the flour into a medium bowl. Make a well in the center. Pour the oil, vinegar, baking powder, salt, and water into the well. Using your hands, gradually draw the flour into the center. Knead until you have a soft, elastic dough. Add more water, if necessary. Divide the dough into small balls, according to the number of phyllo sheets you desire and according to the size of your pan. Place them in a floured pan, next to each other, covered with a damp cloth. Let the dough rest for an hour or two. Flatten each ball with a rolling pin, on a floured board, and roll until very thin. To get the dough extra thin, roll each phyllo sheet around the rolling pin, pressing lightly and rolling backwards and forwards, until it is about 1/8 inch thick or thinner. To prevent the dough from sticking, sprinkle a little flour on the surface of the sheet frequently. For an easier way of making phyllo, flatten the dough balls into small circles and place 3 together, one on top of the other, brushing each generously with oil or melted butter. Roll them out, all together, into a large round sheet. You also can use 5 small circles to make one large, thick sheet. When you place a filling between 2 of these phyllo sheets you have the "vlachiki pita" found in Greek villages. During baking, the 5 layers of phyllo separate as the oil or butter spreads between the layers of dough. This makes the dough very flaky and crisp.

Home-made Egg Noodles
(Hilopites)

Yields 4 lbs
Preparation time 3-4 hours
Drying time 5-6 days

1 cup milk
2 tablespoons salt
1/2 lb fine semolina
3 lbs light rye flour
8 eggs, beaten

Mix the milk, salt, and semolina in a large bowl. Allow the mixture to stand for 1 hour. Add the eggs and enough flour to form a smooth, elastic dough, kneading constantly. Cover and allow to rest for 1 hour. Divide the dough into equal pieces and roll out as thin as possible. Place on a cotton tablecloth and allow to dry for a few minutes. Wrap a pastry sheet around the rolling pin and cut lengthwise. Remove the rolling pin. In this way, you can cut the dough into long strips easily. Cut vertically into 1/2 inch strips. Then cut into small squares. (Greek egg noodles are usually not kept long.) Repeat procedure with the remaining pastry sheets. Spread the noodles on the tablecloth and allow to dry in a cool, well-ventilated place for 5-6 days. Put them in a "tourva" (small bag made of thick cotton) and hang them in a cool place or store them in the refrigerator.

Sour Trahanas
(Trahanas Xinos)

Yields 3 lbs
Preparation time 20 hours
Drying time 5 days

4 quarts whole ewe's milk
3/4 cup yogurt
1 tablespoon salt
coarse semolina (about 3 lbs), or
half semolina and half cracked wheat

Place the milk in a ceramic container or enamel bowl. Add yogurt and mix well with a wooden spoon. Place a thick cotton dish towel on top and cover with a thick blanket. Let stand in a warm place for 18 hours. From time to time stir the mixture with a wooden spoon. Add the semolina or semolina-cracked wheat mixture slowly, until it forms a thick dough. Pinch off pieces and continue as for sweet trahanas.

Boiled Sweet Trahanas
(Trahanas Glikos Vrastos)

Yields 3 lbs
Preparation time 2 hours
Drying time 5 days

4 quarts whole ewe's milk
1 tablespoon salt
coarse semolina (about 3 lbs), or
half semolina and half cracked wheat

Boil the milk, stirring constantly to prevent sticking. When the milk comes to a boil, turn off heat or lower it to the minimum, add salt, and very slowly add the semolina-wheat mixture, stirring constantly, with a wooden spoon, until thick. Remove from the heat and cover with a thick cotton towel. Let it cool. Pinch off small pieces and place them on a thick cotton tablecloth. Put them away in a dark, well-ventilated spot, until dry and ready to crumble. Rub the pieces between your hands and pass through a coarse sieve (in Greece there are sieves made especially for trahana). Put the pellets back on the tablecloth, and leave undisturbed in a cool place for 4-5 days, until completely dry. Place in a "tourva" (small bag made of thick cotton) or jar and store in a cool place or in the refrigerator.

Fried Cheese Pies
(Giouzlemedes)

Yields 16 pieces
Preparation time 1 hour
Frying time 30 minutes

8 phyllo sheets
1/2 lb feta cheese, grated
or finely crumbled
melted butter
or margarine

Brush each phyllo sheet with a little melted butter and spread with feta cheese. Tightly roll the sheet lengthwise. Cut the roll in half. Twist each half into a coil and flatten a little with a rolling pin. Repeat until all 8 phyllo sheets are used and you have 16 small pies. Place the coils on an oiled baking sheet and refrigerate for a few hours. (At this point you can also freeze them.) To serve, fry the coils in a nonstick pan with a small amount of oil or butter. Serve hot.
Alternate: Use a mixture of sugar, cinnamon, and finely chopped walnuts, instead of the cheese, and make sweet giouzlemedes.

Zucchini Rolls
(Striftaria me Kolokithakia)

Yields 12-14 pieces
Preparation time 1 hour
Baking time 50 minutes

3 lbs zucchini
1/2 teaspoon salt
1 cup sugar
3/4 cup coarsely chopped walnuts
1½ teaspoon cinnamon
1/8 teaspoon nutmeg
1/4 cup fine bread crumbs
2 eggs (optional)
1/4 cup melted butter
1/3 cup butter
1/2 cup vegetable oil
1 lb packaged phyllo
confectioners' sugar and cinnamon for dusting

Wash and grate the zucchini. Sprinkle with 1/2 teaspoon salt, rub lightly between your hands, and let drain in a colander. You should have 4 cups of grated zucchini. Mix the zucchini in a bowl with the sugar, walnuts, cinnamon, nutmeg, bread crumbs, eggs (if using), and melted butter. Set aside. Heat the 1/3 cup of butter and vegetable oil together. Brush one half of each phyllo sheet with it and fold the other half over the buttered part. Brush the surface. Place 2-3 tablespoons of the filling lengthwise on the phyllo sheet and roll. Then twist the roll into a coil. Repeat the procedure with the remaining phyllo sheets. Arrange the coils on a buttered baking sheet, one next to the other, leaving small spaces between them so the sides will brown. Brush the surface with butter, preheat oven to 350°F, and bake for about 50 minutes, or until golden brown. Serve hot or cold, dusted with confectioners' sugar and cinnamon.

Alternate: To serve rolls soaked in syrup: boil 2 cups sugar with 1½ cups water and 1 tablespoon lemon juice together for 5 minutes. Pour hot syrup over the rolls as soon as you take them out of the oven. Let them soak until all the syrup is absorbed and the rolls are completely cool. Transfer to a platter.

COILED EGGPLANT PIE, PAGE 59 • ZUCCHINI ROLLS, PAGE 58 • PUFF PASTRY APPLE SQUARES, PAGE 59

Onion Pie (Kremmidopita)

Yields 20 pieces
Preparation time 1 hour
Baking time 1 hour

1 lb packaged phyllo
2/3 cup olive oil or melted butter

the filling
2 lbs onions, sliced
4 eggs, lightly beaten with
1/3 cup light cream or evaporated milk
2/3 lb feta cheese, crumbled
1/2 cup grated kefalotiri or Romano cheese

Cook the onions in a little water for 15 minutes, until tender. Strain and mix the remaining ingredients. Line a buttered baking pan with half the phyllo sheets, one on top of the other, brushing each with olive oil. Spread the onion mixture on top and cover with the remaining phyllo sheets, brushing each with olive oil. Score the surface in serving pieces and brush the surface with the remaining olive oil. (At this stage the pie may be wrapped and frozen, if desired. Let it thaw out before baking.) Preheat oven to 350⁰F and bake for approximately 1 hour, or until golden brown. Do not cover any leftovers or they will become soggy.

Coiled Eggplant Pie
(Melitzanopita Strifti)

Yields 20-24 pieces
Preparation time 1 hour
Baking time 50 minutes

1 lb packaged phyllo
1/2 cup butter or margarine
1/2 cup olive oil

the filling
3 lbs eggplant
salt
lemon juice
1/2 cup butter
1 medium onion, grated
2 tablespoons finely chopped parsley, dill, or mint
1/2 lb feta cheese, grated
1/2 cup light cream or evaporated milk
4 eggs, lightly beaten
1 tablespoon fine bread crumbs
salt and pepper

Peel the eggplant and grate coarsely into a colander. Sprinkle with a little salt and lemon juice and allow to stand for 1 hour. Rinse well and drain. Remove excess water with your hands. Heat 1/2 cup butter in a saucepan and sauté the onion until transparent. Add the grated eggplant and sauté until soft. Remove from

the heat and mix in the remaining ingredients. Alternatively the eggplants may be roasted, as in the recipe for Eggplant Salad (page 29). In that case, peel, chop, and combine the eggplant flesh with the sautéed onion and remaining ingredients. Heat 1/2 cup butter with the oil. Brush one half of each phyllo sheet with the butter and oil mixture. Fold the other half over the buttered part and brush the surface. Spread 2-3 tablespoons of filling lengthwise and roll up the phyllo. Twist the roll into a coil in the center of a buttered, round (14-inch) baking pan. Repeat the procedure with the remaining phyllo sheets and twist the rolls around the center coil until you have covered the whole pan. Brush the top with the remaining butter and oil mixture and sprinkle with a little water. Preheat oven to 350⁰F and bake for 40-50 minutes, or until golden brown. Serve hot or cold. Do not cover leftovers or they will become soggy.

Puff Pastry Apple Squares
(Milopites me Sfoliata)

Yields 16 individual pies
Preparation time 1 hour
Baking time 35 minutes

16 ready-made puff pastry squares or
1 recipe Home-made Puff Pastry (page 56)
1 egg yolk, beaten with a little water

the filling
2 lbs tart apples
2 tablespoons lemon juice
1/2 cup raisins
1/2 cup sugar
1/2 teaspoon cinnamon
1/8 teaspoon grated nutmeg
2 tablespoons bread crumbs
3 tablespoons melted butter

Peel and core the apples. Cut into thick slices. Mix with the lemon juice to prevent discoloring. Wash the raisins and pat dry with paper towels. Add to the apples and toss. Sprinkle with sugar, cinnamon, nutmeg, and bread crumbs. Pour in melted butter and mix lightly. Set aside. Roll out the puff pastry sheets, place 2 tablespoons of the apple filling in the center of each, and bring the top corners together over the filling. Moisten with a little water and press with your fingertips to seal. Brush the top of each pie with a little beaten egg yolk. Cut strips of pastry the width and length of your finger and place 2 strips in the form of an X, on top. Brush the surface of each pie with beaten egg yolk, preheat oven to 400⁰F, and bake for 35-40 minutes, or until golden brown. Dust with confectioners' sugar and a little cinnamon and serve.

salt, rub lightly with your hands, and leave to drain in a colander. Mix the zucchini with all the other filling ingredients in a bowl. Set aside. In a small saucepan, melt the butter combined with the olive oil. On a floured pastry board roll out the 12 balls, one by one, into very thin sheets, just before baking. Line the bottom of a buttered baking pan (12x14 inches), with 5 phyllo sheets, one on top of the other, brushing each one with the oil and butter mixture. Spread half the filling mixture over them. Cover with 2 buttered phyllo sheets. Spread them with the rest of the filling. Cover with the remaining phyllo, brushing again with butter. Press edges firmly together and crimp. Score the pie in serving pieces and brush top with remaining oil-margarine mixture. Sprinkle with a little water, preheat oven to 350⁰F, and bake until golden brown, approximately 1 hour.
Alternate: If using ready-made phyllo, stack half of the sheets one on top of the other buttering each one and spread half the filling along the ends of the sort sides. Roll up both sides until they meet in the center. Repeat the procedure with the remaining sheets and filling.

Béchamel Cheese Pie
(Tiropita me Béchamel)

Yields 20-24 pieces
Preparation time 1 hour
Baking time 50 minutes

1 lb packaged phyllo or
1 recipe, Home-made Phyllo Dough (page 56)
1 1/2 lbs feta cheese, crumbled
1 cup light Béchamel (page 52)
4 eggs, lightly beaten
pinch of pepper
pinch of nutmeg
1 tablespoon grated onion
3/4 cup butter or margarine, melted

Prepare the béchamel, remove from the heat, and stir in pepper, nutmeg, and grated onion. Add the eggs and feta cheese. Mix well. Line a buttered baking pan (12x14 inches) with half the phyllo sheets, one on top of the other, brushing each one with melted butter. Spread the cheese mixture on top and cover with the remaining phyllo, brushing again with butter. Score the top sheets into squares and brush with the remaining butter. (At this stage you may freeze the pie. When ready to bake, let it thaw out first.) Sprinkle with 2 or 3 tablespoons water. Preheat oven to 350⁰F and bake for 40-50 minutes, until golden brown. Serve hot.
Note: If you use home-made phyllo dough, you will need 1 1/2 cups butter to brush the sheets because they are more absorbent.

Zucchini Cheese Pie (Kolokithotiropita)

Yields 20-24 pieces
Preparation time 2 hours
Baking time 1 hour

1 recipe Home-made Phyllo Dough (page 56) or
1 lb packaged phyllo
2/3 cup olive oil
2/3 cup butter

the filling
2 lbs zucchini, grated
1 lb feta cheese, crumbled
5-6 eggs
3 tablespoons cream of wheat or semolina
3 tablespoons melted butter
1/2 cup heavy cream or evaporated milk
1/2 teaspoon freshly ground pepper
1/2 teaspoon cinnamon
1/2 teaspoon sugar
1/2 cup finely chopped parsley or dill

Prepare home-made phyllo dough and divide into 12 balls. Cover with a damp towel, and allow to rest for 1 hour. Sprinkle the grated zucchini with 1/2 teaspoon

Puff Pastry Cheese Pies
(Tiropitakia me Sfoliata)

Yields 30-40 pieces
Preparation time 35 minutes
Baking time 35 minutes

1 lb ready-made puff pastry or
1 recipe, Home-made Puff Pastry (page 56)

the filling
3 cups crumbled feta cheese
1 cup grated Swiss cheese
1/4 cup heavy cream
2 tablespoons melted butter
2 eggs
pinch of pepper
pinch of nutmeg (optional)

the topping
1 egg yolk, beaten with a little water
sesame seeds

Roll puff pastry into a sheet about 1/4 inch thick. Cut small circles or squares about 4x4 inches. Combine all the filling ingredients in a bowl and mix well. Place 1 teaspoon of the cheese filling on each square or circle and fold into triangles or half moons. Moisten edges with water and pinch to seal. Prick the tops with the prongs of a fork. Brush tops with egg yolk mixture and sprinkle with sesame seeds. (At this point the pies may be frozen.) Refrigerate for about 10 minutes while you preheat the oven to 400°F. Bake for about 30-35 minutes, or until light brown. Serve hot.

Sweet Pumpkin Pie
(Kolokithopita Glikia)

Yields 20-24 pieces
Preparation time 1 hour and 30 minutes
Baking time 1 hour

1 lb packaged phyllo or
1 recipe, Homemade Phyllo Dough (page 56)
2 lbs pumpkin
2/3 cup sugar
2 tablespoons cream of wheat or semolina
6 eggs, lightly beaten
1/2 cup heavy cream
1½ teaspoon cinnamon
1/4 teaspoon nutmeg
1 cup melted butter or corn oil
the topping
powdered sugar
powdered cinnamon

Prepare the phyllo dough. Divide into 12 small balls,

cover with a damp cloth, and allow to rest for about 1 hour. Peel and deseed squash and cut in pieces. Steam or boil in a little water until tender. Drain and mash. Put in a bowl with the sugar, eggs, cream, and spices, and set aside. On a floured board, roll out the dough into 5- or 6-inch circles. Stack them in 6 groups, 2 in each, buttering each generously as you stack them. Roll out to 6 sheets, 1-inch wider than the pan. Place 3 sheets on the bottom of a buttered baking pan (14 inches in diameter), brushing each generously with the melted butter or oil. Spread the pumpkin mixture on top and cover with the remaining sheets, brushing again generously. Moisten edges, press firmly together, and crimp. Score the pie in serving pieces and brush the surface with remaining butter. Sprinkle a little water over the top. Preheat oven to 350°F and bake for about 1 hour or until golden brown. Serve hot or cold, sprinkled with powdered sugar and cinnamon. Alternatively, brush one half of each phyllo sheet with the melted butter, fold the other half over it and butter the surface. Spread 1/6 of the filling lengthwise and roll up the phyllo. Twist the roll into a coil in the center of a buttered, round (14-inch) baking pan. Repeat with the remaining sheets, twisting the rolls around the center coil. Brush the top with butter, and sprinkle with water. Bake and serve as it is mentioned above.
Note: If using ready-made phyllo, line the bottom of the baking pan with half the sheets and put the other half on top of the filling, brushing each one with butter. Use only 1 cup of butter to brush the phyllo.

buttered baking pan with half the phyllo sheets, one on top of the other, brushing each one with butter. Sprinkle every two phyllo sheets with cheese. Lay the sheets smoothly, one on top of the other, without pressing down on them. With the aid of a sharp, serrated knife, score the bougatsa into serving pieces, again trying not to flatten the phyllo. Brush the surface with the remaining butter. (At this stage the bougatsa may be wrapped and frozen. When ready to bake, let it thaw out first.) Lightly beat the eggs with the milk and cream and pour the liquid over the bougatsa. Allow to stand, for about 1 hour, until egg mixture soaks in. Preheat oven to 350ºF and bake for approximately 1 hour, or until golden brown. Serve hot.

Apple Pie Rolls (Milopita)

Yields 15-20 pieces
Preparation time 1 hour
Baking time 1 hour

1 cup sugar
1/4 cup fine bread crumbs
1¹/₂ teaspoon cinnamon
1/8 teaspoon nutmeg
4 cups coarsely grated tart apples
1 cup coarsely chopped walnuts
1/2 cup raisins (optional)
1 tablespoon lemon juice
1/2 cup melted butter
1/3 cup corn oil
1 lb packaged phyllo
confectioners' sugar
cinnamon

In a small bowl mix the sugar, bread crumbs, cinnamon, and nutmeg. Set aside. In a large bowl mix the apples, walnuts, and raisins. Sprinkle with lemon juice and toss. Add dry ingredients and mix well. Pour half the melted butter over the mixture and toss. Set aside. Heat the rest of the butter and oil together. Brush half of each phyllo sheet with the mixture, fold the other half over it. Butter the surface. Spread 2-3 tablespoons of apple filling lengthwise and roll up. Arrange rolls in a rectangular, lightly-buttered baking pan just large enough to fit them all. Or twist the rolls into a large coil, covering the bottom of a round (14-inch) baking pan. Brush rolls with remaining butter-oil mixture and sprinkle with 2-3 tablespoons sugar. (At this stage the apple rolls may be wrapped and frozen. When ready to bake, let them thaw out first.) Preheat oven to 350ºF and bake for about 1 hour, or until golden brown. Allow to cool. Cut into pieces and sprinkle with confectioners' sugar and a little cinnamon. Serve warm. Do not cover any leftovers or they will become soggy. They will keep for 2 days, unrefrigerated.

Bougatsa with Cheese
(Bougatsa me Tiri)

Yields 20-24 pieces
Preparation time 1 hour
Baking time 1 hour

1¹/₂ lbs feta cheese, grated
pepper
1 lb packaged phyllo
2/3 cup melted butter or margarine
5 eggs
1 cup milk
1/2 whipping cream

Mix the cheese and pepper in a bowl. (If the cheese is very salty, soak it in cold water for a few hours.) Line a

Kasseri Cheese Pie
(Kasseropita)

Yields 20 pieces
Preparation time 1 hour
Baking time 45 minutes

4 cups grated kasseri cheese
4 cups grated Swiss cheese
pepper and salt (if needed)
1 lb packaged phyllo
1 cup melted butter
6 eggs
1½ cups milk

Mix the two cheeses and season with the pepper and salt, if needed. Set aside. Butter one half of each phyllo sheet and fold the other half over the buttered part. Butter the surface. Sprinkle generously with cheese and roll the phyllo up, lengthwise. Place it in the center of a round, buttered baking pan (14 inches in diameter), and twist it into a coil. Continue rolling and twisting the other sheets until you have a large coil that covers the bottom of the pan. Brush the top with the remaining butter. (At this point you may freeze the pie. When ready to bake, let it thaw out first.) Beat the eggs with the milk and pour the liquid over the pie. Allow to stand for about 1 hour, until the egg mixture has soaked in. Preheat oven to 400°F and bake for about 45 minutes until golden brown. Serve hot.

Shortbread Cheese Pies
(Kouroubougatses)

Yields 20-30 pieces
Preparation time 1 hour
Baking time 40 minutes

the dough
3 cups all-purpose flour
1 teaspoon baking powder
1 teaspoon baking soda
1 teaspoon salt
1/2 cup olive or vegetable oil
1/2 cup shortening
1 egg yolk
1/3 cup cold water

the filling
2 whole eggs
1 egg white
2 cups crumbled feta cheese
1 cup grated Swiss cheese
3 tablespoons butter
3 tablespoons heavy cream

the topping
1 egg yolk, beaten with a little water

Sift together the flour, baking powder, baking soda,

and salt, in a large bowl. Mix the oil and shortening into the flour by hand or with a pastry blender, until coarse crumbs are formed. Lightly beat the egg yolk with cold water and sprinkle it over the mixture. Press the dough crumbs together into a ball. Knead the dough gently, cover, and refrigerate for about 1 hour. Roll out the dough into a rather thick sheet, and cut into 4-inch circles. Lightly mix all the filling ingredients in a bowl. Place 1 tablespoon of the filling on each circle and fold in half. Press edges together to seal. (At this point, you may wrap and freeze the pies. When ready to bake, let them thaw out first.) Brush with egg yolk, preheat oven to 350°F, and bake for 35-40 minutes, until golden brown. Serve hot or cold.
Note: Any left-over dough can be used to wrap small sausages (wieners) or other fillings. If wrapping wieners, brush the dough with mustard and a little ketchup. Place the sausages on top and fold the pastry around them, pressing edges together to seal. Bake as above.

Custard Pie
(Bougatsa me Krema)

Serves 8-10
Preparation time 30 minutes
Baking time 30 minutes

> 4 cups milk
> 1/4 cup butter
> 2/3 cup fine semolina
> 2/3 cup sugar
> 2 whole eggs and 2 egg yolks
> 1 teaspoon vanilla
> 1 lb packaged phyllo
> 2/3 cup melted butter
> confectioners' sugar
> cinnamon

Heat the milk to boiling. In another saucepan heat the butter, pour in the semolina, and sauté for 1-2 minutes. Off the heat, pour in the hot milk all at once, stirring constantly. Return to the heat. Add the sugar. Simmer, stirring, until creamy and thick, the consistency of custard. Remove from the heat. While the custard is cooling for 5 minutes, lightly beat the eggs and egg yolks. Pour the eggs and the vanilla into the custard, stirring constantly until smooth. Set aside. (To prevent a skin forming, place a sheet of plastic wrap on the surface of the cream.) On a lightly buttered baking sheet, the size of the phyllo, lay down a sheet of phyllo, brush with the melted butter, and add another sheet. Repeat until half the phyllo sheets, approximately 10 of them, have been used. (A 1-pound packet of phyllo usually contains 20 sheets.) Pour the custard mixture over them and spread evenly. Cover with the rest of the phyllo, brushing each sheet with melted butter. Preheat oven to 400°F and bake until the phyllo is golden brown. Cut into squares and serve hot, sprinkled with confectioners' sugar and powdered cinnamon.

Pizza Boats (Peinirli)

Yields 12 pieces
Preparation time 1 hour and 30 minutes
Baking time 20 minutes

> 2/3 cup warm water or milk
> 1 block compressed yeast or
> 1 envelope active dry yeast
> 1/2 teaspoon sugar
> 2 cups all-purpose flour
> 1/4 teaspoon salt
> 2 tablespoons oil
>
> *the filling*
> 2 cups grated kasseri or Swiss cheese
> 1 cup grated kefalograviera or Romano cheese
> bacon, ham, or salami
> small wieners, plain or wrapped in bacon

Dissolve the yeast in the warm milk or water along with the sugar. Let stand until bubbly. Sift flour and salt together into a large bowl. Add the yeast and the oil and knead until you have a smooth, elastic dough, adding water as needed. Shape dough into balls the size of a ping-pong ball. Roll out the dough into oval pastry sheets 4-5 inches long. Mix the two cheeses and place 3-4 tablespoons of the cheese mixture in the center of each oval. Moisten the ends of the dough and press them together so that they resemble small boats. Arrange the "peinirli" on a lightly buttered baking sheet, cover, and let stand for 15-20 minutes, until the dough rises. Brush the surface of each boat with a little oil. Preheat the oven to 375°F and bake for about 10 minutes. Remove from the oven and place one of the following ingredients in the middle of each boat: bacon or ham rolls, small wieners, or slices of salami, folded or rolled. Press them in slightly. Bake for another 10 minutes, until the dough is lightly browned. Serve immediately.

Thessaloniki Cheese Pie
(Bougatsa Thessalonikis)

Yields 16 pieces
Preparation time 35 minutes
Baking time 45 minutes

1 recipe Home-made Phyllo Dough (page 56) or
1 lb packaged phyllo
1/2 cup melted butter or
corn oil
2 lbs feta cheese, crumbled
2 egg whites, beaten with
1/2 cup heavy cream or
evaporated milk
freshly ground pepper

Brush half the phyllo sheets with melted butter or oil and place them in a baking dish (12x14 inches). Prepare the filling. Place the cheese in a bowl, add the egg-cream mixture and mix lightly. Spread the filling over the phyllo and sprinkle it with pepper. Butter the remaining phyllo sheets and place them on top. Score the pie in wide strips. Preheat the oven to 350°F and bake for 40 minutes or until the surface is golden brown. Serve hot in bite-sized pieces, if you want to eat it the way they do in Thessaloniki.
Alternate: This pie can also be made with home-made or store-bought puff pastry.

Milk Pie (Galatopita)

Serves 12
Preparation time 15 minutes
Baking time I hour and 10 minutes

8-9 fyllo sheets
1/2 cup butter
1/2 teaspoon cinnamon
4 large eggs
1¼ cups sugar
2 tablespoons cornstarch dissolved in
4 cups hot milk
dash of vanilla
confectioners' sugar and cinnamon for dusting

Butter a round baking pan 10 inches in diameter. One by one, fold the fyllo sheets into pleats, starting with the short side, and lay them loosely in the pan in a circle so that they form deep creases, some large, some small, until you have filled the pan. Melt the butter, skim off the proteins that collect on the surface, and pour off the water that forms at the bottom. With a

pastry brush paint the fyllo sheets with the clarified butter, making sure you coat the inside of the pleats as well as the tops. Sprinkle them with the cinnamon, preheat the oven to 350°F, and bake for 25-30 minutes until the pastry is golden. Meanwhile, beat the eggs with the sugar in a bowl until they are pale yellow and smooth. Gradually pour in the cornstarch-milk mixture, beating continuously, add the vanilla (if powdered, dissolve it in a little cold milk). Take the pan with the baked fyllo out of the oven and fill it with the custard, a spoonful at a time, spreading it evenly over the pastry and into the creases. Replace the pan in the oven and bake for another 25-30 minutes until the custard is firm. Serve the pie hot, dusted with confectioners' sugar and cinnamon. Keep any leftovers in the refrigerator and reheat before serving.

with the beaten eggs. Combine with the cheeses and stir lightly. Line a buttered baking pan with half the phyllo sheets, one on top of the other, brushing each one with butter. Spread the cheese mixture on top and cover with the remaining phyllo, brushing again with butter. Score the pie in serving pieces and brush the surface with remaining butter. (At this stage the pie may be wrapped and frozen, if desired. Let it thaw out before cooking.) Preheat oven to 350°F and bake for approximately 30-40 minutes, or until golden brown. Sprinkle confectioners' sugar and cinnamon, if desired, and serve. Leave any leftovers uncovered, except if refrigerated.

Spinach and Cheese Tarts
(Spanakotiropitakia)

Yields 24 tarts
Preparation time 1 hour and 30 minutes
Baking time 45 minutes

24 ready-made puff pastry circles or
2 recipes Home-made Puff Pastry (page 56)
2 cups Béchamel Sauce (page 52)
2 eggs, lightly beaten

the filling
2 lbs fresh spinach
2/3 lb feta cheese, crumbled
8 spring onions, finely chopped
1/2 cup finely chopped dill
1/2 cup finely chopped parsley
1/4 cup light cream or evaporated milk
4 eggs, lightly beaten
salt and pepper
2 12-cupcake baking pans

Roll out the puff pastry circles and pat them into the cupcake forms. If using home-made puff pastry, roll it to a thickness of about 1/4 inch and cut out circles, using a 5-inch, floured pastry cutter. Wash and finely chop the spinach. Sprinkle with a little salt and knead it until it wilts. Squeeze out all the water. Put it in a bowl with the rest of the filling ingredients and mix well. Put 2 tablespoons of the filling in each pastry shell. (At this stage you may freeze them, sealed in plastic bags. When ready to bake, let them thaw out first.) Prepare 2 cups thick béchamel sauce and fold in the 2 lightly beaten eggs. Pour 2 tablespoons of the sauce in each tart to cover the spinach filling. Preheat oven to 350°F and bake for about 45 minutes. Serve hot.

Sweet Cottage Cheese Pie
(Mizithropita Glikia)

Yields 20 pieces
Preparation time 1 hour
Baking time 30 minutes

1 lb myzithra or cottage cheese
1/2 lb anthotiro or ricotta cheese
4 eggs
3/4 cup sugar
1 tablespoon cornstarch
1 teaspoon vanilla
1/4 cup milk
1 lb packaged phyllo
3/4 cup melted butter
confectioners' sugar
cinnamon (optional)

Crumble and mix both cheeses in a bowl. Set aside. Beat the eggs with sugar until thick and lemon-colored. Dilute cornstarch and vanilla in the milk and mix

Lenten Spinach Pie
(Spanakopita Nistissimi)

Yields 20 pieces
Preparation time 1 hour
Baking time 1 hour

2 lbs fresh spinach or
1 lb frozen spinach
1/3 cup olive oil
3/4 cup grated onion
8 fresh spring onions, finely chopped
1 leek, finely chopped (optional)
1/2 cup finely chopped dill
1/2 cup finely chopped parsley
salt and pepper
1 lb packaged phyllo
3/4 cup oil (half olive, half vegetable)
1/2 cup club soda (carbonated water)

Wash and finely chop the spinach. Sprinkle with a little salt and rub it with your hands until it wilts. Squeeze out all the water. If using frozen spinach, just squeeze out the water. Heat the oil in a saucepan and sauté the onions and leek over high heat. Add the spinach, dill, parsley, salt, and pepper, stir, and remove from the heat. Line a buttered baking pan with half the phyllo sheets, one on top of the other, brushing each one with oil. Spread the spinach mixture evenly on top and cover with the remaining phyllo sheets, brushing each with oil. Score the pie into serving pieces, and brush the surface with the remaining oil. Preheat oven to 400ºF and bake for 15 minutes, remove from the oven, and sprinkle with club soda. Replace the pan in the oven and continue baking for approximately 45 minutes or until golden brown. Serve hot or cold.

Rolled Pastries with Chicken
(Bourekia me Kotopoulo)

Yields 20-24 pieces
Preparation time 1 hour and 30 minutes
Baking time 1 hour

1 small chicken
1 onion, cut in half
salt and pepper
3 hard-boiled eggs, chopped
1 cup finely chopped ham
1 cup crumbled feta cheese
1 cup grated kasseri or Swiss cheese
2 cups Béchamel Sauce (page 52)
2 eggs, lightly beaten
1 lb packaged phyllo
3/4 cup melted butter or margarine
ketchup
1/2 cup grated kefalotiri or Romano cheese

Boil the chicken in a little water, with the onion, salt, and pepper, until tender. When cool, remove skin and bones and cut into small pieces. In a bowl combine the chicken pieces, chopped eggs, ham, and cheeses. Mix well. Prepare 2 cups light béchamel sauce. Fold in the lightly-beaten eggs. Stir the sauce into the chicken mixture, and season to taste. Brush melted butter on half the width of each phyllo sheet. Fold the other half over the buttered part. Brush the surface with butter. Place 2 tablespoons of chicken filling at the center bottom, about 1 inch from the edge. Dot the filling with a drop of ketchup and sprinkle some grated cheese over it. Fold the two sides of the phyllo over the filling, brush again with melted butter, and roll up. Repeat until filling and phyllo sheets are used up. Arrange on a buttered baking sheet and brush with remaining butter. Preheat oven to 350ºF and bake until golden brown, about 1 hour. Serve hot.

Spinach and Cheese Pie
(Spanakotiropita)

Yields 20-24 pieces
Preparation time 1 hour and 30 minutes
Baking time 1 hour

2 lbs fresh spinach
8 spring onions, finely chopped
1/2 cup finely chopped dill
1/2 cup finely chopped parsley
1 lb feta cheese, crumbled
1/2 cup heavy cream
5-6 eggs
1/4 cup melted butter
pepper and salt (if needed)
1 lb packaged phyllo or
1 recipe, Home-made Phyllo Dough (page 56)
3/4 cup oil (half olive oil, half vegetable)

Wash and finely chop the spinach. Sprinkle with a little salt and knead it with your hands until it wilts. Squeeze out all the water. Put the spinach in a bowl with the rest of the filling ingredients and mix well. Line a buttered baking pan with half the phyllo sheets, one on top of the other, brushing each one with oil. Spread the spinach filling evenly on top and cover with the remaining phyllo, again brushing each one with oil. Fold in the edges of the phyllo. Score the pie in serving pieces and brush the top with the remaining oil. Sprinkle with a little water, preheat oven to 350ºF, and bake for about 1 hour, until golden brown. Serve hot or cold.
Alternate: The spinach may be blanched, cooled, and squeezed dry, instead of rubbed with salt.
Note: If using home-made phyllo, use 1/2 cup more oil.

ter, cheese, and season to taste. Fold in the eggs. Line a large, oiled, round (14-inch) baking pan with one (5-layer) phyllo sheet and brush with butter. Place a single sheet over it, brush with butter, sprinkle with bread crumbs, and spread the leek filling evenly on top. Cover with the remaining single sheet, brush with butter, and top with the second 5-layer phyllo sheet. Moisten edges, press firmly together, and crimp. Score the pie into serving pieces, and brush the surface with the remaining butter. (At this point, you may wrap and freeze the pie. When ready to bake, let it thaw out first.) Sprinkle the top with a little water, preheat oven to 350°F and bake for 40-50 minutes, until golden brown. Serve hot or cold. *Alternate:* Use 1 lb leeks and 1 lb spinach. *Note:* If using ready-made phyllo, place half the sheets on the bottom of baking pan and the other half on top of the filling. Brush each sheet with melted butter. Ready-made phyllo dough does not absorb as much butter as homemade.

Ground Meat Pie
(Kreatopita me Kima)

Yields 24 pieces
Preparation time 1 hour
Baking time 30 minutes

1/4 cup butter or margarine
1 cup grated onions
5 spring onions, finely chopped
1 lb ground lean meat (beef or veal)
1 cup beef stock or a beef bouillon cube
salt and pepper
4 eggs, lightly beaten with
1/2 cup light cream or evaporated milk
1/2 cup finely chopped dill
2 lbs ready-made puff pastry or
2 recipes Home-made Puff Pastry (page 56)
1/2 cup grated kefalotiri or Romano cheese
1 egg yolk, beaten with a little milk

Sauté both onions, lightly, in the butter. Add ground meat and sauté until it loses its pinkness. Add the beef stock, season to taste, and simmer, covered, for about 30 minutes until all the liquid has evaporated. Remove from the heat, and fold in the eggs and cream or milk. Add the dill and set aside. Divide the puff pastry dough into two. Roll out each half, with the rolling pin, into a 12x16-inch rectangle. Line an oiled baking pan with half the pastry, spread the meat mixture evenly over it, top with cheese, and cover with the other half of the pastry. Score the top into 24 pieces, brush the surface with beaten egg yolk and milk, preheat the oven to 400°F, and bake for about 30 minutes, or until golden brown. Serve hot.

Leek and Cheese Pie
(Prassotiropita)

Yields 20-24 pieces
Preparation time 1 hour and 30 minutes
Baking time 50 minutes

1 lb packaged phyllo dough or
1 recipe, Home-made Phyllo Dough (page 56)
2 lbs leeks, chopped
1 cup milk
1/2 cup chopped parsley or mint
1/4 cup melted butter
1 lb feta cheese, crumbled
6 eggs, lightly beaten
salt and pepper to taste
1 tablespoon fine bread crumbs
2/3 cup olive oil

Divide the dough into 12 balls and roll out according to the recipe for Meat Pie Country Style (page 69). Blanch the leeks and drain. Put them in a saucepan with the milk and simmer, covered, until the leeks are tender and the sauce is thick. Remove from the heat, add parsley, but-

Meat Pie Country-Style
(Kreatopita Vlachiki)

Yields 20-24 pieces
Preparation time 2 hours
Baking time 1 hour

1 recipe, Homemade Phyllo Dough (page 56)
1¹/₃ cups melted butter or (half butter, half olive oil)

the filling
3 large onions, thinly sliced
2 leeks, chopped
1/2 cup olive oil
4 lbs boneless veal or other tender meat
salt and pepper
2-3 allspice berries
cinnamon (optional)
5 eggs, lightly beaten

Prepare the phyllo dough, divide into 12 balls, cover with a damp cloth, and set aside. Steam the sliced onions and the chopped leeks and drain. Heat the olive oil in a saucepan and sauté the meat until browned all over. Add the steamed onions and leeks and the remaining ingredients except for the eggs. Cover and simmer, until the meat is tender and juices are reduced to about a cup. When cool, discard the allspice, cut the meat into small pieces, and fold in the eggs. Set aside. Roll out the dough balls into 6-inch circles. Brush circles generously with butter. Stack 5, one on top of the other, and roll out into a rather thick sheet. Repeat with another 5 stacked circles. Roll the remaining 2 circles, individually, into very thin circles. Grease a round (14-inch) baking pan, line it with one 5-layer sheet, brush with butter. Place a single sheet over it and brush generously with butter. Spread the meat mixture evenly on top and cover with the remaining single sheet. Brush with butter and top with the other 5-layer sheet. Moisten edges, press firmly together, and crimp. Score the pie in serving pieces and brush the top with the remaining butter. At this point either wrap and freeze, or preheat oven to 350°F and bake for about 1 hour, until golden brown. Serve hot.

Alternate: Chicken can be used in place of veal. The pie may also be made with puff pastry (in this case do not use any butter) or with packaged phyllo, which requires less melted butter than homemade dough.

Vegetables
(Ladera)

Though few Greeks would call themselves vegetarians, they have always given vegetables priority. You could even say that vegetable dishes are the mainstay of Greek cuisine. This is one of the few countries in the world where vegetables dishes are main courses, not side dishes or garnitures for meat, fish, or poultry, but taking pride of place on the table with no apologies. We could not be farther from the Anglo-Saxon tradition of meat and two veg, and no Greek would ever confuse ketchup with a vegetable either.

There are two main reasons for this widespread appreciation of the fruits of the earth. The first is that through the ages meat was never abundant, given the relative lack of pastureland in this mountainous country. Scarcity meant that it was considered food fit for the gods and reserved for celebrations. Ordinary people had to make do with what they could gather or grow. And curiously, many of the vegetables and fruits – tomatoes, peppers, eggplant, potatoes – we think of as quintessentially Mediterranean were nowhere to be found, being much later imports from the New World or South Asia. Even the lemon, such a prevalent flavoring in Greek food, had yet to be brought from the Holy Land. Nevertheless, in early antiquity Greeks were eating many of the staples they still enjoy today: onions, garlic, leeks, beets, lettuce, lentils, chick-peas, broad beans, and the whole wealth of nutritious greens in all their diversity gathered from the great outdoors. Moreover, they were seasoning their dishes with many of the same herbs: celery, fennel, dill, cumin, and mint. They obviously knew what to do with these foods, because by the time the Romans took over, every aristocrat wanted to employ a Greek cook.

Meanwhile, with the adoption of Christianity as the official religion in the Roman and then Byzantine empires came the practice of fasting. Not fasting as in the sense of eating only bread and water, but rather restricting one's consumption of animal products. At first the discipline concerned a few days just preceding Easter, but eventually, in the Greek Orthodox Church at least, it was imposed during several other periods. In time, the year held almost as many fasting days – 40 days before Easter and Christmas, some weeks before Pentecost and the Assumption of the Virgin, but also regularly on Wednesdays and Fridays – as non-fasting days. Because eggs, dairy products, and fish were also forbidden, this meant that Greeks had to rely on vegetables, fresh and dried, wheat, nuts, and the occasional seafood for all their nourishment, even if they could afford meat and poultry. Coincidentally or not, fasting was an excellent way of conserving less plentiful resources, as well as introducing a beneficent balance to the diet.

As a result of these constraints, over the centuries, the Greeks developed vegetable dishes that were so hearty and satisfying that meat seems superfluous. Of course, a major reason why these dishes are so delicious not to mention healthful is that they are cooked with plenty of olive oil, one of the most important components of the Mediterranean Diet. Indeed, these dishes are called ladera, meaning cooked with olive oil (not "Oily Dishes" as is sometimes seen on Greek taverna menus), and they truly express the genius of Greek cooking, revealing both originality and nutritional wisdom. These are the dishes that scientists who "discovered" the Mediterranean Diet point to when they describe good eating habits to Northern Europeans and Americans. But they have absolutely nothing in common with the depressing food we usually associate with a diet. Greeks love to eat them at home but they are equally common on taverna menus. There is no trace of self-denial in classic dishes like Imam Bayildi, eggplant stuffed with meltingly sweet onion; Anginares ala Polita, lemony artichokes Constantinople-style; and Briami, a baked vegetable casserole.

BAKED MIXED VEGETABLES, PAGE 73 • SPINACH WITH RICE, PAGE 84 • ARTICHOKES CONSTANTINOPLE-STYLE, PAGE 76

Apart from being healthy and good to eat, they are also appealing to the eye, often combining ingredients of contrasting or complementary colors as, for example, in Artichokes Constantinople-Style. Here green artichokes, orange carrots, and white potatoes are made even more enticing with the addition of brighter green accents of fresh dill, spring onions, and peas. Vegetable dishes are invariably seasoned with aromatic fresh herbs. Favorite combinations are chopped flat leaf parsley and mint or chopped spring onions and dill. Tomato sauces, on the other hand, often contain a cinnamon stick to make them richer.

Besides the ladera dishes, there are a host of other imaginative ways of using vegetables. Greeks are fond of grating them, molding them into balls, and frying them. Zucchini, eggplant, tomatoes, greens, and potatoes are particularly adapted to this treatment. They also love to sauté vegetables – spinach or leeks, for example – with rice, producing easy meals which are comforting in the extreme. In addition, they have mastered the art of stuffing any vegetable that can be hollowed out and of wrapping leaves (cabbage, vine leaves, lettuce) around a stuffing. These stuffings are usually rice-based, seasoned with herbs and onions plus raisins and pine nuts, if the recipe comes from Asia Minor. Many recipes for stuffed or wrapped vegetables come in two versions, with meat and without, for the fasting periods. The latter are commonly called orfana or "orphans", but you will probably find that it would take more than meatlessness to make these orphans sad.

This chapter includes a wide variety of recipes for the most typical vegetable dishes in the Greek repertoire. Some of them are meals in themselves, some are side dishes, and some can even be served as appetizers. Vegetarians will love them, but even if you are a dedicated carnivore, you may end up appreciating the Greek approach to vegetable cooking much more than you could have anticipated.

General Instructions

The basic ingredients that go into most Greek vegetable dishes, apart from the vegetables themselves, are olive oil, onions, tomato purée or paste, and fresh and dried herbs. Among these herbs are parsley, dill, mint, basil, oregano, thyme, and bay leaves. A few dishes may be made with butter, but in every other case the oil called for is olive oil, unless otherwise specified, usually extra virgin. You may be tempted to economize by substituting some other kind of oil, but the taste and richness imparted by olive oil cannot be duplicated. And by now it has been proven that olive oil is far healthier than corn, peanut, or sunflower oil. In all recipes, fresh tomatoes can be replaced by canned tomatoes or tomato purée or tomato paste diluted in water. Two tablespoons of tomato paste diluted in one cup of water is equal to one cup of tomato juice or puréed ripe tomatoes. Fresh tomatoes should only be used if they are in season and sun-ripened. Although thanks to refrigeration, speedy transport and greenhouses, you can find most vegetables year-round in the supermarket, you will have better results with these recipes if you use only vegetables in season that you have bought from the farmers' market or organic produce shop. And don't store them for too long. The longer they sit in your refrigerator, the greater their loss of flavor, firmness and nutritional value.

Another way to conserve these qualities is not to overcook them. Dishes cooked with olive oil are tastier when most of the liquid has been boiled off and a thick sauce remains. For this reason, do not add too much water when preparing them. Simmer the vegetables and let them cook slowly in a pot with the lid slightly askew to allow steam to escape. If you haven't cooked Greek vegetable dishes before, measure the oil carefully. Too little oil and the food will be tasteless; too much and it will be unappetizingly rich and heavy.

Many of these recipes call for chopped or grated onion. Before you sauté it, grate it into a colander, sprinkle a little salt over it, rinse it with a little water, and squeeze out the extra moisture your hands. This reduces some of onion's pungency and makes the dish lighter. In addition, do not brown the onion when sautéing it; just cook it gently in hot oil until it is soft and translucent. This way your dish will be much lighter and better for you.

When cooking these dishes, add salt and pepper towards the end, when the meal is almost done. Salt has the property of drawing the water or liquid out of foods being cooked, making them too dry. Pepper is added to food to season it, not to make it hot. Lengthy cooking causes it to lose its delicate aroma and taste.

Once you learn to make these olive oil-based dishes as the Greeks do, you may find you also like to eat them the way they do: at room temperature rather than piping hot. And, if there any leftovers, you will also discover an added bonus: they are even more delicious the next day.

Baked Mixed Vegetables (Briami)

Serves 6
Preparation time 1 hour and 30 minutes
Cooking time 40 minutes

1 lb eggplant
1 lb zucchini
1/2 lb fresh green beans, stringed and cut in thirds
2 large potatoes, peeled and cut in large chunks
2 large carrots, peeled and cut in chunks
2 medium green bell peppers, seeded and sliced
6-8 large, fresh mushrooms, wiped clean and quartered
2 lbs fresh, ripe tomatoes, chopped
1/2 cup olive oil
2 medium onions, sliced
salt and pepper
2-3 garlic cloves, sliced (optional)
1/2 cup chopped parsley
1/2 cup grated kefalotiri or Romano cheese
oil for frying

Wash and trim the eggplant and zucchini. Cut them in large chunks. Salt both generously and let stand in separate colanders for about 1-2 hours. Rinse in plenty of water and squeeze out excess. Heat half the olive oil and fry them, lightly. Set aside. In the same pan sauté the beans, potatoes, carrots, peppers, and mushrooms lightly in hot oil. Set aside. Heat the rest of the oil in a deeper saucepan and sauté the onions and garlic. Add the tomatoes and simmer for about 10 minutes. Add the parsley and seasonings, stir well, and remove the pan from the heat. Put all the fried vegetables into a large clay or ovenproof dish and toss gently. Pour the sauce over the dish and cover with aluminum foil. Preheat the oven to 350°F and bake for about 40 minutes. Remove the foil, sprinkle the top with grated cheese, and brown for about 10 minutes more. Serve hot or cold.

Roast Potatoes (Patates Fournou)

Serves 5-6
Preparation time 1 hour
Cooking time 1 hour and 30 minutes

4 lbs potatoes
1/3 cup lemon juice or
2 cups tomato purée
salt, pepper, and oregano
1 garlic clove, finely chopped (optional)
1/3 cup olive oil
1/3 cup butter or margarine

Wash and peel the potatoes. Cut into fourths or sixths, depending on their size. For lemon-roasted potatoes, combine them with lemon juice, salt, pepper, oregano, and garlic. Let them stand for 1 hour. Transfer to a clay or glass baking dish. Sprinkle with oil, dot with butter, cover with aluminum foil, preheat oven to 350°F, and bake for 1 hour. Remove foil and continue baking for about 30 more minutes, turning occasionally, until the potatoes are soft and lightly browned all over. For tomato-roasted potatoes, pour the tomato purée over them, combine with remaining ingredients, and stir well. Bake for 40 minutes, covered, and 40 minutes, uncovered, or until the potatoes are soft and the sauce is thick. Serve hot. Excellent with roast meats.

Braised Potatoes
(Patates Yachni)

Serves 4-6
Preparation time 30 minutes
Cooking time 45 minutes

3 lbs potatoes
1 tablespoon lemon juice
2/3 cup olive oil
2/3 cup grated onion
1 garlic clove, chopped
2 lbs fresh tomatoes, puréed or
1 lb can tomato purée
1 teaspoon sugar
1 bay leaf
3-4 allspice berries (optional)
1 cup beef stock, beef bouillon cube, or water
salt and pepper
1/2 cup finely chopped parsley

Wash and peel the potatoes. Cut into fourths or sixths, depending on their size. Sprinkle with lemon juice and toss. Heat the oil in a saucepan and gently sauté the onion and garlic until transparent. Add the tomatoes, the potatoes, and the remaining ingredients. Stir well, cover, and simmer until the potatoes are soft and the sauce is thick. Do not stir or the potatoes will crumble. To prevent sticking, shake the pan every now and then during cooking. Before serving discard the allspice and bay leaf. Equally good hot or cold, accompanied by black olives or feta cheese.

Fried Potatoes
(Patates Tiganites)

Serves 4-5
Preparation time 15 minutes
Cooking time 15 minutes

4 lbs potatoes
oil for frying
salt or
1/2 cup grated kefalotiri or Romano chesse

Wash and peel the potatoes. Cut in thin slices. If not to be eaten immediately, set aside, covered with cold water to prevent discoloring. Dry well. Cover the bottom of a frying pan with 1/3 inch of oil and heat. When very hot, fry the potatoes, a handful at a time, until crisp and lightly browned on both sides. Remove with a slotted spoon and drain on absorbent paper. Sprinkle with salt or plenty of grated cheese and serve immediately. An excellent garnish for souvlakia, meatballs, or any roast.

Buttered Peas and Carrots
(Arakas ke Karota Voutirou)

Serves 5-6
Preparation time 45 minutes
Cooking time 30 minutes

2 lbs fresh peas or
1 lb frozen peas
3-4 fresh carrots, cubed or
1 lb frozen carrot cubes
1/2 cup butter or margarine or
mixture of both in equal quantities
salt and pepper
2 tablespoons lemon juice

Drop the peas and carrots, separately, in rapidly boiling water and boil, uncovered, 8-10 minutes or until done to your taste. Drain. Toss the vegetables in a pan over high heat until any water clinging to them evaporates. Add small pieces of butter or margarine and toss the vegetables until coated with melted butter. Remove from the heat, sprinkle with lemon juice, salt, and pepper, and serve at once. Excellent garnish for roast meat or chicken.
Alternate: Following the same procedure, butter canned or fresh artichoke bottoms and fill them with the carrots and peas. Use to garnish meat or fish dishes at buffets.

Peas and Fava Beans
(Arakas me Koukia)

Serves 5-6
Preparation time 1 hour
Cooking time 45-60 minutes

2 lbs fresh fava beans or
1 lb frozen
2 lbs fresh peas or
1 lb frozen
1 cup olive oil
8 spring onions, finely chopped
1/2 cup finely chopped dill
3 tablespoons lemon juice

Shell the fava beans. If the pods are young and tender, simply string them and cut in half or thirds. Otherwise discard the pods. Wash and drain. Shell, wash, and drain the peas. Heat the oil in a large saucepan and quickly sauté the spring onions. Add the fava beans and peas, salt, pepper, and 1 cup of water. Cover and simmer until the vegetables are tender and most of the liquid has been absorbed. Add a little more water if they start to stick. Remove from the heat and add the lemon juice. Shake to distribute the juice. Delicious either hot or at room temperature.

Braised Peas
(Arakas Laderos)

Serves 5-6
Preparation time 45 minutes
Cooking time 45-60 minutes

4 lbs fresh peas or
2 lbs frozen peas
2/3 cup olive oil
8 spring onions, finely chopped
1½ lbs fresh tomatoes, puréed or
1lb can tomato purée
1/2 cup finely chopped dill
salt and pepper

Shell and wash the peas. Heat the oil in a large saucepan and lightly sauté the spring onions. Add the peas, the remaining ingredients, and 1 cup water. Stir well, season with salt and pepper, and simmer, covered, until the peas are tender and the sauce is thick. Add more water if the dish seems dry. Serve hot or cold, accompanied by Greek Village Salad.

Artichokes Constantinople-Style
(Anginares Politikes)

Serves 4
Preparation time 30 minutes
Cooking time 30 minutes

8 fresh or frozen artichokes
2/3 cup olive oil
1 medium onion, grated
4 fresh spring onions, chopped
2 large carrots, sliced
3 large potatoes, cut in quarters
1/4 lb frozen peas (optional)
1/2 cup finely chopped dill
salt and pepper
1 egg
1/4 cup lemon juice

If using fresh artichokes, wash them well. Cut off the stem and peel off the dark green outer leaves. Depending on the tenderness of the leaves, remove 1/3 to 2/3 of each artichoke and cut off the tops, about an inch or two from the bottom. Scrape out the fuzzy choke from the center with a teaspoon. Rub each artichoke heart with lemon and place in a bowl with some water, a little flour, and lemon juice to prevent discoloring. Gently heat the oil in a shallow pan and sauté the onions. Add the carrots and sauté lightly. Arrange the artichokes in the pan, add the potatoes, peas, dill, seasonings, and 1 cup hot water. Cover and simmer for about 30 minutes until the artichokes and potatoes are tender and the sauce is reduced. Add some more water during the cooking time, if necessary. Beat the egg with lemon juice in a bowl. Slowly add a few tablespoons of the pan juices, beating continuously, and pour the sauce back into the pan. Shake the pan to incorporate the egg and lemon sauce.
Alternate: Plain lemon juice may be substituted for the egg and lemon sauce. Serve hot or cold.

Artichokes and Fava Beans
(Anginares ke Koukia)

Serves 6
Preparation time 1 hour
Cooking time 30 minutes

3 lbs young, fresh fava beans
6 artichokes
1 cup olive oil
8 spring onions, finely chopped
1/2 cup finely chopped dill
salt and pepper
2 tablespoons lemon juice

Trim the ends of the fava beans and destring. Wash in cold water, drain, and cut in half. Discard any tough pods. Prepare the artichokes according to the recipe for Artichokes Constantinople Style (page 76). Gently heat the oil in a saucepan and sauté the onions. Add the beans, artichokes, dill, salt, pepper, and 1 cup water. Cover and simmer until the beans and artichokes are tender and the sauce thickens. Remove from the heat and sprinkle with the lemon juice. Shake the pan to distribute the juice. Serve hot or at room temperature with feta cheese and a green salad. The dish is also delicious made with fava beans on their own.
Note: If desired, add one ripe, finely chopped tomato to the other ingredients.

Assorted Rice-Stuffed Vegetables
(Yemista Tourlou)

Serves 6
Preparation time 1 hour
Baking time 1 hour and 45 minutes

3 large tomatoes
3 large green bell peppers
2 large eggplants
1 large zucchini
4 large potatoes
1½ cups olive oil
1 cup finely chopped onions
1½ cups short-grain rice
1/2 cup finely chopped mint leaves
3 tablespoons tomato paste
1 teaspoon sugar
salt and pepper
cumin (optional)
1/2 cup tomato purée

Wash and dry the vegetables well. Slice off the tops of tomatoes and peppers, reserving them. Scoop out the pulp and seeds, as in the recipe for Rice-Stuffed Tomatoes and Peppers (page 85). Set aside. Cut eggplants and zucchini lengthwise in half, and scoop out enough of the centers to form 6 cases (4 eggplants and 2 zucchini). Parboil them for 5 minutes and drain. Arrange the hollowed vegetables in a baking pan or ovenproof dish. Wash the rice in a colander until the water runs clear. Drain and set aside. Heat half the oil in a saucepan, add the onions and sauté lightly. Finely chop the pulp from the eggplant, half of the zucchini, and all the tomatoes. Add to the onions and cook the pulp over moderate heat for 10 minutes, stirring frequently. Remove from the heat, add the rice and all other ingredients except for the tomato purée. Mix well and fill each hollowed vegetable with the mixture. Do not overfill. Replace the tops on the tomatoes and peppers, and place a tomato slice on top of each stuffed eggplant and zucchini case. Cut the potatoes into large pieces and place among the vegetables. Pour the tomato purée over the potatoes and sprinkle with salt and pepper. Spoon the remaining oil over the vegetables and potatoes. Cover the dish loosely with aluminum foil, preheat the oven to 350°F, and bake for 1 hour. Remove the foil and continue baking, uncovered, for about 45 minutes, or until tops are brown. The sauce should be thick. Add water if necessary to prevent the food from sticking to the pan. Serve hot or cold.

Buttered Asparagus
(Sparangia Voutirou)

Serves 4
Preparation time 15 minutes
Cooking time 10-15 minutes

1 lb fresh, tender asparagus
1/3 cup butter or margarine
salt and freshly ground pepper
2 tablespoons lemon juice

Snap off and discard the tough ends. Wash and drain the asparagus. To prevent spears from falling apart while cooking, tie the asparagus in bundles and lower them, holding the end of the string, into a deep pan of gently boiling water. Simmer the spears for 5-8 minutes, depending on their thickness. Do not overcook. To remove, hook a fork under the string and lift the asparagus bundles out of the water. Cut the string and spread the stalks on a dish towel to dry. Melt the butter or margarine in a shallow flameproof dish and place the asparagus in it. Season with salt and pepper, and simmer, uncovered, until all the liquid evaporates. Sprinkle with lemon juice and serve at once. Exceptional with fish or meat.

Braised Okra (Bamies Yiachni)

Serves 4
Preparation time 30-40 minutes
Cooking time 15 minutes

1 lb fresh or frozen okra
vinegar or lemon juice
3/4 cup olive oil
1 medium onion, grated
1 lb fresh or canned tomatoes, puréed
6 tablespoons finely chopped parsley
1/8 teaspoon sugar
salt and pepper
3 lemon slices, peeled
1 ripe tomato, sliced

Wash fresh okra and carefully trim the cone-shaped stem end, taking care not to pierce it. Dip trimmed top in salt. Leave the okra to stand in a colander for a half hour. Frozen okra need no trimming. Rinse fresh or frozen okra with water and a little vinegar or lemon juice. Heat the oil in a shallow pan, add the onion, and sauté until transparent. Add tomatoes, parsley, sugar, pepper, and lemon slices, cover, and simmer for 10 minutes. Add okra, stir gently into the sauce, and place the tomato slices on top, sprinkled with a little salt and pepper. Cover and bring to a boil over medium heat. Reduce heat and simmer for about 15 minutes. Do not overcook. Add water only if the dish seems dry. Correct seasonings but do not stir the okra while they're cooking, as they are delicate; just shake the pot a few times.

Eggplant and Peppers with Cheese (Melitzanes ke Piperies me Tiri)

Serves 6
Preparation time 2 hours and 30 minutes
Baking time 30 minutes

4 lbs eggplant
2 lbs long green peppers
oil for frying
2 lbs fresh ripe tomatoes, puréed
salt, pepper, and oregano
1 lb feta cheese, crumbled

Wash, peel, and cut the eggplant into thick slices. Sprinkle with salt and let stand in a colander for 2 hours. Rinse well and pat firmly with paper towels to remove excess liquid. Wash and deseed the peppers. If the peppers are large, cut them into wide strips. Deep fry the sliced eggplant and peppers and drain well on paper towels. Pour a few tablespoons of the frying oil into a saucepan. Add the tomatoes, salt, pepper, and oregano and simmer until the sauce is thick. Layer the sliced eggplant and peppers in a clay or glass baking dish and pour half the sauce over them. Spread the crumbled cheese on top and sprinkle on the remaining sauce. Preheat oven to 350°F and bake for about 20 minutes, until the top is lightly browned. Serve hot.

Zucchini Souffle (Kolokithofai)

Serves 6
Preparation time 30 minutes
Cooking time 1 hour

2 lbs zucchini
salt
1/2 cup butter
1/4 cup all-purpose flour
2 cups warm milk
4 eggs, lightly beaten

1/2 lb feta cheese, crumbled
1/2 cup finely chopped dill
4 tablespoons fine bread crumbs
pepper to taste

Wash and grate the zucchini into a colander, sprinkle generously with salt, and let drain for 1-2 hours. Take handfuls of the grated zucchini and squeeze hard to remove excess liquid. Heat the butter in a saucepan over moderate heat, add the zucchini, and sauté for about 10 minutes, tossing frequently. Stir in the flour and cook for 5 minutes. Add the warm milk and simmer, stirring until the mixture thickens into a béchamel sauce. Remove from the heat and allow to cool. Fold in the eggs, cheese, dill, and pepper. Do not add salt as the zucchini and cheese will contribute sufficient salt. Butter a large souffle dish, sprinkle it with half the bread crumbs, and pour in the zucchini mixture. Smooth the surface with a wooden spoon and sprinkle with the remaining bread crumbs. Dot with butter, preheat the oven to 350⁰F, and bake for about 1 hour. Serve hot.

Split Pea Purée (Fava)

Serves 6
Preparation time 10 minutes
Cooking time 1 hour

1 lb green or yellow split peas
1/2 cup olive oil
1 small onion, grated
salt and pepper
3 tablespoons finely chopped parsley or dill
oregano (optional)
4 spring onions, chopped
olive oil for dressing
lemon juice for dressing

Wash the split peas in a colander and allow to drain. In a large pot bring 5 cups of water to the boil. Add the split peas and return to the boil slowly, skimming off the scum that rises. Cover and simmer for about 35 minutes. Meanwhile, in a saucepan, gently sauté the onion in the oil until soft but not brown. Add to the split peas and mix well. Add salt, pepper, and a pinch of oregano, if desired. Simmer for another 30 minutes, or until the peas have disintegrated. Remove from the heat, stir rapidly with a wooden spoon until smooth. Empty into 6 small bowls and sprinkle with the parsley, onions, a little olive oil, and lemon juice. The purée will set as it cools. Serve hot or cold.
Note: You can also serve it in one larger bowl as an appetizer dip for a party.

Chick-Peas with Eggplant
(Revithia me Melitzanes)

Serves 6
Preparation time 12 hours
Cooking time 45 minutes

1 lb chick-peas
1 tablespoon salt
1 medium onion, finely chopped
2 medium tomatoes, chopped
1/3 cup olive oil
2 lbs eggplant
salt and pepper
paprika

Soak the chick-peas overnight in water and salt. Drain and rub the peas between your palms to remove most of the skins. Rinse well and boil in a shallow pan with water to cover. Skim off the foam, add the onion, tomatoes, oil, salt, pepper, and a pinch of paprika. Cover and simmer until tender and the sauce has thickened. In the meantime, prepare the eggplant as for frying. Fry in hot oil until golden brown and drain on paper towels. Arrange the eggplant slices in the pan on top of the chick-peas and continue cooking for 5-10 minutes more. Serve hot.
Alternate: Place the boiled chick-peas in a clay baking dish and arrange the sliced eggplant on top of them. Cover with thinly sliced tomatoes and sprinkle with a little oil, salt, pepper, and oregano. Preheat oven to 350⁰F and bake for 20 minutes. Serve hot.

Baked Eggplant
(Kapakoti)

Serves 4-6
Preparation time 2 hours
Baking time 2 hours

4 lbs eggplant
1/4 cup olive oil
1 large onion, sliced
1 lb chopped fresh or canned tomatoes
salt and pepper
1 long green chili pepper, sliced (optional)
2 tablespoons finely chopped parsley

Wash and peel the eggplants. Cut them lengthwise into 4-6 slices depending on their thickness. Sprinkle with salt and set aside in a colander for 2 hours. Rinse thoroughly and remove excess water by pressing firmly with paper towels. Fry the slices lightly and drain on absorbent paper. Heat the oil in a saucepan and sauté the onion. Add the tomatoes, salt, and pepper, and cook for a few minutes. Layer the eggplant slices in a clay or glass baking dish, scatter the sliced chili pepper over them, and pour the sauce on top. Cover with aluminum foil, preheat oven to 250°F, and bake for about 2 hours. Serve at room temperature sprinkled with the parsley.

Garlic-Stuffed Zucchini
(Kolokithakia me Skordo)

Serves 4-5
Preparation time 45 minutes
Baking time 1 hour and 30 minutes

12-14 small zucchini (2 lbs)
18 garlic cloves, sliced
1 cup finely chopped parsley
salt and pepper
1 teaspoon paprika
2/3 cup olive oil
14 small slices feta cheese
flour

Scrub the zucchini. Lop off both tips. Using a sharp knife, make 4 incisions lengthwise in each zucchini, making sure not to cut all the way to the end. Mix the garlic, parsley, salt, pepper, paprika, and half the oil in a bowl. Insert the garlic mixture into the zucchini incisions, pressing with your thumb. Arrange the zucchini in a clay or glass baking dish and place a slice of feta cheese over the top incision of each zucchini. Pour the remaining oil over zucchini and sprinkle with a little flour. Cover with aluminum foil, preheat oven to 350°F, and bake for about 1 hour and 30 minutes until the zucchini are tender and the sauce is thick. Serve hot or cold. Delicious with ouzo.

Onion-Stuffed Eggplant
(Melitzanes Imam)

Serves 4-5
Preparation time 1 hour and 30 minutes
Cooking time 1 hour

8 medium eggplants (3 lbs)
4 large onions, quartered
8 garlic cloves, sliced
2/3 cup olive oil
1³/₄ cups puréed fresh or canned tomatoes
1/2 cup finely chopped parsley
salt and pepper

Wash the eggplants and lop off the tops and bottoms. Pare them lengthwise in strips, leaving about an inch of skin in between. Using a sharp knife, make two incisions lengthwise in each eggplant, making sure not to cut all the way to the end. Sprinkle the eggplant with plenty of salt and set aside for 1-2 hours in a colander. Rinse under running water, squeeze out excess liquid with your hands, and pat dry. Heat half the oil in a frying pan and sauté the eggplants a few at a time, turning them several times, until lightly browned all over. Transfer to a baking pan, side by side. Sauté the onions and garlic in the hot oil, for about 5 minutes, until transparent. Add the tomatoes, parsley, and seasonings. Cook for about 10 minutes. To stuff the eggplant, spoon the mixture between the incisions, pressing it in with your fingers or the back of a spoon. Pour any remaining sauce over the eggplant. Drizzle the remaining fresh oil on top, sprinkle with a few gratings of pepper, preheat oven to 350⁰F, and bake for about 1 hour. Add a little water if the dish seems too dry. Serve hot or cold.

Macaroni and Cheese Casserole
(Pastitsio me Tiria)

Serves 5-6
Preparation time 30 minutes
Baking time 30 minutes

1/2 lb thick macaroni (ziti, penne)
1/4 cup butter or margarine, melted
3 cups soft feta cheese, crumbled
2 cups grated kasseri or Swiss cheese
salt and pepper
2 cups thick Béchamel (page 52)
2 eggs
1 cup heavy cream
1 cup grated kefalotiri or Romano cheese

3 tablespoons fine bread crumbs

Cook macaroni in boiling water according to package directions and drain. Allow to cool slightly. Mix the pasta with half the melted butter, the crumbled feta, grated kasseri, pepper, and a pinch of salt, unless the cheese is salty. Set aside. Prepare 2 cups thick white sauce, stir in the eggs, cream, and grated kefalotiri cheese. Butter an ovenproof baking dish and sprinkle it with breadcrumbs. Spread half the pasta mixture over the bottom of the dish, and pour half the white sauce over it. Do the same with the remaining pasta and cover with the rest of the sauce. Smooth the surface, preheat oven to 350⁰F, and bake about 30 minutes until the surface is golden brown.
Alternate: Chop 5-6 slices ham or bacon and add them to the basic pasta cheese mixture.

Rice Stuffed Zucchini
(Kolokithakia Yemista me Rizi)

Serve 4
Preparation time 45 minutes
Cooking time 1 hour

8 medium zucchini
1/4 cup butter or margarine
1/2 cup grated onion
1 cup crumbled feta cheese
1/4 cup short-grain rice
3 tablespoons finely chopped parsley
1 egg, lightly beaten
1¹/₂ cups puréed fresh or canned tomatoes
1/2 teaspoon sugar
1/2 cup olive oil
freshly ground pepper

Remove stems and ends of zucchini. Wash and parboil for 5 minutes. Drain in a colander and allow to cool. Scoop out centers with a potato peeler or a teaspoon, leaving only a thin layer next to the skin. Finely chop half the scooped-out zucchini flesh and sprinkle it with a little salt. Allow to stand in a colander for 1 hour. Squeeze out excess water with your hands. Set aside. Sauté the onion in the butter, add the chopped zucchini, and stir over moderate heat, until any liquid has evaporated. Remove from the heat, allow to cool, and stir in the cheese, rice, parsley, and egg. Fill the hollowed zucchini with the mixture, and arrange them in a shallow pan just large enough to hold them. Mix the tomatoes, oil, and sugar, and pour the sauce over the zucchini. Sprinkle with a little freshly ground pepper and simmer, covered, for about 1 hour, or until the zucchini are soft and the sauce is thick. Add a little hot water if the dish seems dry. Serve hot, sprinkled with freshly ground pepper.

Eggplant Patties (Melitzanokeftedes)

Serves 4-5
Preparation time 1 hour
Frying time 15-20 minutes

4 lbs eggplant (2 cups eggplant purée)
1 cup bread crumbs
1 cup grated kefalotiri or Romano cheese
1 garlic clove, crushed
2 eggs
1 teaspoon baking powder
1/4 cup finely chopped parsley
2 tablespoons minced onion
salt and pepper
fine bread crumbs for dredging
oil for frying

Wash the eggplants, dry, and broil according to the recipe for Eggplant Salad (page 29). Purée in a food processor. In a mixing bowl, combine the eggplant purée with the remaining ingredients. Mix well and refrigerate the mixture for about 1 hour. Form into patties and roll them in fine bread crumbs. Pour oil into a frying pan to a depth of 1/3 inch and heat the oil until it reaches the smoking point. Slip in the patties a few at a time and fry until browned on both sides. Remove with a slotted spoon and drain on paper towels. Serve with Tzatziki and Beet Salad.

Potato Patties (Patatokeftedes)

Serves 4-5
Preparation time 2 hours
Frying time 30 minutes

2 lbs potatoes
1 egg and 2 egg yolks, lightly beaten
3/4 cup grated kefalotiri or Romano cheese
2 tablespoons finely chopped parsley
2 tablespoons minced onion
salt and pepper
fine bread crumbs or flour for dredging
oil for frying

Wash the potatoes well and boil them in their skins. Peel and while still hot, purée them in a food processor. In a mixing bowl combine the potato purée with the beaten eggs, cheese, parsley, onion, salt, and pepper. Mix well, cover, and let the mixture rest in the refrigerator for 1-2 hours. Shape into patties, coat with fine bread crumbs or flour, and deep fry in hot oil until brown on both sides.
Alternate: Make fish roe patties (taramokeftedes) by substituting 1/3 tarama paste for the cheese and 2 teaspoons of oregano for parsley. Do not salt; the fish roe is very salty. Delicious with ouzo.

Zucchini Fritters
(Keftedes me Kolokithakia)

Serves 4-5
Preparation time 30 minutes
Frying time 30 minutes

2 lbs medium zucchini
1/4 cup grated onion
1/4 cup olive oil
1 cup grated kefalotiri or Romano cheese
3/4 cup dry breadcrumbs
3/4 cup self-raising flour
3 eggs
1/4 cup finely chopped dill or mint
salt and pepper
oil for frying

Wash and grate the zucchini into a colander. Sprinkle them with 1/2 teaspoon salt and let drain for an hour or so. You should have about 4 cups of grated zucchini. Meanwhile, lightly sauté the onion in the oil. Squeeze the zucchini dry, a handful at a time. In a bowl combine the zucchini with all the other ingredients, including the onion, and mix well. Heat an inch or more of oil in a large frying pan until almost smoking. Drop tablespoonfuls of the mixture, a few at a time, into the hot oil and fry until browned and crisp on both sides. Drain on paper towels and serve hot, accompanied by Tzatziki or Garlic Sauce.

Braised Kidney Beans (Barbounofasoula)

Serves 6
Preparation time 30 minutes
Cooking time 1-2 hours

3/4 cup olive oil
1 medium onion, grated
2 lbs fresh or dried shelled kidney beans
1 lb fresh or canned tomatoes, puréed
1 tablespoon tomato paste (optional)
1 tablespoon ketchup
1/2 cup finely chopped parsley
1 small, long green pepper, chopped
salt and pepper

In a large pan, gently sauté the onion in the oil until soft but not brown. Add all the other ingredients along with 2 cups hot water. Depending on the quality of the beans, cook slowly for 1-2 hours, until the beans are soft and the sauce is thick. Add a little hot water if the dish seems dry. Serve hot or cold, accompanied by feta cheese and salad.

Pumpkin Fritters
(Keftedes me Kitrino Kolokithi)

Serves 6
Preparation time 2 hours
Frying time 15 minutes

2 lbs pumpkin or other yellow squash
1 cup finely chopped spinach
3-4 fresh garlic stems, finely chopped or
1 small garlic clove, finely chopped
1/2 cup finely chopped spring onion
1/3 cup finely chopped dill
1/3 cup finely chopped fennel tips
1/4 cup finely chopped mint
3 eggs, lightly beaten
1/2 lb grated feta or other mild grating cheese
1/8 teaspoon cumin (optional)
1/8 teaspoon cinnamon (optional)
1 cup dry breadcrumbs
salt and freshly ground pepper
flour for dredging
oil for frying

Cut the pumpkin into pieces and grate into a colander. Sprinkle a little salt over them and let drain for 1-2 hours. Squeeze dry with your hands. Mix the spinach with the garlic, onion, and herbs, sprinkle with salt, and knead the mixture lightly to bruise it. Combine the spinach with the drained pumpkin and the remaining ingredients, adding the breadcrumbs gradually until you can form patties with the mixture. Let stand 30 minutes in the refrigerator. Shape large round patties, dredge them in flour, and flatten them with your palms. Heat at least 1 inch oil in a heavy-bottomed frying pan and fry the patties, a few at a time, over medium heat until they are browned on both sides. Drain on paper towels. Delicious either hot or cold, accompanied by Tzatziki, Garlic Sauce, or Eggplant Salad.

Greens Fritters (Hortokeftedes)

Yields 30 fritters
Preparation time 20 minutes
Frying time 8-10 minutes

1 lb various greens (spinach, nettles, chard)
1 cup self-raising flour
1/2 cup chopped onion
1/4 cup finely chopped spring onion
2 eggs
1/4 cup finely chopped fennel tips or dill
1/4 cup finely chopped dill or parsley
salt and freshly ground pepper
oil for frying

Trim and wash the greens carefully, discarding any tough stems or withered leaves. Chop finely, salt, and rub them with your hands to wilt them. Mix them with the remaining ingredients, adding a little water until you have a thick batter. Heat at least 1 inch oil in a frying pan and fry tablespoonfuls of the mixture, a few at a time, browning them on both sides. Drain on paper towels and serve either hot or cold.
Alternate: You may also add 1 cup grated feta cheese to the batter.

Place a thick piece of absorbent paper or a clean dish towel between the pot and the lid to absorb the steam. After 10-15 minutes, sprinkle with freshly ground pepper and serve the dish with black olives and feta cheese. Also delicious served cold the next day.

Leeks with Rice (Prassorizo)

Serves 4-6
Preparation time 30 minutes
Cooking time 1 hour

3 lbs tender leeks
2/3 cup olive oil
1 medium onion, grated
1 cup tomato purée or water
salt and pepper
1/3 cup short-grain rice
2 celery stalks, sliced
3 tablespoons finely chopped parsley
1 small green pepper, chopped
2 tablespoons lemon juice

Wash the leeks thoroughly and trim off the tops and all the tough leaves. Chop coarsely and blanch in boiling water for 5 minutes. Drain in a colander. In a heavy-bottomed pan gently sauté the onion in oil, until transparent. Add the leeks, the tomato purée or water, and seasonings. Cover and simmer until the leeks are half done, adding a little water, if necessary. Add the rice, celery, parsley, and pepper. Stir and simmer, covered, until the leeks are soft but firm and the rice is done. Remove from the heat. Sprinkle with lemon juice and freshly ground pepper. Accompany with feta cheese and olives or Greek Village Salad.

Spinach with Rice (Spanakorizo)

Serves 4
Preparation time 30 minutes
Cooking time 20 minutes

3 lbs fresh spinach
1 cup olive oil
1 small onion, finely chopped
1/2 cup chopped spring onions
1 cup tomato juice or hot water
1 cup finely chopped dill
salt and pepper
1/3 cup short-grain rice

Wash the spinach and trim off the tough stems. Reserve a few large leaves. Coarsely chop and blanch the spinach in boiling water. Drain and set aside. Heat the oil in a saucepan and gently sauté the onions together. Add the tomato juice or water, spinach, dill, seasonings, and stir. Spread the spinach mixture evenly over the bottom of the pan, with a wooden spoon, making hollows here and there. Wash the rice in a strainer, until the water runs clear. Fill the hollows with small portions of rice and cover them with the reserved spinach leaves. Simmer, covered, for about 15-20 minutes, until the rice swells and most of the liquid is absorbed. Do not stir while cooking. Turn off the heat.

Rice with Tomatoes (Domatorizo)

Serves 5-6
Preparation time 15 minutes
Cooking time 20 minutes

2/3 cup olive oil
3 garlic cloves, sliced
4 lbs fresh or canned tomatoes, chopped
2 tablespoons ketchup (optional)
1 teaspoon sugar
3 tablespoons finely chopped parsley
1 cup hot meat stock
1 cup hot water
2 teaspoons salt
2 cups short-grain rice
freshly ground pepper

Heat the oil in a pan and lightly sauté the garlic. Add the tomatoes, ketchup, sugar, and parsley. Simmer for 15-20 minutes, or until the tomatoes are a thick pulp. Add the meat stock, the water and stir in the rice. Simmer, covered, for about 20 minutes, until all the water has evaporated and the rice is soft. Sprinkle with freshly ground pepper and serve hot or cold, accompanied by feta cheese and Greek Village Salad.

Buttered Green Beans
(Fasolakia Voutirou)

Serves 4-5
Preparation time 30 minutes
Cooking time 1 hour

2 lbs fresh green beans or
1 lb frozen green beans
1/4 cup butter or margarine
salt and freshly ground pepper
2 tablespoons finely chopped parsley

Follow the recipe for Green Bean Salad (page 35) through the stage of dipping them in cold water. Drain them well and refrigerate, covered, until ready to serve. Shortly before serving, heat the butter or margarine in a saucepan, add the beans and toss them lightly, for 2-3 minutes, over medium heat. Serve them hot, sprinkled with a little salt, freshly ground pepper, and chopped parsley. Delicious with meat or poultry.

Rice-Stuffed Tomatoes and Peppers
(Domatopiperies Yemistes)

Serves 6
Preparation time 1 hour
Cooking time 1 hour and 40 minutes

6 large tomatoes
6 large green peppers
2 tablespoons ketchup
2 tablespoons tomato paste
1 1/2 cups short-grain rice
1 1/4 cups olive oil
1 cup grated onion
salt and pepper
2/3 cup finely chopped parsley
2 tablespoons finely chopped mint
4 large potatoes

Choose firm round tomatoes and peppers. Wash and wipe dry. Slice off the stem ends of the tomatoes and carefully scoop out most of the pulp, leaving only a thin layer next to the skin. Slice off pepper tops leaving the stalks intact, and remove the seeds. Reserve both sets of tops. Set aside. Purée the tomato pulp and mix with the ketchup and tomato paste. Wash the rice in a strainer until the water runs clear. Set aside. Heat half the oil in a saucepan, add the onion, and sauté until transparent. Pour in 2/3 of the tomato purée, add seasonings, and boil for 10 minutes, over medium heat. Remove from the heat. Add the rice, parsley, and mint. Mix well. Loosely stuff the tomatoes and peppers two-thirds full with the rice mixture. Pack them close together in a shallow baking pan. Replace the tops of each tomato and pepper. Peel and cut the potatoes into eighths and place them between the stuffed vegetables. Pour the remaining tomato purée over the potatoes, and sprinkle with a little salt and pepper. Spoon the rest of the oil over the stuffed vegetables and potatoes. Preheat oven to 350ºF and bake for about 1 hour and 40 minutes. Add a little water, if necessary, while baking. Serve hot or cold.

Rice-Stuffed Cabbage Rolls
(Lachanodolmades me Rizi)

Serves 4-6
Preparation time 1 hour
Cooking time 30-40 minutes

1 medium cabbage
1 1/2 cups olive oil
1 cup onion, grated
1 cup finely chopped spring onions
1 large carrot, grated
2 tablespoons lemon juice
1/2 cup finely chopped parsley or dill
salt and freshly ground pepper
3 tablespoons pine nuts
1/4 teaspoon cayenne
2 cups tomato juice
1 1/2 cups short-grain rice

Prepare cabbage and separate the leaves as in the recipe for Meat-Stuffed Cabbage Rolls (page 99). Heat the oil in a saucepan, add the onion, and sauté lightly. Add the tomato juice and the remaining ingredients, except for the rice. Boil the sauce for 10 minutes. Remove from the heat and stir in the rice. Strain the mixture through a sieve, reserving the sauce. Stuff the cabbage leaves with the rice mixture, making small rolls. Pack the stuffed cabbage leaves into a large pan in layers, seam side down. Pour the sauce over them, cover, and simmer, until the rice is soft and the sauce has reduced. Add some hot water, if needed. Serve hot or cold, sprinkled with freshly ground pepper and accompanied by feta cheese.
Alternate: Prepare the dish with water instead of tomato juice. Add 1/2 cup raisins and sprinkle 2-3 tablespoons extra lemon juice on top just before serving.

Leeks and Celery
with Egg-Lemon Sauce
(Prassoselino Avgolemono)

Serves 4-5
Preparation time 15 minutes
Cooking time 45 minutes

3 lbs leeks, washed, thoroughly trimmed
and cut into 2-inch pieces
1 lb celery root, trimmed
and cut in chunks
3/4 cup olive oil
salt and freshly ground pepper
2 eggs
1/3 cup lemon juice

Blanch the leeks and celery root, separately, in boiling water for about 10 minutes and drain. Set aside. Heat the oil in a heavy-bottomed casserole over high heat, add the leeks, and sauté lightly. Pour 1/2 cup water over them and simmer, covered, until the leeks are half done. Add the celery root, salt, and pepper. Stir and continue simmering, until the vegetables are tender but firm and the sauce is thick. Add a little water if the dish seems dry. To make the egg-lemon sauce, lightly beat the eggs in a bowl and add the lemon juice, a little at a time, beating continuously. Gradually add a few tablespoons of the pan juices, beating all the time. Pour the mixture over the dish, shaking the pan gently

to distribute the sauce. Serve hot, sprinkled with freshly ground pepper. Excellent with roast meat.

Braised Green Beans
(Fasolakia Yiachni)

Serves 5-6
Preparation time 45 minutes
Cooking time 1 hour

3 lbs fresh or 2 lbs frozen green beans
2/3 cup olive oil
1 small onion, grated
4 spring onions, finely chopped
3 garlic cloves, sliced
1 1/2 cups chopped fresh or canned tomatoes
1/2 cup finely chopped parsley
1/2 teaspoon sugar
salt and pepper

String the beans and cut off the tips. Wash in cold water and drain. Snap the beans in half, slice lengthwise, or leave whole. Heat the oil in a large pan and gently sauté the onions and garlic until soft but not brown. Add the tomatoes and sauté for a few more minutes over high heat. Add the beans and the remaining ingredients. Pour 1/2 cup water over them and stir well. Simmer, covered, for about 1 hour, or until the beans are tender and the sauce is thick. Serve the beans hot or cold, accompanied by Tzatziki or Beet Salad with Garlic Sauce.

Mushrooms with Garlic
(Manitaria me Skordo)

Serves 4
Preparation time 10 minutes
Cooking time 1 hour

2 lbs fresh mushrooms
1 lb fresh tomatoes, peeled and chopped
10 whole garlic cloves
2/3 cup olive oil
salt, pepper, and oregano
2 tablespoons lemon juice

Trim and discard raggedy or tough mushroom stems. Wipe clean with a damp cloth. Slice any large mushrooms in half. Place the mushrooms in a clay or glass ovenproof dish. Add the remaining ingredients and mix well. Preheat oven to 350°F and bake for about 1 hour, or until the mushrooms are soft and the liquid is reduced. Baste them now and then with the pan juices. Serve hot.

Mushrooms Greek-Style
(Manitaria Ellinika)

Serves 4
Preparation time 15 minutes
Cooking time 15 minutes

1/4 cup olive oil
1 small onion, finely chopped
1 garlic clove, sliced (optional)
1 lb fresh mushrooms or
1 lb can mushrooms, drained
1 tablespoon tomato paste
2 bay leaves
1/4 cup white wine
1/2 cup Chicken Stock (page 44)
salt and freshly ground pepper
2 tablespoons finely chopped parsley

Heat the oil in a saucepan, add the onion and garlic and sauté, until transparent. If using canned mushrooms, add them and the rest of the ingredients, except for the parsley, and stir well. Cover and simmer until the sauce thickens. Remove from the heat and discard the bay leaves. Stir in the parsley, sprinkle with freshly ground pepper, and serve hot or cold.
Note: If using fresh mushrooms, wipe them clean with a damp cloth. Add them to the sautéed onion and garlic, and sauté until their liquid is released and reabsorbed. Add the rest of the ingredients except for the parsley and continue cooking as above.

Mushroom Omelet
(Omeleta me Manitaria)

Serves 2
Preparation time 5 minutes
Frying time 10 minutes

1/2 lb small fresh mushrooms
2 tablespoons olive oil
2 tablespoons butter or margarine
4 eggs
1/4 cup milk or light cream
salt and pepper
5-6 drops Tabasco (optional) or
1/4 teaspoon cayenne

Trim raggedy or tough mushroom stems and discard. Wipe clean with a damp cloth. Slice the mushrooms in half or in quarters. Heat the oil and butter in a heavy-bottomed skillet, add the mushrooms, and sauté until juices are released and reabsorbed. Remove with a slotted spoon and set aside. Beat the eggs lightly with milk or cream, and Tabasco, if using. Pour the egg mixture into the skillet, scatter the mushrooms on top, and sprinkle with salt and pepper. When the eggs begin to set, flip the omelet with a spatula. Cook and brown the omelet to your liking. Transfer to a plate and serve immediately.

Fried Mushrooms
(Manitaria Tiganita)

Serves 4
Preparation time 15 minutes
Frying time 15 minutes

1 lb fresh mushrooms
flour for dredging
oil for frying
salt and freshly ground pepper

Trim and discard ragged or tough stem ends. Wipe clean with a damp cloth. In a plastic bag put enough flour to coat the mushrooms. Add them a few at a time and shake well. Transfer to a sieve or a colander and shake off the excess flour. Cover the bottom of a frying pan with 1/3 inch of oil. When hot, fry a handful at a time, turning frequently until crisp. Remove with a slotted spoon and drain on absorbent paper. Serve immediately, sprinkled with a little salt and freshly ground pepper.

Meats (Kreata)

In antiquity, the Greeks were known for their great love of meat. Because they valued meat so highly, they sacrificed it to the gods. But because the gods were ethereal, they also knew the delicious aroma of roasting meat would be sufficient to placate their lusty appetites. With the gods satisfied by the ritual, their worshippers were free to enjoy the succulent flesh. Even today, a lamb or kid roasted on the spit is the apex of festive dining. And since it has always been a luxury, a whole animal or joint is still associated with important feast days or special events.

Greece is a mountainous country, more suited to the raising of sheep and goats than cattle. As a consequence, lamb and kid have traditionally been preferred over beef and veal. In addition, in the old days every family kept a pig, which they would slaughter before Christmas and preserve for eating throughout the winter. Rural families also relied on game – rabbit and hare, venison and wild boar – to supplement their diet.

Generally speaking, meat – no matter what kind – was scarce and expensive, something to be reserved for special occasions or used sparingly to flavor a dish of vegetables, pasta, or rice. Until the 1960's, a roast might reach the dinner table five or six times a year in poorer areas, while even in more prosperous homes meat on its own was rarely more than a weekly event.

Nevertheless, small amounts of less choice cuts were affordable and Greek housewives became ingenious in making a little go a long way. They particularly had and have a way with ground meat, whether on its own or kneaded with onions, spices, or herbs. Every family has treasured recipes for meatballs – fried as keftedes, sauced as tsoutzoukakia, or even boiled as yiouvarlakia, not to mention grilled biftekia, which are akin to hamburgers. But in combination with vegetables, rice or pasta, some of their ground-meat inventions have become legendary classics of Greek cuisine. Among the more famous, Moussaka, Pastitsio, Dolmadakia (Stuffed Vine Leaves), and Yemista (Stuffed Tomatoes and Peppers) are often found on international menus.

Other dishes, less well known but every bit as delectable, are the marriages of inexpensive cuts of meat and vegetables that once tried will be cooked again and again. Favorite such stews are lamb with artichokes, pork with celery, or veal with zucchini, bathed in an egg-and-lemon or tomato sauce. Pot roasts, braised in a little liquid on top of the stove, are also more common than in some other cultures because ovens are a fairly recent phenomenon in Greece. Wood-burning ovens were used chiefly for baking bread, but only a few times a month since they consumed so much wood and required so much attention. Most food was cooked in a heavy pot suspended over the fire in the hearth or in a clay pot buried in the ashes.

General Instructions

In Greece, meat is invariably served well-done, regardless of how it is prepared. Most Greeks are horrified by rare meat and prefer the melt-in-your-mouth tenderness of slow-cooked lamb, pork, or veal. They have many ways of cooking it: roasted in the oven or on the spit, grilled over charcoal or under the broiler, fried with a little fat or oil, braised or stewed or baked in wine, broth, lemon, or tomato juice.

The way meat is produced and consumed has changed radically in recent years. The recommendations of nutritionists and doctors that we reduce our intake of ani-

mal fats has led to a demand for lean beef and pork, which is reflected in the raising of "designer breeds" with a far lower proportion of fat than in the past. It is estimated that the meat sold today is 27 percent less fatty than it was twenty years ago. But because fat is essentially what makes a cut tastier, juicier, and more tempting, these leaner meats need to be treated differently to keep them moist.

Meat consists of muscle tissue. Well protected muscles that are rarely used, such as the filet or the loin, have a smooth texture with few fibers. These are the tenderest but also the most expensive parts of the animal. The meat from young animals tends to be more tender than that of older ones, but that of more mature animals usually has a richer taste. Regardless of its age, meat from the ribs – lamb, kid, and pork chops, beef and veal steaks – is the best for grilling. These cuts are usually marinated beforehand in olive oil and lemon juice and seasoned with herbs such as oregano, thyme, or rosemary.

The most common cuts for roasting are the leg or shoulder of lamb, kid, or pork. Greeks consume very little aged beef nor do they have a habit of eating milk-fed veal. Most of the beef used is from a yearling steer; it is red in color but more delicate than beef. It is rarely hung but sold quite fresh so that it is apt to be tough and is more commonly found in stews than as steaks or roasts. On the other hand, Greeks are extremely fond of roast lamb, kid, and pork, which they often rub with dried herbs and leave to marinate overnight in the refrigerator for added flavor. The favorite herb in this case is oregano, but thyme and rosemary, or a mixture of the two, is also typical. Another dry marinade that penetrates deeper into the flesh is a mixture of herbs and finely chopped garlic inserted into gashes or slits made in the surface of the roast. As for salt, there is some disagreement whether meat should be salted before or after roasting, but I always sprinkle on a little salt in the beginning, because in small quantities it barely affects the moisture, while it does bring out the natural flavors. Pepper, on the other hand, loses its potency and aroma with long cooking, so I add it in two doses, before and after cooking – the first dose to permeate the meat, the second to give it the characteristic perfume and taste of freshly ground pepper.

Greeks love to eat roasted or grilled meats when they go out, but at home the traditional and most common way of preparing meat is braising or stewing with vegetables, pasta, or rice in a pot on top of the stove. For these dishes, meat from muscles that are well used, such as the neck, shoulder, or leg, are the most suitable. Being generally coarser and more fibrous, these cuts benefit from slow cooking over low heat. Although they may be tough, they can be extremely tasty and succulent when properly cooked. Cooking these cuts at high temperatures will make them even tougher, although you should brown the meat quickly in oil so that a crust is formed which seals in the juices. To sauté meat correctly, first wipe each piece with paper towels and heat the oil in a heavy-bottomed pan until it is almost smoking. Resist the temptation to add too many pieces at a time, because crowding the pan lowers the temperature and the meat tends to boil rather than brown and the juices escape. After browning, the meat is simmered slowly. The amount of water or liquid needed for cooking will depend on the type of pot you use and on the quality of the ingredients. Always pour in less water than the recipe suggests and add a little more while the dish is cooking, if necessary. Always add hot water so as not to interrupt the boiling process. When making meat and vegetable stews, partly cook the meat before adding the vegetables. The approximate time will depend on the freshness and type of the vegetable(s) used.

Fresh meat decays rapidly, so be sure to keep it in a very cold spot in the refrigerator at a temperature of 1°-4° C (under 40°F). Ground meat spoils even more quickly and should be cooked within a day or two of purchasing. Larger cuts and roasts will keep from three to five days. Although frozen meat can be stored for up to a year, ground meat for three months, for the sake of taste and texture, it is preferable not to leave it for more than one month. Never refreeze defrosted meat. The safest way to defrost meat is to leave it in the refrigerator for as long as it takes. While steaks and chops need only one day, larger cuts may need as many as three or four days. In all the recipes in this chapter, the bone is included with the meat for extra flavor unless otherwise specified.

Lamb on the Spit
(Arni sti Souvla)

The most representative traditional feast in Greece is Easter, especially Easter in the countryside. Village streets are lined with spits and the smell of young lambs roasting on charcoal fills the air. Even in the cities, anyone with a patch of open space or some kind of courtyard may be found roasting a lamb on the spit. Preparing and skewering the lamb is a difficult task which can take several hours to perform. All the preliminaries should be carried out the day before. Only young spring lambs weighing not more than 26 pounds should be cooked in this way.

1. Have the butcher remove the larynx and all the entrails, except the kidneys. Reserve them for your Easter soup (see page 48).
2. Sprinkle the stomach with plenty of salt and pepper and a little oregano, if desired.
3. Pass the spit through the lamb along the spinal cord, taking care that the backbone does not bend. Make sure that the spit passes through the center of the head, if your lamb has one. (Headless lambs are the norm outside Greece.)
4. Secure the lamb by passing a soft wire in two or three places around the spinal cord and the spit and pull to tighten and straighten the backbone.
5. Firmly tie and secure the lamb's neck onto the spit with wire.
6. Pull the lamb's legs up on the spit towards the backbone and cross the ankles, tying them firmly to the spit with wire.
7. Lace up the stomach opening of the lamb carefully with sturdy string and a poultry needle.

8. Rub the outside of the lamb with lemon juice mixed with salt and pepper. At this point the lamb is ready for roasting.

The day before, dig a pit in the ground slightly longer than the spitted lamb. Pound a forked, upright stake at either end of the pit, tall enough so that the spit holding the lamb will be 16 to 20 inches above the fire. Line the pit with aluminum foil – this will reduce the cooking time – and put plenty of charcoal on top of it. Light the fire and when the coals are white, lower the skewered lamb onto the stakes. Have plenty more charcoal at hand to keep the fire hot.

To roast the lamb, turn the spit slowly and constantly. The fire, at first, should be spread the length of the lamb, concentrated on the legs and shoulders. Baste the lamb from time to time with a marinade of oil and lemon juice, salt, pepper, and oregano or thyme, if desired. To baste the lamb, use a long stick with a wad of cotton tied tightly to the end with string and a double piece of cheese cloth. The roasting time will depend on the weight of the lamb. A lamb weighing from 22 to 26 pounds needs at least 5 hours cooking time to be well-done. One hour before it is done, lower the spit closer to the fire, drawing the coals under the parts that need more roasting. The lamb will be ready when the skin starts splitting open around the legs and the back and when the meat separates from the bone so that the bone shows through in several places. When a lamb is as well-done as the Greeks like it, it does not need to be carved. Simply remove the spit to a large table, spread with a plastic sheet. With a single tap of the spit, the meat will fall apart off the bones. Be sure not to let it get cold. This is a treat that is best piping hot.

Kali Orexi (Good Appetite)

Meat Kebabs
(Souvlakia)

Serves 4-5
Preparation time 6 hours
Grilling time 15-20 minutes

*3 lbs beef filet or sirloin or other tender parts of lamb,
pork, or veal, cut into 1¹/₂ inch cubes
salt, pepper, and oregano
2-3 tablespoons olive oil
1-2 tablespoons lemon juice
small wooden skewers
2 onions, quartered
2 green peppers, cut into 1-inch squares
2 firm tomatoes, cut into 1-inch squares or
whole cherry tomatoes*

Place the cubed meat in a large bowl, sprinkle with pepper, oregano, oil, and lemon juice. Mix well. Cover and marinate in the refrigerator for 6 hours, or overnight, turning the meat from time to time to keep it well moistened. Thread the meat onto the skewers, separating the cubes with pieces of vegetable, arranged alternately. If the meat is lean, thread small pieces of lard next to the meat. This will make the "souvlakia" tastier and more tender. Brush the souvlakia with oil and sprinkle with a little more oregano. Grill them, preferably over charcoal, turning and basting frequently, for about 15 minutes, or until the meat is done to your taste. Sprinkle with salt to prevent the meat from drying out and serve immediately, garnished with spring onions, sliced tomatoes, and lemon halves. Accompany with a green salad and french fried potatoes.

MEAT KEBABS, PAGE 92 • MEATBALLS WRAPPED IN CAUL, PAGE 25 • BAKED INNARD BUNDLES, PAGE 27

Spit-Roasted Pork Kebabs
(Kondosouvli)

Serves 6-8
Preparation time 6 hours
Grilling time 2 hours

4 lbs boneless pork, loin or leg, cut into serving portions
salt, pepper, and oregano
4-5 tablespoons olive oil
3-4 tablespoons lemon juice
1 small spit
2-3 large green bell peppers, seeded and halved
2-3 large firm tomatoes, halved
1 large onion, halved and separated into layers

In a large bowl combine the meat with salt, pepper, and oregano to taste. Toss with oil and lemon juice to coat. Mix well, cover, and marinate in the refrigerator from 6 hours to overnight, turning the meat from time to time. Thread the marinated meat onto the spit, alternating with pepper and tomato halves and onion layers. Grill slowly over charcoal, turning the spit continuously and basting the meat occasionally with the oil-lemon mixture and oregano. Grill 1-2 hours or until the meat is done to your taste.

Pork Chops in Wine
(Brizoles Hirines Krassates)

Serves 4
Preparation time 5 minutes
Cooking time 35 minutes

4 large loin or rib pork chops,
cut 1-inch thick
salt and pepper
3 tablespoons olive oil
1/2 dry white or red wine

Season the chops with salt and pepper. Heat the oil in a skillet large enough to hold all 4 chops. Fry the chops over medium heat, moistening with 1-2 tablespoons water when the juices boil down. Fry until the chops are cooked through, approximately 20 minutes. Then raise the heat and brown them quickly. Pour in the wine and boil briskly for 1-2 minutes, until most of the wine evaporates. Transfer the chops with a slotted spoon onto a platter. Stir the pan juices and pour the sauce over the chops. Serve immediately with fried potatoes and Boiled Greens.
Note: The chops also can be served with pitted green or black Greek olives preserved in brine. Use 1/3 of a pound and blanch them in boiling water for 5 min-

utes. Allow to stand 5 minutes more in the hot water, then rinse and drain. Add to the pan with the chops after most of the wine has evaporated and simmer, covered, 5-8 minutes.

Grilled Veal or
Pork Chops (Brizoles sti Skara)

Serves 4
Preparation time 12 hours
Grilling time 20 minutes

4 large veal or pork chops
salt, pepper, and oregano
olive oil
1 lemon, cut in wedges

Sprinkle the chops with pepper and oregano and brush with oil. Place them in a deep platter, cover, and marinate in the refrigerator for 12 hours. Grill the chops, preferably over charcoal, for about 20 minutes, basting with oil and turning frequently, until the meat is done to your taste. When they are nearly cooked, after about 15 minutes, season with salt, a little more oregano, and freshly ground pepper. Remove from the grill and serve at once. Garnish with lemon wedges and accompany with Buttered Vegetables and Greek Village Salad.

Grilled Lamb Chops
(Brizoles Arnisies sti Skara)

Serves 4
Preparation time 6 hours
Grilling time 20 minutes

1/4 cup olive oil
2 tablespoons lemon juice
oregano
2 lbs lamb chops
salt and pepper

Mix oil, lemon juice, and oregano. Rub the mixture onto both sides of the chops. Arrange them in a deep platter, cover, and marinate for several hours in the refrigerator. Grill, preferably over charcoal, taking care to place the chops about 2 inches from the heat. Turn the chops frequently. After about 15 minutes, when the chops are nearly cooked, season with salt and pepper. Remove from the grill and serve at once, garnished with lemon wedges. Accompany with fried potatoes and Greek Village Salad.
Note: The lamb chops can also be fried for a very tasty but much heavier meal.

Lamb Parcels (Arni Kleftiko)

Serves 6
Preparation time 1 hour
Baking time 50 minutes

2 lbs boneless lamb, cut in small cubes
salt, pepper, and oregano
2 tablespoons lemon juice mixed with
2-3 tablespoons olive oil
1/2 lb frozen peas
3 medium carrots, sliced
3 tablespoons butter, clarified
1/3 cup olive oil
2 garlic cloves, sliced
3 large potatoes, diced
2 large tomatoes, each cut in 6 slices
12 phyllo sheets
oil for brushing
1/2 lb kefalotiri or pecorino cheese, diced

Season the meat lightly with pepper and oregano. Toss with lemon juice and oil to coat. Cover and marinate for 1-2 hours in the refrigerator. Meanwhile, blanch the peas and carrots in lightly salted water for

5 minutes and drain. Toss with the butter. Heat half the oil in a heavy-bottomed saucepan. Add the meat cubes and sauté until lightly browned all over. Add the garlic, season lightly with salt, and set aside. Half fry the potatoes in a fryer and allow to drain on paper towels. Heat the rest of the oil in a large skillet and fry the tomato slices on both sides. Brush the top half of each phyllo sheet with oil and fold the other half over it. Brush again with oil. Do the same with the other phyllo sheets and put each two together. Distribute the lamb pieces, vegetables, and cheese evenly among them. Top with 2 slices of tomato and sprinkle with oregano and freshly ground pepper. Do not add salt, as the cheese is quite salty. Wrap and tie the phyllo with thick cotton string as if making 6 beggar's purses. Preheat oven to 350°F, place in a roasting pan, and bake for about 50 minutes. Serve immediately accompanied with Lettuce and Dill Salad.

Stuffed Breast of Lamb
(Stithos Arniou Yemisto)

Serves 8-10
Preparation time 30 minutes
Roasting time 2 hours and 30 minutes

1 tender lamb breast from the saddle up
1/3 cup lemon juice
the lamb's liver and innards
salt and freshly ground pepper
1 lb ground beef or
another lamb's liver and innards
1 large onion, finely chopped
1/2 cup olive oil
1 cup Carolina rice
1/2 cup finely chopped dill
1/2 cup finely chopped parsley

Parboil the liver and innards (which in Greece are sold as a unit) and chop them finely. Wash the lamb breast inside and out, rub it with lemon juice, and sprinkle with salt and pepper. Heat half the oil in a large frying pan and sauté the onion until translucent. Add the chopped organ meats, ground beef, salt, and pepper, and sauté, stirring, until all the liquid evaporates. Remove from the heat, add the remaining ingredients, and mix well. Fill the breast with the mixture and sew up the opening with kitchen thread. Preheat the oven to 425°F, place the breast in a baking pan, upright, and pour the rest of the oil and 1 cup water over it. Roast for 30 minutes and then reduce the heat to 350°F and continue roasting for two more hours or until the meat is thoroughly cooked. Baste occasionally with the pan juices. If you wish, strew some potatoes around the meat after the first hour. Sprinkle with salt, pepper, and pan juices and let roast along with the lamb until they are soft and lightly browned.

Lamb's Head Roasted in Paper
(Kefalaki sto Ladoharto)

Serves 1
Preparation time 5 minutes
Roasting time 1 hour and 30 minutes

1 or more lamb heads
salt, pepper, and oregano
olive oil
lemon juice

Clean and wash the head well. Wipe with damp paper towels and place on a double sheet of greaseproof paper, which you have brushed with a little oil to prevent burning. Season the lamb's head with salt and pepper, brush with oil, and sprinkle with lemon juice and oregano. Wrap carefully in the paper and tie the ends with string. Place in an oiled roasting pan. Preheat oven to 350ºF and roast for about 1 hour and 30 minutes. Remove from the oven and serve immediately with mustard sauce and a green salad.

Breaded Lamb Cutlets
(Brizolakia Arnisia Pané)

Serves 4
Preparation time 6 hours
Cooking time 10 minutes

2 lbs lamb cutlets
1/4 cup olive oil
2 tablespoons vinegar
1/2 cup dry white wine
2 tablespoons lemon juice
oregano (optional)
10 peppercorns
1 garlic clove, sliced (optional)
salt and pepper
2 eggs, lightly beaten
flour and fine bread crumbs
oil or margarine for frying

With a sharp knife trim any excess fat from each cutlet. Pare off the meat and fat from the last 2 inches of the rib bone, so that it is completely clean. Arrange the cutlets in a deep platter. Mix the oil, vinegar, wine, lemon juice, oregano, peppercorns, and garlic, and pour the mixture over them. Refrigerate and marinate for 6 hours. Remove from the marinade and drain well. Dip both sides of the cutlets into the flour, then into the beaten eggs, and finally into the bread crumbs. Arrange them on waxpaper and allow the coating to set for 30-40 minutes in the refrigerator. In a large skillet heat oil or margarine to a depth of 1/3 inch. Fry the cutlets, a few at a time, 4 minutes on each side, until the coating is crisp and brown. Garnish with lemon wedges and chopped parsley. Serve immediately with Buttered Vegetables and Cucumber-Tomato Salad.

Roast Leg of Lamb in Paper
(Bouti Arnisio sto Ladoharto)

Serves 6-7
Preparation time 30 minutes
Roasting time 2 hours and 30 minutes

1 leg of lamb (5 lbs)
3-4 garlic cloves, slivered
salt and pepper, oregano (optional)
2 tablespoons lemon juice
olive oil

Wipe the leg with damp paper towels. Sprinkle the slivers of garlic with salt, pepper, and oregano, pressing to make the seasonings stick. With the point of a sharp knife, make 20-25 slits in the meat and insert the coated garlic slivers into them. Rub the leg with lemon juice and brush with oil. Thoroughly butter a piece of greaseproof paper, large enough to cover the meat completely, and carefully wrap the leg in it. Tie the ends with string. Place in an oiled roasting pan and brush the paper with a little oil to prevent burning. Preheat the oven to 350ºF and roast for about 2 hours and 30 minutes. Serve with Lemon-Roasted Potatoes and mustard sauce.

Pot-Roasted Lamb with Lemon Sauce
(Arni Lemonato Katsarolas)

Serves 5-6
Preparation time 15 minutes
Cooking time 1 hour and 30 minutes

1/3 cup olive oil
3 lbs lamb, kid, or veal, cut into portions
1/3 cup lemon juice
salt and pepper
oregano (optional)

Heat the oil in a heavy-bottomed cooking pan over high heat, add the meat portions and brown them lightly all over. Pour the lemon juice and 1/2 cup hot water over them, add seasonings, and oregano, if desired. Cover and simmer, over a moderate heat, moistening with 2-3 tablespoons more water when the juices boil down, until the meat is tender and the sauce is reduced and thick. Serve with Potato Croquettes or Buttered Vegetables.
Alternate: When the meat is nearly cooked, add 2 lbs peeled potatoes, cut in pieces. Pour in enough hot water to cover the potatoes and simmer until the meat and potatoes are done, and the sauce is reduced and thick.

Roast Lamb with Potatoes
(Arni sto Fourno me Patates)

Serves 6
Preparation time 30 minutes
Cooking time 3 hours and 30 minutes

1 leg of lamb (4 lbs)
1/3 cup lemon juice
1/3 cup olive oil
4 lbs potatoes, peeled and quartered
1/3 cup margarine or butter
salt, pepper, and oregano

Wash the meat and place it in a roasting pan. Rub it with lemon juice, reserving any left over, and sprinkle with salt and pepper. Add a little water to the pan and pour the oil over the meat. Preheat the oven to 300°F, cover with the meat with aluminum foil, and roast for about 2 hours, basting now and then with the pan juices. Turn the meat over a few times to keep it moist. Add a little water when the juices boil down. Remove from the oven, surround the meat with the potatoes, season the potatoes with salt, pepper, and oregano, dot with the butter, and sprinkle with the reserved lemon juice. Raise the oven temperature to 350°F, return the pan to the oven, and roast for 1 hour and 30 minutes more, until the meat is tender and the potatoes are soft and lightly browned. Half an hour before serving time, take off the aluminum foil to brown the skin, or set the meat under the broiler for a few minutes. Let the meat rest for 5 or 10 minutes before carving.
Note: If desired, rub the leg of lamb with 3 cloves of crushed garlic, or cut the garlic into slivers and insert them into slits made all over the meat.

Lamb and Rice Casserole
(Arni Yiouvetsi me Rizi)

Serves 6
Preparation time 15 minutes
Baking time 2 hour and 30 minutes

3 lbs lamb shoulder
lemon juice
2 garlic cloves
salt and pepper
olive oil for brushing
1/4 cup butter or margarine
1½ cups long-grain rice
4½ cups hot water or meat stock
freshly ground pepper
kefalotiri or Romano cheese, grated

Rub the meat with lemon juice and garlic. Season with salt and pepper, brush with oil, and place in a clay or glass ovenproof dish with a small amount of water. Preheat oven to 300°F, cover dish with aluminum foil, and bake for about 1 hour and 30 minutes, or until the meat is tender. In the meantime, heat the butter or margarine in a saucepan over high heat, add the rice and sauté lightly. Transfer the rice from the saucepan to the baking dish with the meat, add the stock, put back the foil, and bake for another 20 minutes. Remove the foil, sprinkle the top with freshly ground pepper and grated cheese, and bake for 10-15 minutes more. Serve hot, accompanied by Tzatziki.

Baked Lamb with Orzo (Arni Yiouvetsi)

Serves 6
Preparation time 30 minutes
Cooking time 2 hours

1/2 cup olive oil
3 lbs stewing lamb, cut into portions
3 cups puréed fresh or canned tomatoes
4 garlic cloves, sliced
1/2 teaspoon sugar
salt and pepper
1/2 cup butter or margarine
1 lb orzo
2 medium tomatoes, thinly sliced
1/2 cup grated kefalotiri or Romano cheese,
plus more for the table

Heat the oil in a large heavy-bottomed pan. Add the lamb and lightly brown the pieces all over. Add the tomatoes, garlic, sugar, and seasonings to taste. Cover and simmer for 1 hour. Meanwhile heat the butter in a frying pan and sauté the orzo for a few minutes over high heat, until golden. Transfer to an ovenproof dish. In Greece a special clay pot, called "yiouvetsi," is used. Six individual glass or glazed ceramic pots could also be used. Arrange the lamb portions on the orzo and pour the sauce over them. Add 3 cups of hot water and cover the dish. Preheat the oven to 350°F and bake for 1 hour, or until all the water has been absorbed and the pasta is soft. Add extra hot water, if necessary, if the dish seems too dry. Fifteen minutes before it is completely cooked, remove the lid, arrange the tomato slices on top, and sprinkle with the grated cheese. Continue to bake, uncovered, until the cheese has melted and is lightly browned. Serve hot with additional grated cheese.
Alternate: The lamb in this recipe can be replaced by veal or other tender meat.

Kebabs with Yogurt and Tomato Sauce (Souvlakia me Yiaourti ke Saltsa Domatas)

Serves 5
Preparation time 1 hour
Cooking time 1 hour

1¹/₂ cups Beef Stock (page 44)
3 lbs boneless pork, cubed
pepper and oregano
olive oil

for the sauce
3 tablespoons butter
1 garlic clove, chopped
1¹/₂ cups puréed fresh tomatoes or 1¹/₂ oz can tomato purée
2 teaspoons sugar
salt, pepper, and cayenne
5 tablespoons margarine
10 Middle Eastern pita breads
1 lb strained yogurt

The day before: a) Prepare the Beef Stock (page 44) b) Thread the meat cubes onto 10 wooden skewers, arrange on a platter, and sprinkle with pepper and oregano. Brush the meat with oil, cover, and refrigerate. c) Prepare the sauce. Melt the butter in a saucepan and gently sauté the garlic. Add the tomato, sugar, pepper, and a pinch of cayenne, cover, and simmer, until you have a thick sauce. Allow to cool and refrigerate. The next day, one hour before serving, melt the margarine and brush the pita breads on both sides. Grill them lightly over charcoal or under the broiler. Then grill or broil the kebabs, basting with oil and turning them frequently, until the meat is done to taste. In the meantime, heat the beef stock and tomato sauce. Cut the grilled pitas into pieces and distribute evenly in 5 soup plates. Spoon 5-6 tablespoons hot beef stock over each and spread 2-3 tablespoons yogurt on top. With the help of a fork slide the meat off two skewers onto each plate and spoon 3-4 tablespoons tomato sauce over the meat. Sprinkle with freshly ground pepper and cayenne. Serve immediately.

Lamb with Curly Endive
(Arnaki me Andidia)

Serves 5-6
Preparation time 1 hour
Cooking time 1 hour and 30 minutes

2/3 cup olive oil
3 lbs lamb or kid shoulder, cut into serving portions
1/3 cup grated onion
salt and freshly ground pepper
3 lbs curly endive or escarole
1/2 cup finely chopped parsley
2 eggs
1/3 cup lemon juice

Heat the oil in a heavy-bottomed cooking pan over high heat, add the meat portions, and brown them lightly. Add the onion and, as it begins to brown, pour in a half cup hot water, season, and simmer, covered, until the meat is done and the sauce is thick. Add more water, if necessary if the meat seems dry. In the meantime, trim and wash the endives, chop coarsely, and parboil for 5 minutes. Drain well. Add the endives and parsley to the pan with the meat and continue simmering for about 15 minutes, or until the endives are tender but firm. To prepare the egg-lemon sauce, beat the eggs lightly in a bowl, slowly add the lemon juice and 5-6 tablespoons of the hot sauce, beating all the time. Pour the mixture into the pan, shaking it gently to distribute the sauce. Allow the dish to stand 5 minutes before serving. Sprinkle with some freshly ground pepper and serve accompanied by Greek Village Salad. *Alternate:* Substitute quartered artichoke bottoms for the endives. To prevent the artichoke bottoms from discoloring, immerse them in a bowl of water and lemon juice, to which you have added a little flour, until ready to use.

Lamb Fricassee
(Arnaki Fricasse)

Serves 6
Preparation time 1 hour
Cooking time 1 hour and 30 minutes

2/3 cup olive oil
4 lbs lamb, cut into portions
salt and pepper
2 lbs spring onions
1 lb romaine lettuce
1/2 cup finely chopped dill
1/2 cup finely chopped parsley
2 eggs
1/2 cup lemon juice

In a heavy-bottomed stew pot sauté the meat portions in the oil, over high heat, until lightly browned all over. Pour in 1 cup hot water, add seasonings, and simmer, covered, for about 40 minutes, until the meat is half done. In the meantime, trim and wash the spring onions and the lettuce, chop coarsely, and drain. Add them along with the chopped dill and parsley to the casserole with the meat. Cover and cook gently, until the meat is tender and the vegetables are tender but firm. To prepare the egg-lemon sauce, lightly beat the eggs in a bowl, add the lemon juice, a little at a time, beating continuously. Gradually add a few tablespoons of the lamb broth, beating all the while. Then pour the mixture back in the pot. Shake the pot gently to distribute the sauce. Serve immediately.
Note: Spring onions may be parboiled and drained before being added to the meat. For a less caloric dish, substitute plain lemon juice for the egg-lemon sauce. Simply sprinkle it over the lamb and swirl the pot to mix it in.

Meat-Stuffed Cabbage Rolls
(Dolmades me Lachano, Yiabrakia)

Serves 6-8
Preparation time 1 hour
Cooking time 30-40 minutes

1 large green cabbage
1 lb ground beef
1 lb ground pork
1 cup grated onion
1/2 cup short-grain rice
1/2 cup finely chopped parsley
salt and pepper
1/2 cup olive oil
1/2 cup butter or margarine
Egg-Lemon Sauce (page 52) or
Egg-Lemon Cream Sauce (page 52)

Choose a cabbage with loose leaves. Wash well and, with a sharp, pointed knife, cut deeply around the core, and remove it to make the leaves separate more easily. Blanch the cabbage in lightly salted water for 10-15 minutes, until the outer leaves are soft and sup-

ple. Remove the cabbage, drain and, when cool enough to handle, carefully remove all the soft leaves, which should detach easily. Blanch the rest of the cabbage, until the remaining leaves are soft and separated. Trim the hard stems off the leaves and cut each into 2-3 pieces, large enough to roll. In a mixing bowl combine the meat, onion, rice, parsley, seasonings, and oil, and mix well. Line the bottom of a large shallow pan with 1-2 cabbage leaves that are torn. Place 1 tablespoon stuffing at the base of each leaf, fold the bottom over it, then fold in the sides, and roll the leaf up. Pack the rolls tightly into the pan, seam side down, in more than one layer, if necessary. Pour 1 cup boiling water over the rolls and dot with margarine or butter. Place a heavy plate upside down over the rolls to keep them in shape while cooking. Cover and simmer for 30-40 minutes, until the leaves are tender and the sauce reduced. Add more water if the dish seems dry. When ready, prepare the egg-lemon sauce, or egg-lemon cream sauce, and pour it over the rolls. For a less caloric dish, substitute plain lemon juice for the egg-lemon sauce. Simply sprinkle it over the pan and shake to distribute evenly. Season with more freshly ground pepper and serve hot.

Meat-Stuffed Tomatoes and Peppers
(Domatopiperies me Kima)

Serves 6
Preparation time 1 hour and 30 minutes
Baking time 1 hour and 30 minutes

> 6 large tomatoes
> 6 large green bell peppers
> 1 cup olive oil
> 1½ lbs ground lean meat (beef or veal)
> 1 medium onion, finely chopped
> 2 tablespoons tomato paste
> 1 tablespoon ketchup
> salt and pepper
> 1/2 cup short-grain rice
> 1/2 cup finely chopped parsley
> 1 tablespoon finely chopped mint (optional)
> 4 large potatoes
> 1 cup tomato juice
> 1/4 cup butter

Wash and wipe dry the tomatoes and peppers. Slice off pepper tops and discard the seeds. Slice off the tops of tomatoes, and carefully scoop out most of the pulp, leaving only a thin layer next to the skin. Reserve the sliced-off tops. Purée the tomato pulp and mix with the sugar and tomato paste. Heat the oil in a large pan.

Add the ground meat and the onion. Sauté for 10-15 minutes. Pour in the tomato purée and seasonings, and cook over medium heat, until the sauce becomes very thick, approximately 15 minutes. Remove from the heat, add the rice, parsley, and mint, and stir well. Transfer to a strainer and reserve the juice. Stuff the peppers and tomatoes 2/3 full with the meat mixture and pack them closely in a shallow baking pan. Replace the sliced-off tops on the stuffed vegetables. Peel and cut the potatoes into eighths. Place them around and between the tomatoes and peppers. Spoon the reserved juice and tomato juice over the potatoes and sprinkle with a little salt and pepper. Brush the vegetable cases with a little olive oil, and dot the potatoes with butter. Preheat oven to 350ºF and bake for about 1 hour and 30 minutes until done and tops are brown. Add some hot water during the baking, if necessary. Serve hot.

Meat Rolls Smyrna-Style
(Soutzoukakia Smyrneika)

Serves 4
Preparation time 30 minutes
Cooking time 45 minutes

> 2 thick slices day-old country bread (crusts removed)
> 1/2 cup dry red wine
> 1 lb ground lean meat (beef or veal)
> 1/2 cup finely chopped onion
> 2 garlic cloves, crushed
> 1 egg
> 3 tablespoons chopped parsley
> 1/2 teaspoon ground cumin
> salt and pepper
> flour for coating
> 1/2 cup olive oil

> the sauce
> 1 lbs fresh tomatoes
> 1 tablespoon vinegar
> 1 garlic clove, chopped
> 1 bay leaf
> 1/2 teaspoon sugar

Soak the bread in the wine for about 5 minutes, or until thoroughly softened. Then squeeze out and reserve the excess wine. In a large bowl combine the ground meat with the wine-soaked bread, onion, garlic, egg, parsley, cumin, and seasonings to taste. Mix the ingredients with a wooden spoon until thoroughly blended. Cover and chill for 1 to 2 hours. Dampen your hands, pinch off walnut-size portions of the meat mixture, and shape into 20 oval rolls. Roll them in flour. Heat the olive oil in a large frying pan. Slip in the meat rolls and fry until browned all over, turning occasionally and allowing time for the meat to cook thoroughly. Remove from the pan using a slotted spoon and set aside. Strain the frying fat through a fine sieve into a sauce pan. Add all the sauce ingredients and the reserved wine. Bring to a boil and simmer until the sauce is thick. Drop in the meat rolls, spoon some sauce over them, and simmer, covered, for 15 minutes. Serve hot, with rice or french fried or mashed potatoes.

Veal Corfu-Style
(Sofrito Kerkiras)

Serves 6
Preparation time 40 minutes
Cooking time 50 minutes

3 lbs thick veal flank or loin, cut into 10 slices 1/3 inch
thick, and pounded to 1/4 inch
salt and pepper
flour for dredging
1/2 cup olive oil
5-6 garlic cloves, finely chopped
1/3 cup finely chopped parsley
1/3 cup vinegar
oil for frying

Season the veal slices with salt and pepper, dip them in flour, and shake off the excess. Heat the oil in a large frying pan. Add the veal slices 3 to 4 at a time and brown them over high heat for about 3 minutes on each side. Transfer the veal to a platter. Add the garlic to the frying pan and stir for a few seconds, add 1/4 cup water and the vinegar, and boil briskly for 1-2 minutes, scraping up any glaze from the pan sides and bottom. Return the veal to the skillet and add the parsley. Cover and simmer for 10-15 minutes, basting the meat occasionally with the pan juices. Serve hot with potato purée or rice pilaf.

Greek Hamburgers (Biftekia)

Serves 4
Preparation time 30 minutes
Cooking time 15 minutes

1 lb ground meat (beef or veal)
1 large onion, chopped
1 medium tomato, seeded and finely chopped (optional)
1-2 teaspoons oregano
1 egg
3 tablespoons bread crumbs
2 tablespoons grated kefalotiri or Romano cheese
1/4 cup olive oil
1 tablespoon vinegar
salt and pepper

In a large bowl, combine the meat with the onion and all the other ingredients. Knead for 2 minutes. The mixture should be moist and malleable. Add a few tablespoons of water or beer, if necessary, to soften the mixture. Cover and chill for 1-2 hours. Dampen your hands and shape the meat into four patties. Brush them with oil and grill, preferably over charcoal, turning frequently, for about 15 minutes, or until the meat is done to your taste. Serve hot. Greek hamburgers are delicious accompanied with Eggplant Salad, Tzatziki, or Taramosalata.

Noodles or Spaghetti with Meat Sauce
(Hilopites i Makaronia me Kima)

Serves 4-5
Preparation time 15 minutes
Cooking time 1 hour

1 recipe, Meat Sauce (page 53)
1 lb egg noodles or spaghetti
2 tablespoons olive oil
1 tablespoon salt
kefalotiri or Romano cheese, grated

Prepare the Meat Sauce according to the recipe on page 53. When the sauce is almost ready, bring plenty of water to a boil in a large pot, add the oil and salt. When the water is boiling rapidly, drop in the pasta. Stir to keep the strands from sticking together. Cook the pasta on medium heat for about 8 to 15 minutes, depending on package directions. When cooked al dente, drain and place in a heated bowl, add the sauce and the cheese, toss thoroughly, and serve.

GREEK HAMBURGERS, PAGE 101 • MEAT ROLLS SMYRNA-STYLE, PAGE 100

Baked Pasta Greek-Style
(Pastitsio)

Serves 8-10
Preparation time 1 hour
Baking time 1 hour

1/2 cup olive oil
1 medium onion, chopped
2 lbs ground meat (beef or veal)
2 cups puréed fresh or canned tomatoes
1 tablespoon tomato paste
2 tablespoons ketchup
3 tablespoons finely chopped parsley
salt and pepper
1 egg, lightly beaten
1 lb ziti or thick spaghetti
1/4 cup melted butter
4 cups grated cheese (Swiss,
Gouda, or Cheddar)
2 tablespoons fine bread crumbs

4 cups light Béchamel (page 52)
4 eggyolks, lightly beaten
nutmeg
1/2 cup grated pecorino cheese

Heat the oil in a saucepan and sauté the onion until transparent. Stir in the ground meat and sauté 10-15 minutes until slightly browned. Mix the tomato purée, tomato paste, sugar, and parsley, and pour it over the meat. Cover and simmer until all the liquid is absorbed. Remove from the heat, and allow to cool 5 minutes. Fold in the egg and 1/2 cup of the grated cheeses. Taste and season with salt and pepper. Set aside. Boil the pasta in lightly salted water until tender. Strain and toss with melted butter. When cool, mix in remaining cheeses, and set aside. Prepare 4 cups light béchamel and fold in the 4 lightly-beaten eggyolks. Add salt, pepper, and a pinch of nutmeg. Butter an ovenproof dish (12x14 inches), sprinkle the bottom with fine bread crumbs, and spread half the pasta over them. Place the meat mixture on top and cover with the remaining pasta. Pour the béchamel over the dish, and sprinkle with the grated pecorino cheese. Preheat the oven to 350°F, and bake for about 1 hour, until golden brown. Allow the dish to stand 10 minutes, then cut into portions, and serve hot accompanied by Greek Village Salad.

Zucchini Quiche
(Tarta me Kolokithakia)

Serves 8-10
Preparation time 30 minutes
Cooking time 40 minutes

2 lbs fresh zucchini
1/4 cup butter or margarine
3 tablespoons grated onion
10 bacon slices, coarsely chopped
2 tablespoons finely chopped parsley
3 eggs, lightly beaten
1 cup heavy cream
1 cup grated kefalotiri or pecorino cheese
2 tablespoons fine bread crumbs
salt and pepper
4-5 sheets phyllo
melted butter for brushing

Wash and grate the zucchini, sprinkle generously with salt, and drain in a colander for an hour or two. Remove as much of their liquid as possible by squeezing handfuls of grated zucchini between your palms. Sauté the onion in the butter or margarine until transparent. Add the zucchini and cook over moderate heat, for 8-10 minutes, tossing frequently. When the zucchini begin to brown, remove the pan from the heat and set aside. Broil the bacon until crisp and drain off fat on paper towels. Discard the fat. Mix the bacon and parsley with the zucchini. Beat the eggs with the cream and fold in the grated cheese, bread crumbs, and zucchini mixture. Season with pepper only. The zucchini will contribute sufficient salt. Cut the phyllo the size and shape of 1 12-inch quiche baking dish. Brush each sheet with melted butter and place them on the bottom of the dish. Spoon the zucchini mixture over the phyllo, smooth the surface, preheat the oven to 400°F, and bake for about 40 minutes, until the surface is golden brown. Serve at once.

Moussaka
(Moussakas)

Serves 8-10
Preparation time 2 hours
Cooking time 35-40 minutes

5 lbs round eggplant
1/3 cup olive oil
1 large onion, grated
2 garlic cloves, sliced
1½ lbs ground lean meat (beef or veal)
3 cups puréed fresh or
canned tomatoes
2 tablespoons ketchup
salt and pepper
2 eggs whites, lightly beaten
1/2 cup finely chopped parsley
6 tablespoons fine bread crumbs
1½ cups grated kefalotiri or
pecorino cheese
4 cups light Béchamel (page 52)
1/2 cup heavy cream
4 eggyolks, lightly beaten

Wash and trim the eggplant. Slice into 1/2-inch thick rounds. Sprinkle generously with salt and leave them to drain in a colander for 2 hours. Rinse, squeeze gently, and pat them dry with paper towels. Fry in hot oil until lightly browned on both sides. Drain and set aside. Heat the oil in a heavy-bottomed saucepan and sauté the onion and garlic until transparent. Add the meat and stir for 10 minutes until it begins to brown. Add the tomatoes and the ketchup, and season to taste. Simmer covered, until all the liquid evaporates. Allow to cool, and mix in the lightly-beaten egg whites and the chopped parsley. Sprinkle the bottom of a 12x14- inch, buttered ovenproof dish with 2 tablespoons bread crumbs, arrange half the eggplant slices in a layer on top, and spread half the meat sauce over the eggplant. Sprinkle with half the grated cheese and 2 more tablespoons of bread crumbs. Cover with the remaining eggplant slices, the remaining meat sauce, and sprinkle the top with the rest of grated cheese and the remaining bread crumbs. (At this stage you may freeze the dish, covered tightly. When ready to bake, let it thaw out first.) Prepare 4 cups light béchamel sauce, stir in the cream and eggyolks. Preheat the oven to 400°F, pour the sauce over the moussaka and bake for about 45 minutes until nicely browned. Let the dish stand for 15 minutes before serving. Serve with Greek Village Salad.

Alternate: Replace half or all the eggplant with sliced potatoes, or substitute zucchini for the eggplant. A combination of eggplant, zucchini, and potatoes can also be used.

ing a thin layer next to the skin. Reserve the flesh for a zucchini souffle or quiche (pages 78, 102). Gently heat the oil in a saucepan and sauté the onion, until transparent. Remove from the heat and mix with the ground meat, rice, parsley, salt, and pepper. Loosely fill the hollowed zucchini with the meat mixture, leaving room for expansion while cooking. Pack the stuffed zucchini closely into a heavy-bottomed, shallow pan and pour in 1½ cups hot water and the melted margarine. Cover and simmer for about 1 hour and 30 minutes, or until the meat is tender and the sauce reduced. Add a little more water if the dish seems dry. When ready, prepare the Egg-Lemon Sauce (page 52) and pour it over the dish, shaking the pan gently to distribute the sauce. For a lighter version, sprinkle the stuffed zucchini with plain lemon juice instead of the egg-lemon sauce. Season with freshly ground pepper and serve hot, accompanied by Cucumber-Tomato Salad or Greek Village Salad.
Alternate: Cook the stuffed zucchini in tomato sauce. Add a large peeled and chopped tomato to the meat mixture, and substitute 1½ cups tomato purée for the hot water. Cook slowly until the meat is done and the sauce is thick. Omit the egg-lemon sauce.

Meatballs with Egg-Lemon Sauce
(Keftedakia me Avgolemono)

Serve 4-5
Preparation time 1 hour
Cooking time 35 minutes

> *1 recipe, Meatballs (page 20)*
> *oil for frying*
> *1/4 cup olive oil*
> *1 large onion, finely chopped*
> *1 tablespoon flour*
> *2 cups Meat Stock (page 44) or water*
> *1/2 teaspoon tomato paste*
> *2 eggs*
> *1/4 cup lemon juice*
> *salt and pepper*

Meat-Stuffed Zucchini
(Kolokithakia me Kima)

Serves 6
Preparation time 1 hour
Cooking time 1 hour and 30 minutes

> *12 medium zucchini (about 4 lbs)*
> *1/2 cup olive oil*
> *1/2 cup grated onion*
> *1 lb ground beef*
> *1/2 cup short-grain rice*
> *1/2 cup finely chopped parsley*
> *salt and freshly ground pepper*
> *1/2 cup melted margarine*
> *1-2 eggs*
> *1/2 cup lemon juice*

Wash the zucchini and slice off both ends. Blanch them in lightly salted boiling water and drain. Using a potato peeler or a teaspoon scoop out most of the flesh, leav-

Prepare the recipe for Meatballs, adding mint leaves and 1/2 teaspoon ground allspice for flavoring. Omit the oregano. Fry the meatballs in hot oil, browning them lightly all over. Drain and set aside. Heat the oil in a heavy-bottomed pan and sauté the onions until transparent. Sprinkle with the flour and stir for about 1 minute. Add the meat stock or water, salt and pepper, and the tomato paste dissolved in a little water. Boil gently, uncovered, for about 30 minutes, until the sauce has reduced. Put the meatballs in the sauce, stir, and simmer together for 5 minutes. To prepare the egg-lemon sauce, lightly beat the eggs in a bowl, gradually add the lemon juice and a few tablespoons of the hot sauce, beating all the time. Pour the egg-lemon sauce over the meatballs, shaking the pan to distribute the sauce. Serve with Boiled Vegetables and Greek Village Salad.

Meat-Stuffed Artichoke Bottoms
(Anginares Yemistes)

Serves 6
Preparation time 1 hour
Cooking time 45 minutes

1/2 recipe, Meat Sauce (page 53)
1 egg, lightly beaten
12 frozen or fresh artichoke bottoms
1/3 cup butter or margarine
1/4 cup lemon juice
1 cup thick Béchamel Sauce (page 52)
1 egg, lightly beaten
3 tablespoons heavy cream
1 cup grated kefalotiri or Romano cheese

Prepare the Meat Sauce. When ready, let it cool slightly, and stir in the beaten egg. Set aside. If you are using fresh artichokes, trim and prepare according to the recipe for Artichokes Constantinople Style (page 76). Heat the butter in a saucepan and sauté the artichoke bottoms on all sides, until shiny. Sprinkle them with the lemon juice and remove from the heat. Allow to cool and place the artichokes in a baking pan or flame-proof baking dish just big enough to hold them. Spoon the juices over them. Fill each artichoke bottom with 2-3 tablespoons of the meat sauce and top with grated kefalotiri or Romano cheese. Prepare 1 cup thick béchamel sauce and fold in the beaten egg, the cream, and some of the grated cheese. Cover each artichoke with a smooth layer of béchamel sauce. Preheat the oven to 350°F, sprinkle the dish with the remaining grated cheeses, and bake until golden brown. Serve hot with Cucumber and Tomato Salad. Ideal for a buffet party.

Meat Loaf (Rolo me Kima)

Serves 8
Preparation time 1 hour
Cooking time 1 hour and 30 minutes

2 lbs ground beef or ground pork or
1 lb of each
2 eggs, lightly beaten
1 medium onion, grated
3 tablespoons finely chopped parsley or mint
salt and pepper
4 tablespoons dry bread crumbs
4-5 hard-boiled eggs

Combine the ground meat with the beaten eggs, onion, parsley or mint, salt, pepper, and bread crumbs, in a large bowl. Knead well. On a floured surface flatten the meat mixture, shaping it into a rectangle of approximately 6x12 inches. Shell the cooked eggs and arrange them along the rectangle, lengthwise. Fold the meat over the eggs, shaping it into a loaf. Seal well by patting the loaf with both hands. Coat with flour and cook the meat loaf in either of the following ways:
a) Heat 4 tablespoons of butter in a shallow heavy-bottomed pan over high heat and brown the loaf all over. Add 2 cups tomato purée, 2 bay leaves, 3-4 allspice berries, 2 cloves, and season to taste. Simmer covered, for about 1 hour and 30 minutes, or until the meat is tender and the sauce reduced. Add a little water, if needed. Serve accompanied by Mushrooms Greek Style or Rice Pilaf.
b) Place the loaf in a baking pan with 4 lbs potatoes, peeled and sliced. Add one cup water. Sprinkle the potatoes with 3 tablespoons lemon juice, season with salt, pepper, and a little oregano, and dot with 1/2 cup butter or margarine. Brush the meat loaf all over with a little oil, preheat the oven to 350°F, and bake for about 1 hour and 30 minutes, until the loaf is well browned, the potatoes are thoroughly cooked, and the sauce is almost completely absorbed. Serve hot.

Meat-Stuffed Eggplant
(Melitzanes Papoutsakia)

Serves 5-6
Preparation time 2 hours
Baking time 1 hour

6 medium eggplants (2¹/₂ lbs)
1 lb ground lean meat (beef or veal)
3 spring onions, finely chopped
1 medium onion, grated
1/2 cup finely chopped parsley
2 cups chopped fresh or canned tomatoes
salt and freshly ground pepper
1/2 cup olive oil
1 egg
3 tablespoons heavy cream
1¹/₂ cups thick Béchamel (page 52)
2 egg yolks, lightly beaten
1 cup grated pecorino cheese
2 tomatoes, thinly sliced

Choose elongated eggplants. Wash, wipe dry, and cut off the stems. Halve the eggplants lengthwise, sprinkle liberally with salt and place in a colander for 1-2 hours.

Rinse with cold water and squeeze out the excess water with your hands. In a large frying pan, fry the eggplants in olive oil over medium heat, until they are golden brown. Arrange them closely in an oiled oven-proof dish, flesh side up, and set aside. Sauté the onion in the oil, until transparent, mix in the ground meat, and sauté until lightly colored, approximately 10 minutes. Add the tomatoes, parsley, seasonings, and toss briefly over high heat. Then reduce the heat and simmer, covered, until the sauce is very thick. Remove from the heat and allow the mixture to cool slightly. Beat the egg and cream lightly, and mix into the meat mixture. With the back of a large spoon, press down the flesh of the eggplant halves, making space for the stuffing. Put 2-3 tablespoons of meat mixture in each half eggplant and spread evenly. Prepare the béchamel and fold in the egg yolks and half the grated cheese. Spoon a small amount of béchamel sauce over the meat, smooth the surface, and place a tomato slice on top. Sprinkle with the remaining grated cheese and a dash of freshly ground pepper. Pour a little water into the baking dish, preheat the oven to 350°F, and bake for about 1 hour, until the tops are golden brown. Serve hot, accompanied by Salad-Filled Tomato Cups.

Veal Stew with Potatoes
(Moschari Kokkinisto me Patates)

Serves 5-6
Preparation time 30 minutes
Cooking time 1 hour and 30 minutes

4 lbs potatoes
1 recipe, Veal or Beef Stew (page 111)
1/2 cup olive oil
3-4 allspice berries
1 garlic clove, sliced
1 bay leaf

Peel and cut the potatoes into four or six pieces, depending on their size. Soak them in cold water while you prepare the Veal Stew according to the recipe on page 111, with the addition of the extra olive oil, allspice, garlic, and bay leaf. When the meat is nearly cooked, add the potatoes and enough water to cover them. Stir gently and simmer, covered, until the meat and potatoes are tender and the sauce is reduced. Add a little water if the dish seems dry. Serve hot, accompanied by a green salad.
Note: For a tastier but richer dish, lightly fry the potatoes before adding them to the meat. In this case use only 1/4 cup butter.

Meat-Stuffed Vine Leaves
(Dolmadakia me Kima)

Serves 6
Preparation time 2 hours
Cooking time 40 minutes

1 lb fresh or preserved vine leaves
1 lb ground beef
1 lb ground pork
1 large onion, finely chopped
1/2 cup finely chopped parsley
1/2 cup finely chopped fresh dill or mint
1/2 cup short-grain rice
1 cup olive oil
1/4 cup butter or margarine
2 eggs
1/3 cup lemon juice
salt and pepper

Wash the vine leaves and trim off the stems. Blanch them, a few at a time, in boiling water. Drain and cool. Mix the ground meat thoroughly with the onion, herbs, rice, seasonings, and half the oil. Line the bottom of a casserole with any torn or damaged vine leaves. Lay out a vine leaf flat (dull side up) and place about a tablespoon of the meat mixture in the middle of it. Fold over the sides, then roll up into a neat parcel. Repeat, until all the filling is used. Arrange the stuffed vine leaves in the pot, packing them in tightly,

seam side down, to keep from unraveling while cooking. A second or more layers may be necessary. Pour in the remaining oil and 1 cup boiling water. Dot with the butter or margarine. Place a heavy plate upside down on top of the vine leaves to keep them in shape as they cook. Cover and simmer for 30-40 minutes or until the liquid is reduced by one third and the leaves are tender. Lightly beat the eggs in a bowl, add the lemon juice gradually, and continue beating. Very slowly pour 2-3 ladlefuls of hot liquid from the vine leaves into the egg mixture, beating all the time. Pour the egg-lemon sauce back over the stuffed vine leaves, shaking the pan gently to distribute it. Remove from the heat. Allow to stand for 15 minutes before serving. Sprinkle with freshly ground black pepper.
Alternate: The egg and lemon sauce, which is part of this recipe, can be replaced by a light savory White Sauce or an Egg-Lemon Cream Sauce (page 52).

Meat-Stuffed Onions
(Kremmidia Yemista)

Serves 6-8
Preparation time 1 hour
Cooking time 1 hour

4 lbs large sweet onions
1/2 cup olive oil
1 small onion, finely chopped
1 lb ground beef, 1 lb ground pork
1 cup canned tomato purée
salt and pepper
1/2 cup short-grain rice
1/2 cup finely chopped dill
1/2 cup butter or margarine
Egg-Lemon Cream Sauce (page 52)
kefalotiri or pecorino cheese, grated

In a large saucepan bring 4 pints water to a boil. In the meantime, peel and slit the onions, half way, from top to bottom. Drop them into the boiling water. Boil for about 15 minutes. Drain them in a colander, allow to cool, and separate the onion layers. Set aside. Heat the oil in a saucepan and sauté the grated onion lightly. Add the ground meats and sauté for 10 minutes more. Add the tomato purée and seasonings, cover, and simmer for about 10 minutes. Remove from the heat; stir in the rice and dill. Place 1 tablespoon of stuffing in each onion layer and roll. Pack the stuffed onion layers tightly together in a baking dish, to keep them from unraveling while cooking. Pour 1/2 cup boiling water over them, and dot with butter or margarine. Preheat oven to 400°F, cover, and bake for about 1 hour. There should be very little juice by the end. Prepare Egg-Lemon Cream Sauce, or Egg-Lemon Sauce, pour it over the onions and sprinkle with kefalotiri or Romano grated cheese. Serve hot.

Roast Leg of Pork
(Bouti Hirino sto Fourno)

Serves 20-30 (for buffet dinners)
Preparation time 30 minutes
Roasting time 7 hours

1 leg of pork, rind removed (16 lbs)
1/2 cup lemon juice
1/2 cup orange juice
1/2 cup pineapple juice
whole cloves
salt and pepper

Wash the meat well, drain, and pat dry with paper towels. Rub it all over with lemon juice, salt, and pepper. With a sharp knife score the top in diamond shapes and stud each diamond with a clove, first making an opening with a hard, pointed skewer. Place the pork in a roasting pan on a wire rack. Pour the orange and pineapple juices over the meat, cover with aluminum foil, and tuck it around the rim of the roasting pan. Preheat the oven to 275°F and roast the leg for 6-7 hours. Remove the foil, increase the temperature to 400°F, and roast the meat for about 1 hour more, basting frequently with the pan juices until well browned. Serve the roast hot, accompanied by quince, prunes, and apricots, prepared as in the recipe for Stuffed Turkey Greek-Style (page 152), or cut thick slices and serve cold with mustard.

Pork with Beans (Hirino me Fasolia)

Serves 6
Preparation time 12 hours
Cooking time 2 hours

1 lb dried white beans
3/4 cup olive oil
3 lbs boned pork shoulder or chuck, cubed
1/2 cup grated onion
2 garlic cloves, sliced (optional)
1½ cups tomato purée
1 tablespoon tomato paste
1 small green chili pepper, finely chopped
3 tablespoons finely chopped parsley
1/4 teaspoon cayenne (optional)
salt and freshly ground pepper

Soak the beans in water overnight and drain. Put them in a large kettle, add enough hot water to cover and cook until tender. Drain and set aside. Heat the oil in a large heavy-bottomed pan, and sauté the meat, until lightly browned all over. Add the onion and garlic and sauté lightly. Add the rest of the ingredients, except for the beans. Stir well, cover, and simmer, until the meat is almost tender. Add the beans and 1 cup hot water, cover, and simmer until the meat is soft and the sauce is thick. Add a little more water during the cooking time, if necessary. Serve hot.

Garlic-Flavored Leg of Pork
(Bouti Hirino Skordato)

Serves 20-30 (for buffet dinners)
Preparation time 30 minutes
Roasting time 6-7 hours

1 leg of pork, rind removed (14 lbs)
1/2 cup lemon juice
8-10 garlic cloves, slivered
salt and pepper

Sprinkle the slivers of garlic with salt and pepper and press the slivers with your fingers to make the seasonings stick. With the point of a sharp knife, make small incisions all over the meat, and insert the coated garlic slivers into them. Preheat the oven to 275°. Place the leg in a roasting pan on a wire rack, add 1 cup water, and roast, covered with aluminum foil, for about 6 hours. Baste frequently with the pan juices. Remove the foil, increase the heat to 400°F, and continue to bake, basting regularly for about 1 hour more, or until the pork is well browned. Let stand for 15 minutes before carving into thick slices and serve hot or cold with mustard sauce.

the mushrooms on a platter surrounded by the sliced tongue, and serve accompanied by Boiled Cauliflower.

Veal Tongue in Wine Sauce
(Glossa Moscharisia Krassati)

Serves 6
Preparation time 30 minutes
Cooking time 1 hour and 30 minutes

1 veal tongue (2 lbs)
1/2 cup vegetable oil or
1/2 cup margarine plus 1 tablespoon
1/3 cup olive oil
1/4 cup brandy or
1/4 cup whiskey
1 cup dry white wine
2 tablespoons lemon juice
salt and pepper
oregano and thyme
2 strips bacon, chopped
1 lb fresh or canned mushrooms

Wash and trim the tongue. Rub it with a little salt and lemon juice and cut in slices. Heat margarine or vegetable oil in a large, heavy-bottomed shallow pan, add the tongue, a few slices at a time, and sauté, until lightly browned on both sides. Drain and discard the cooking fat. Add the olive oil and heat to sizzling point. Pour on the brandy or whiskey and ignite. Shake the pan to keep the alcohol burning. When the flames die down, pour on the wine, lemon juice, and seasonings. Boil briskly until most of the wine evaporates. Add enough hot water to cover the tongue and simmer, covered, until tender. In a separate frying pan heat 1 tablespoon margarine and sauté the bacon and mushrooms. Add them to the pan with the tongue, cover, and simmer 5-8 minutes. Arrange

Veal Tongue with Rice
(Glossa Moscharisia me Pilafi)

Serves 6
Preparation time 30 minutes
Cooking time 2 hours

1 veal tongue (2 lbs)
salt and peppercorns
1 lemon, halved
2 carrots
1 small onion
1 celery stalk
1/4 cup butter
1 1/2 cups long-grain rice
1 green bell pepper, chopped

Rub the tongue with salt and lemon. Rinse well, put in a kettle, add enough water to cover, and bring to a boil. Discard the water and rinse the tongue. Put it in a pan of hot water along with the carrots, onion, celery, salt, and peppercorns. Cover and simmer for about 2 hours, until the tongue is tender. Remove from the heat and leave the tongue to cool in the liquid. Remove, peel off the skin, and cut in thin slices. Pour some stock over the slices to keep warm and moist. Strain the remaining stock (about 4 cups) through a fine sieve. Prepare the rice pilaf according to the recipe for Mussel Pilaf on page 130. Add the chopped green pepper to the rice along with the stock. When the rice is cooked, pack it into a mold, and turn onto a platter. Arrange the tongue slices around the pilaf. Slice the cooked carrots, sauté them lightly in a small amount of butter, and decorate the tongue and rice. Serve hot.

Pork with Cabbage
(Hirino me Lachano)

Serves 6
Preparation time 30 minutes
Cooking time 1 hour and 30 minutes

4 lbs cabbage
1 cup olive oil
3 lbs boned pork shoulder, cubed
1/2 cup grated onion (optional)
2 cups tomato purée
salt and freshly ground pepper
1/4 teaspoon cayenne
2-3 tablespoons vinegar

Discard the outer leaves of the cabbage and trim off the core. Cut the cabbage into pieces and wash. Parboil for 5 minutes in lightly salted water, drain, and set aside. In a heavy-bottomed saucepan, sauté the meat in oil over high heat, until lightly browned all over. Add the onion and sauté lightly. Pour in the tomato. Add the seasonings and simmer, covered, until the meat is almost tender. Add the cabbage and vinegar, and continue simmering until the cabbage is soft and the sauce is reduced. Add a little water if the dish seems dry. Serve hot.
Note: Other meats can be substituted for the pork. If the meat is lean, add 1/2 cup more oil.

Pork with Celery and Egg-Lemon Sauce
(Hirino me Selino Avgolemono)

Serves 6
Preparation time 30 minutes
Cooking time 1 hour and 30 minutes

3 lbs celery roots or stalks
3/4 cup olive oil
3 lbs pork shoulder, cut into serving portions
1/2 cup grated onion
salt and freshly ground pepper
2 eggs
1/3 cup lemon juice

Wash and trim the celery. If using celery roots, clean and cut in quarters. If celery stalks are used, cut into pieces. Blanch the celery in lightly salted boiling water, 8-10 minutes, and drain. Set aside. Heat the oil in a large pan over high heat, and sauté the meat until lightly browned all over. Add the onions and, as they begin to brown, pour in 2 cups hot water. Add seasonings, cover, and simmer until the meat is tender and most of the water has evaporated. About 30 minutes before the meat is completely cooked, add the celery and continue to simmer until the celery is soft but firm. Do not overcook. To make the egg-lemon sauce, lightly beat the eggs in a bowl, then add the

lemon juice, a little at a time, beating continuously. Gradually add a few tablespoons of the pan juices, beating all the time. Pour the mixture over the dish, shaking the pan gently to distribute the sauce. Allow the dish to stand 5 minutes before serving. Sprinkle with ground pepper and serve with feta cheese.
Note: Other meats may be substituted for the pork.

Pork with Leeks
(Hirino me Prassa)

Serves 6
Preparation time 30 minutes
Cooking time 1 hour and 30 minutes

4 lbs leeks
3/4 cup olive oil
3 lbs pork shoulder or leg, cut into serving portions
1/2 cup grated onion
2 cups tomato purée
1 celery stalk, finely chopped
salt and freshly ground pepper

Trim and wash the leeks well. Discard any tough dark green leaves. Cut the leeks into 2-inch pieces. Blanch them in lightly salted boiling water for about 10 minutes and drain. Set aside. Heat the oil in a heavy-bottomed casserole and sauté the meat over high heat until lightly browned all over. Add the onion and sauté lightly. Add the tomato, celery, and seasonings. Cover and simmer until the meat is partially cooked. Add the leeks and continue simmering, until the meat and leeks are tender and the sauce is reduced and thick. Add a little water if the dish seems dry. Serve hot, sprinkled with freshly ground pepper.

Veal Stew with Peas
(Moschari Kokkinisto me Araka)

Serves 5-6
Preparation time 1 hour
Cooking time 1 hour and 30 minutes

3 lbs fresh peas or 1 1/2 lbs frozen
1 recipe, Veal or Beef Stew (page 111)
1/2 cup olive oil
1/2 cup finely chopped parsley

Shell the peas, rinse, and drain. Prepare the Veal Stew according to the recipe on page 111, adding 1/2 cup more olive oil. When the meat is nearly cooked, add the peas, parsley, and 1 1/2 cups water. Stir lightly and simmer, covered, until the meat and peas are tender and the sauce is reduced. Add more hot water during the cooking time, if the stew seems dry. Serve hot, accompanied by Greek Village Salad.

Veal or Beef Stew
(Moschari Kokkinisto)

Serves 5-6
Preparation time 30 minutes
Cooking time 1 hour and 30 minutes

1/3 cup olive oil
3 lbs veal or tenderloin beef, cut into portions
1 medium onion, finely chopped
3 cups puréed fresh or canned tomatoes
4 tablespoons finely chopped parsley (optional)
2 tablespoons ketchup
salt and pepper

Heat the oil in a heavy-bottomed pan. Add the meat, a few pieces at a time, and sauté until lightly browned all over. Add the onion and sauté 2-3 minutes until transparent. Add the tomatoes, parsley, ketchup, salt, and pepper. Stir and simmer, covered, for about 90 minutes, or until the meat is tender and the sauce is thick. Add a small amount of hot water if the dish seems too dry. Serve accompanied by french fried potatoes, pasta, or rice and a green salad.
Alternate: This dish is equally good with lamb or pork.

Veal Stew with Green Beans
(Moschari Kokkinisto me Fasolakia)

Serves 5-6
Preparation time 1 hour
Cooking time 1 hour and 30 minutes

2 lbs fresh green beans or
1½ lbs frozen
1 recipe, Veal or Beef Stew (page 111)
1/2 cup olive oil
2 garlic cloves
1/2 cup finely chopped parsley

If using fresh beans, cut off both ends and string them. Wash in cold water and drain. Snap the beans in half. Set aside. Prepare the preceding Veal Stew, adding the garlic cloves and 1/2 cup more oil. When the meat is nearly cooked, add the green beans (fresh or frozen), parsley, and 1 cup hot water. Cover and simmer, until the meat and beans are tender and the sauce is reduced. Add more hot water during the cooking time, as needed. Serve the stew hot, accompanied by Greek Village Salad and Tzatziki.

GREEK VILLAGE SALAD, PAGE 32 • CUCUMBER AND YOGURT SALAD, PAGE 29 • VEAL STEW WITH GREEN BEANS, PAGE 111

Veal Stew with Eggplant
(Moschari Kokkinisto me Melitzanes)

Serves 5-6
Preparation time 2 hours
Cooking time 1 hour and 30 minutes

1/2 cup olive oil
3 lbs tenderloin beef or veal, cut into cubes
1 medium onion, finely chopped
2 lbs fresh or canned tomatoes, puréed
1/2 cup finely chopped parsley
1 teaspoon sugar
salt and pepper
4 lbs eggplant
olive oil and vegetable oil for frying
1 red bell pepper, cut in small squares
1 green bell pepper, cut in small squares

Prepare the complete recipe for Veal or Beef Stew (page 111). In the meantime, wash, trim, and cut the eggplant, in round or lengthwise slices, according to your preference. Sprinkle them generously with salt and allow to stand for about 2 hours in a colander. Then rinse them under the tap, squeeze out the water with your hands, and fry them in hot oil until light brown. Place the fried eggplant in the pot with the meat, fold in carefully, and simmer, covered, over low heat, for about 10 minutes. For a more festive presentation, lay two long, fried eggplant slices one on top of the other

to form a X, place one cube of the cooked meat in the center, and fold the ends of the eggplant slices over the meat, to make a parcel. Put a piece of red and a piece of green pepper on top and secure them with a wooden toothpick. Repeat the process until all the meat cubes or the eggplant slices are used. Arrange the small parcels closely in a shallow glass baking dish and pour over the sauce. Sprinkle with a little seasoning. Preheat oven to 400°F and bake for 15-20 minutes.

Veal Stew with Spinach
(Moschari Kokkinisto me Spanaki)

Serves 5-6
Preparation time 30 minutes
Cooking time 1 hour and 30 minutes

3 lbs fresh spinach or 1 lb frozen
1 recipe Veal or Beef Stew (page 111)
1/2 cup olive oil
1/2 cup finely chopped parsley or dill

Wash the spinach and trim off the tough stems. Chop coarsely and blanch in boiling water for 5 minutes. Drain and set aside. Prepare the Veal Stew according to the recipe on page 111, adding 1/2 cup more olive oil. When the meat is nearly tender and the sauce is thick, add the spinach and parsley, stir gently, cover, and sim-

EGGPLANT STUFFED WITH ONIONS, PAGE 81 • VEAL AND ONION STEW, PAGE 113 • VEAL STEW WITH ZUCCHINI, PAGE 113

sauce in a bowl, reserving the spices. Cut off the tops and tails of the onions, blanch for about 1 minute, drain, and peel. Heat the oil in a large heavy-bottomed pot, and sauté the onions in batches until lightly browned. Remove each batch with a slotted spoon. In the same pot, brown the meat lightly all over. Pour in the reserved marinade and season to taste. From the reserved spices, add 2 bay leaves, 6 peppercorns, and 6 allspice. Add the tomatoes, cover, and bring to a boil. Then reduce the heat and simmer for about 30 minutes. Add the sautéed onions and 3 of the reserved garlic cloves. Cover and continue simmering, for about 90 minutes, or until the meat and onions are tender and the sauce is very thick. If, when the onions and meat are ready, the sauce has not reduced to the required consistency, strain and boil it down rapidly. Pour it back over the stew. Serve hot with Boiled Beets.

Veal Stew with Zucchini
(Moschari Kokkinisto me Kolokithia)

Serves 5-6
Preparation time 30 minutes
Cooking time 1 hour and 30 minutes

2¹/₂ lbs small zucchini
1 recipe Veal or Beef Stew (page 111)
1/2 cup finely chopped parsley
1/2 cup butter or margarine for frying

Trim the zucchini, wash, and drain well. Prepare the Veal Stew according to the recipe on page 111. In the meantime, heat the butter in a large skillet, add the zucchini, a few at a time, and sauté until lightly browned. When the meat is tender and the sauce is thick, add the sautéed zucchini along with the pan juices and the parsley. Fold lightly, cover, and simmer for 10-15 minutes. Serve hot, accompanied by Cucumber and Tomato Salad.

mer for approximately 15 minutes. Do not add water, the water clinging to the spinach leaves will be sufficient. Do not overcook. Serve with Greek Village Salad.

Veal and Onion Stew
(Moschari Stifado)

Serve 6
Preparation time 24-48 hours
Cooking time 2 hours

2 lbs veal or beef tenderloin, cut into portions
1 cup olive oil
4 lbs stewing or pearl onions
salt and pepper
3 cups puréed fresh or canned tomatoes

the marinade
1/2 cup olive oil
1 cup dry red wine
2 tablespoons vinegar
3 bay leaves
20 peppercorns
10 allspice berries
4 garlic cloves

Combine the marinade ingredients in a large bowl. Place the meat in the marinade, cover, and refrigerate, for 1 to 2 days. Turn and baste the meat 3-4 times. Remove the meat from the marinade and strain the

Veal with Zucchini and Egg-Lemon Sauce
(Moschari me Kolokithakia Avgolemono)

Serves 5-6
Preparation time 30 minutes
Cooking time 1 hour and 30 minutes

3/4 cup olive oil
3 lbs veal tenderloin, cut into portions
1 large onion, grated
2^1/$_2$ lbs small zucchini
1/2 cup finely chopped dill
2 eggs
salt and pepper
1 teaspoon flour
1/3 cup lemon juice

Heat the oil in a large frying pan and sauté the veal over high heat, until golden brown. For a less pungent flavor, put the grated onion in a strainer, sprinkle with salt, and rub it between your fingertips. Rinse and drain well. Add the onion to the meat and sauté lightly 3-4 minutes. Add 1 cup hot water, season with salt and pepper, and simmer, covered, until the meat is partially cooked. In the meantime, trim the zucchini, wash, and drain. Cut any large zucchini in 2-3 pieces. Add the zucchini and dill to the pan with the meat and stir well. Cover the pan and continue simmering, until the meat is cooked and the zucchini are tender but firm. Do not overcook the zucchini. Beat the eggs together with the flour, slowly add the lemon juice, followed by 5-6 tablespoons of the pan juices, beating all the time. Pour the egg-lemon sauce over the meat and vegetables, shaking the pan vigorously. Serve at once.

Boiled Beef or Veal
(Vodino i Moschari Vrasto)

Serves 5-6
Preparation time 30 minutes
Cooking time 3 hours

4 lbs beef neck, chuck, or blade
3-4 carrots, cut into 2-inch pieces
2-3 zucchini, cut into 2-inch pieces
1-2 leeks, cut into 2-inch pieces
1 celery root, cut in pieces
2-3 potatoes, cut in pieces (optional)
2 small whole onions
2-3 parsley sprigs
3 cloves, stuck in one of the onions
10 peppercorns

freshly ground pepper

Place the meat in a pot, add salt and water to cover. Bring slowly to a boil, skimming off the scum that rises to the top. Slow heating of the liquid is important to the clarity of the broth. Meat penetrated gradually by the heat releases scum which will cloud the broth if it is not removed. When the liquid starts to boil, add 3-4 tablespoons cold water to lower the temperature. Continue skimming the surface until no more scum rises. Cover and simmer the meat for about 2 hours and 30 minutes. Add the vegetables, cloves, and peppercorns. Cover and simmer for another 30 minutes, until the vegetables are tender but firm. Lift the meat out and put it in the center of a large platter. Remove the vegetables with a slotted spoon and place them around the meat. Serve the meat hot or cold with mustard sauce. Strain the broth through a fine sieve, adjust the seasoning, and serve in soup plates, sprinkled with freshly ground pepper and grated kefalotiri cheese. Otherwise, use the broth to make soup or to prepare a rice pilaf.

Veal Stew with Eggplant Purée
(Moschari Kokkinisto me Poure Melitzanes)

Serves 5-6
Preparation time 1 hour
Cooking time 1 hour and 30 minutes

1 recipe, Veal or Beef Stew (page 111)
3-4 allspice berries
5-6 peppercorns
6 large eggplants (4 lbs)
1 cup light Béchamel Sauce (page 52)
salt and pepper
nutmeg
1 cup grated kefalotiri or Romano cheese

Prepare Veal Stew (page 111), adding the allspice and peppercorns. Cook until done. Meanwhile, prepare and roast the eggplant as in the recipe for Eggplant Salad (page 29). Peel, cut, and mash them. Prepare 1 cup light béchamel sauce, add a few gratings of nutmeg, and pour the sauce onto the mashed eggplant. Mix and stir over medium heat for 5-6 minutes. Turn off the heat, add the grated cheese, and stir until it is well blended. Adjust the seasonings and transfer onto a serving platter. Spoon some of the sauce over the purée and surround with the meat. Pass the remaining sauce in a heated gravy boat and accompany with a green salad.

Peppers and Sausages in Tomato Sauce (Spetzofai)

Serves 4
Preparation time 2 hours
Cooking time 15 minutes

3 lbs eggplant
1 lb long green peppers
oil for frying
1 lb hot, fresh pork sausages
1/2 cup olive oil
2 lbs fresh tomatoes, puréed

Wash, trim, and slice the eggplants into 1/2-inch-thick rounds. Sprinkle generously with salt and let them stand for about 2 hours in a colander. Rinse them under running water to remove the salt and squeeze out the excess water with your hands. Wash the peppers, trim off the tops, and remove the seeds. Fry the eggplant and peppers until lightly browned. Slice the sausages and brown them lightly in a skillet over medium heat. Drain and discard the fat. Replace the fat with the olive oil and finish frying. Add the tomatoes and cook for 20 minutes, until the sauce is thick. Remove the sausages with a slotted spoon and mound them in the center of a round platter. Surround with the fried eggplant and peppers, and spoon the remaining sauce over them. Sprinkle with a little freshly ground pepper, cover with aluminum foil, preheat the oven to 350⁰F, and bake for about 15 minutes. Serve hot.

Pork in Aspic (Pikti)

Serves 20
Preparation time 2 hours
Cooking time 3-4 hours

1 pig's head, about 6 lbs
salt
2-3 small onions, peeled
3-4 carrots, peeled
1 celery root, peeled and cut in chunks
4 parsley sprigs
4-5 garlic cloves
1-2 bay leaves
10 peppercorns
2-3 tablespoons capers
1/4 cup chopped cucumber pickles
1/3 cup vinegar

Ask the butcher to cut the pig's head into several pieces and to remove the eyes and brain. Wash and let the meat stand in lightly salted water, covered, for about 1-2 hours in the refrigerator, to remove all blood. Change the water every 15-20 minutes. Drain, rinse, and place in a pot. Cover with water, add salt, and bring slowly to a boil, skimming frequently. To slow down the boiling, add 3-4 tablespoons cold water and continue skimming. Add the vegetables, garlic, bay leaves, and peppercorns, and skim off any more scum that rises. Cover and simmer for 2-3 hours. Place in a colander and strain into a clean pot. Separate the bones from the meat. Return the bones to the stock. Cut the meat into small pieces, slice the carrots, and combine in a large mixing bowl with the capers and pickles. Arrange the mixture in a large rectangular mold. Cook the stock for 30-40 minutes longer. Strain into a clean saucepan, skim the fat from the top, add the vinegar, and boil for 5 minutes. You should have about 5-6 cups of stock. Strain again through a sieve covered with damp muslin and allow to cool. If a small amount of stock on a saucer does not set to a jelly in the refrigerator, reheat the stock and reduce over high heat, until it reaches the required consistency. Remove from the heat and allow to cool. When the stock is beginning to thicken, but has not yet jellied, spoon it over the pork into the mold. Refrigerate until set. Serve cold, cut in slices.
Note: This dish can also be made with a kilo of pork shoulder instead of a head, but in this case you will have to add 2 tablespoons of gelatine to the stock.

Veal and Noodle Casseroles
(Moschari Yiouvetsi me Hilopites)

Serves 5-6
Preparation time 30 minutes
Cooking time 2 hours

1 lb Homemade Noodles (page 56)
1 recipe, Veal or Beef Stew (page 111)
1 garlic clove, sliced
3 small tomatoes
1/3 cup butter
1 cup grated kefalotiri or Romano cheese
5-6 small ceramic pots

Prepare the Veal Stew according to the recipe on page 111, adding the garlic clove as well. When the meat is partially cooked, remove from the heat. Cook the noodles with a small amount of water over moderate heat. When the noodles are soft but firm and most of the water is absorbed, remove from the heat and divide them among 5-6 individual ceramic pots. Then place one serving of meat in each pot and cover with sauce. Cut the tomatoes into halves, remove seeds and drain. Melt the butter in a frying pan and sauté the tomato halves for about 2 minutes on each side. Place a half tomato on top of each ceramic dish, and spoon the butter over them all. Preheat the oven to 350°F, sprinkle with grated cheese, and bake for 15-20 minutes, until the meat and noodles are completely cooked and the sauce is absorbed. Serve immediately, with Cucumber and Tomato Salad.

Pot-Roasted Beef or Veal
(Moschari Psito Katsarolas)

Serves 6
Preparation time 30 minutes
Roasting time 2 hours

2 lbs sirloin or rump of beef
salt and pepper
1/3 cup olive oil
2 tablespoons finely chopped onion (optional)
1/2 cup dry red wine
1/4 cup lemon juice
1 teaspoon cornstarch

Wash the meat, drain, and pat dry with a paper towel. Tie up with kitchen string so that it holds its shape while cooking. Season with salt and pepper. In a large heavy-bottomed casserole heat the oil, and sauté the meat until browned. Remove the meat and in the same pan sauté the onions until they are light brown. Return the meat to the pan, add the wine and lemon juice, cover, and simmer over the lowest possible heat, for about 2 hours, occasionally moistening with a few tablespoons of water. When the meat is tender, remove it from the casserole, and discard the string. Slice and arrange the meat on a platter. Keep it hot in a low oven while you strain the sauce through a fine sieve, pressing the solids firmly with a pestle or wooden spoon to extract all the juices. You should have 1 cup of sauce. Return it to the casserole, stir in the cornstarch, dissolved in a little cold water, and simmer 3-4 minutes, until the sauce is thick and glossy. Pour the sauce over the meat, serve with Fried Potatoes or Buttered Peas and Carrots.

Stuffed Veal Breast
(Moschari Rolo)

Serves 6-7
Preparation time 1 hour
Cooking time 2 hours

3 lbs breast of veal, boned
2 tablespoons butter
1 small onion, finely chopped
1/2 lb ground beef
1 tablespoon ketchup
1 tablespoon mustard
1/4 cup pistachio nuts, coarsely chopped
1 egg
salt and pepper
1/3 cup olive oil
1/4 cup brandy
1/4 cup lemon juice

Ask your butcher to remove the bones and prepare the breast for rolling. To make the stuffing, heat the butter and gently sauté the onion until transparent. Mix it in a bowl with the ground meat, ketchup, mustard, pistachio nuts, salt, and pepper. Combine the mixture with a raw egg, until thoroughly blended. Shape the mixture into a long roll, as long as the veal breast, and place it on the meat. Draw the two long edges of the breast together over the stuffing and tie up the veal roll with string. Season the roll lightly with salt and pepper. Heat the oil in a casserole large enough to hold the roll comfortably, and brown it on all sides over high heat. Reduce the heat to low. Cover and continue to simmer, moistening occasionally with a few tablespoons of a mixture of brandy, lemon juice, and water. When cooked, after about 2 hours, lift out the roll, remove the string, slice, and place on a hot serving platter. Strain the sauce through a fine sieve and pour it over the meat. Serve immediately, accompanied by Buttered Artichoke Bottoms filled with Buttered Peas and Carrots. An excellent choice for a buffet.

Veal Roll Wrapped in Phyllo
(Moschari Rolo se Phyllo)

Serves 6-8
Preparation time 1 hour
Baking time 1 hour

1/3 cup butter or margarine

2 lbs boneless veal, cut into small cubes
1 large onion, finely chopped
2 tablespoons flour
1½ cups Beef Stock (page 44)
salt and pepper
3 boiled carrots, cubed (optional)
2 hard-boiled eggs, chopped
2 cups grated cheese (Swiss, Gouda or Cheddar)
1/2 lb ham, cubed
3 tablespoons finely chopped parsley or dill
2 eggs, lightly beaten
8 sheets phyllo
1/3 cup butter or margarine, melted

Heat the butter in a large saucepan and sauté the meat cubes over high heat, until lightly browned all over. Remove the meat with a slotted spoon onto a plate. In the same pan, sauté the onion, until lightly browned. Sprinkle with the flour and stir for 1 minute. Return the meat to the pan, pour in the beef stock, add the seasonings, and simmer, covered, for about 40 minutes, or until the veal is nearly cooked and the sauce is reduced. Remove from the heat, allow to cool slightly, and mix in the carrots, chopped eggs, cheese, ham, and parsley. Bind the mixture with the beaten eggs. On a floured board place the phyllo sheets one on top of the other, brushing each one with melted butter. Arrange the meat mixture lengthwise over the phyllo sheets and fold, shaping into a thick roll. Wet the edges of the phyllo and press them together to seal, place the roll in a buttered baking pan, brush it with butter, and score 3-4 times, to allow steam to escape while baking. Preheat oven to 350°F and bake for about 1 hour, until golden brown. Serve hot, cut in thick slices, accompanied by Lemon-Roasted Potatoes.

Veal Stew with Quinces
(Moschari me Kidonia)

Serves 5-6
Preparation time 1 hour
Cooking time 1 hour and 30 minutes

2/3 cup butter or margarine
3 lbs tenderloin of veal, cut into large chunks
1 medium onion, grated
1½ cups fresh or canned puréed tomatoes
2 teaspoons sugar
salt and freshly ground pepper
5 allspice berries
3 lbs quince
2 tablespoons lemon juice
nutmeg

Heat half the butter or margarine in a heavy-bottomed pan, add the meat, and brown lightly. Add the onion and, as it begins to brown, pour in 1/2 cup water and the tomatoes. Add the sugar and seasonings. Cover and simmer until the meat is cooked and the sauce is reduced. In the meantime, peel and cut the quinces into pieces, remove the hard cores and seeds, and sprinkle with lemon juice to prevent discoloring. Heat the remaining butter in a frying pan and sauté the quinces over medium heat, until lightly browned. Add the fruit and 1/2 cup hot water to the pan with the meat. Stir lightly and simmer, until the quinces are soft but firm and the sauce is reduced. Do not stir the food during the cooking. Shake the pan occasionally to avoid sticking. Sprinkle with a few gratings of nutmeg and freshly ground pepper and serve hot, accompanied by a green salad or Carrot Salad.

Pelion Sausage
(Pelioritiko Boubari)

Serves 5-6
Preparation time 1 hour
Baking time 1 hour and 30 minutes

1 long, thick piece of lamb
or kid intestine or sausage casing
vinegar
1 heart and liver of a spring lamb or kid
1 cup olive oil
2 medium onions, chopped
1 lb ground meat (beef or pork)
1½ cups chopped fresh or canned tomatoes
1/3 cup short-grain rice
1/2 cup finely chopped dill
2 lbs potatoes, quartered
salt and pepper

Wash the intestine very well inside and out. Rinse with vinegar. Parboil the heart and liver, rinse, and chop in small pieces. Heat the oil in a saucepan and sauté the onion, the heart and liver pieces, and the ground meat for about 15 minutes. Add the tomatoes, stir, and cook for a few minutes more. Remove from the heat, add the rice, dill, salt, and pepper. Stir well and strain through a fine sieve, reserving the liquid. Stuff the intestine with the meat mixture. Do not overstuff. Twist the stuffed intestine over the bottom of a large baking pan, shaping it into a loose coil. Add the potato quarters in between and around the boubari. Pierce the boubari in several places so that the steam can escape while baking. Spoon the reserved liquid over the potatoes and sprinkle with salt and freshly ground pepper. Preheat the oven to 350°F, add 1/2 cup water, and bake, uncovered, for 45 minutes. Cover the meat with aluminum foil to keep it moist and bake for another 45 minutes or until done. Serve hot with a Lettuce and Dill Salad.

Lamb with Vegetables
(Arni me Lachanika)

Serves 5-6
Preparation time 1 hour
Cooking time 2 hours

1/3 cup olive oil
2 lbs boneless lamb, cubed
2 medium onions, sliced
1 leek, cut in pieces
3 carrots, sliced
4 medium potatoes, sliced
1 cup beef stock
salt and pepper
1/3 cup butter or margarine
2 tablespoons finely chopped parsley

Heat the olive oil in a saucepan over high heat and sauté the meat cubes, until lightly browned. Remove them with a slotted spoon. In the same pan sauté the onions and leek, until they are soft but not brown. In a clay or glass baking dish arrange half the meat cubes, then half the carrots, and half the potatoes. Spread half the sautéed onions and leek on top. Continue layering the remaining meat, carrots, potatoes, and onion and leek mixture. Sprinkle with parsley and season with salt and pepper. Pour the stock into the frying pan, stir to scrape up any glaze, bring to a simmer, and pour it over the meat and vegetables. Preheat the oven to 350°F. Dot the baking dish with slivers of butter, cover tightly, and bake for about 2 hours, or until the meat and vegetables are tender. Serve straight from the oven, sprinkled with freshly ground pepper.

Easter Eggs (Paskalina Avga)

Traditionally, Greek Easter eggs are colored red and decorated with small stickers containing Easter motifs. Many years ago, when stickers did not exist, housewives used to decorate the eggs with patterns from the leaves of various plants. They would wrap tulle around the egg and leaf before placing the eggs in a pot of red dye. Nowadays some households have adopted the multicolored dyes available, but red eggs – symbolizing the blood of Christ – are still the norm in Greece. They are customarily dyed on Holy Thursday and cracked and eaten to break the Lenten fast after the midnight mass on Holy Saturday.

To dye eggs the Greek way, place them in a large pot covered with cold water and bring them slowly to the boil. When the water starts to boil, lower the heat and simmer for 10 minutes. Remove them with a slotted spoon, a few at a time, and dip them in the dye that you have previously prepared, according to the package directions, in another pot. Let them stay 4-5 minutes. Do not layer the eggs. It is better to repeat the process than crowd them and risk cracking.

Remove the eggs from the dye and leave to drain on paper towels. Before the eggs are completely cool, polish them with a soft cloth dipped in olive oil.

With this method you need dye only the uncracked ones. When eggs boil in the dye from the beginning, they often develop miniscule cracks, and the dye penetrates the whites. Any cracked eggs should of course be eaten first, because they are more perishable.

To decorate eggs in the traditional way our grandmothers did, choose small, pretty leaves from different plants (parsley, fern, basil, etc.). Place one leaf on each egg, after boiling, first in plain water. Wrap and tie it tightly in a piece of tulle or sheer hose. Dip them in the dye for 4-5 minutes. Take them out of the dye, and let them drain on paper towels. Cut the tulle or hose open, and remove it with the leaf. The imprint of the leaf will remain on the egg.

Fish and Seafood
(Psaria ke Thalassina)

From time immemorial fish and seafood have been a fundamental part of the Greek diet – small wonder since we are a nation of islands and even the mainland is surrounded on three sides by the Mediterranean. Every Greek waterfront has its fish markets, while some fish are sold straight from the caique as quickly as they are pried from the net. Among my earliest memories are the times I used to go off with my father in his little dinghy and he would catch the fish my mother would prepare for our meals. It did not occur to us to buy our fish, so lucky were we. Nowadays, depleted stocks mean that fish is much more of a luxury, but fish farms have sprung up at dozens of coves in the islands and along the mainland which produce several species of fish and mussels at more economical prices, while small-er fish still abound for soups and frying.

For centuries, even millennia, Greek fishermen have been sailing out in their caiques, equipped with nets, bright lanterns, and lines with a hundred hooks, and bringing the bounty of the sea to the Greek dinner table. Even when the catch was small, there were always octopus to be harpooned just offshore or clams to be dug from the sand. Meanwhile, Greek housewives, always conscious of the need to feed large families, would devise ways to make these treats go further. While nothing can improve on the simplest methods – grilling, poaching, frying – if a fish is fresh, seafood – shellfish and cephalopods, particularly – lends itself to stewing with dif-ferent combinations of vegetables.

Whether baked or broiled, fried or poached, Greek fish and seafood dishes are considered some of the most exquisite and delicate in our cuisine.

This chapter contains both traditional and modern recipes, for parties and for every day. A typical party dish nowadays, lobster, for example, used to be so com-mon in some parts of Greece – the island of Skyros, for example – that no one except foreigners would eat it. It was so cheap forty years ago that they could have it for breakfast, lunch, and dinner without thinking about the consequences to their wallets. Since then, however, lobster has been discovered as a delicacy and its price and rarity have risen accordingly. On the other hand, some humble, traditional dishes, such as baked anchovies with or without tomato, are so delicious and attractive, they can easily be served at a party. Also do not be afraid of tackling octopus, squid, and cuttlefish. Their flesh could not be sweeter (octopus is the poor man's lobster) and they are very versatile, changing a simple vegetable dish into a original, special treat.

General Instructions
The recipes included in this chapter have been arranged according to fish type

and the method of cooking most appropriate to that type. Other fish may be sub-stituted provided they are of similar size, taste, and texture.

Like meat, fish and seafood may be grilled, baked, stewed, fried, and poached. Since fish is much more tender, it does not need long cooking. There is nothing less appetizing than overcooked, dried out fish. Let's approach baking and grilling first. In the oven, the higher the temperature, the shorter the cooking time. Naturally, temperatures will vary, depending on the recipe and the size and weight of the fish. Larger fish need longer times and lower temperatures (approximately 350°F). Smaller fish need less time but higher temperatures (400°-450°F). Generally speak-ing, all fish should be covered with vegetables, foil, or liquid to protect their flesh from direct oven heat. To test whether a fish is done or not, place the tip of a knife on the thickest part of the back of the fish. The flesh should separate from the bone easily. Any fish, from the largest to the smallest, can be cooked in the oven. Oily fish such as tuna, mackerel, grey mullet, and the like are ideal for baking with onions, plenty of parsley, and olive oil. Medium-sized fish are best suited for grilling.

Grilling, the oldest and simplest way of cooking, can be traced back to the dis-covery of fire, but there have been a few refinements since then. Try marinating your fish or brushing it with lemon juice and olive oil and herbs before grilling over charcoal or under the broiler. Do not use herbs with an intense aroma or they will overpower the taste of the fish. Rosemary, for example, is best with oily fish like mackerel or tuna. Slash each fish lengthwise along the backbone on both sides before you marinate so that the flavors penetrate the flesh and the fish cooks more quickly. Another tip: always oil the grill lightly and heat it before you place the fish on it. This will prevent it from sticking. Whether you marinate or simply baste, the grilling time is short, with the fish close enough to the source of heat to cook through without charring or becoming dry. The smoky flavor of slightly scorched skin permeates the flesh. Grilling over charcoal is the simplest and best method of cooking fresh, medium-sized fish from Greek waters. Served with an oil-lemon dressing and some finely chopped parsley, few things are more delectable.

Small fish, such as anchovies, sardines, picarel, red mullet, are the most suited to frying. If you want to fry large fish, fillet them first or cut them into one-inch slices. Fish or seafood destined for the frying pan should be dredged in flour or rolled in bread crumbs and cooked quickly in very hot oil. A coating of flour or bread crumbs creates a tasty crust which, on the one hand, gives the fish a unique taste and, on the other, protects it from drying by sealing in the juices. The most suitable oil for frying is vegetable oil because it can be heated to high temperatures without burn-ing. Most vegetable oils are tasteless and do not affect the flavor of the fish.

Large fish are also delicious poached or steamed. The best liquid for this type of cooking is a court bouillon or vegetable stock; it gives a special aroma to the fish. To prevent the skin of the fish from splitting open, the poaching liquid should be kept below a simmer; it may tremble but never bubble. When poaching large fish, start them off in cold liquid, so that the flesh cooks evenly. During steaming, the fish should barely touch the surface of the liquid. Fish and shellfish recommended for poaching are sole, trout, cod, grouper, salmon, lobster, shrimp, mussels, and crab.

Because fish spoils much faster than meat, only buy fish which is very fresh. Fresh fish has a pleasant, balmy smell of seawater, its skin is shiny, and its scales sparkle. The flesh is firm, the gills pink, and the eyes glisten. If your fish dealer hasn't cleaned it, scale and eviscerate it as soon as you get it home, sprinkle it with lemon juice, place it in a covered containers and refrigerate it. Fish will not keep for more than a day. Frozen, it will keep for 6 months.

Other types of seafood, such as lobster, shrimp, crab, and mussels, are even more delicate and perishable than fish and for this reason are sold either alive or frozen. When choosing a lobster, make sure it is alive and heavy for its size. A large but lightweight lobster might have been left in the fish farm for days without food or it might have recently shed its shell and had no time to fill up the new one with solid flesh. Shellfish, of course, are delicious raw, so long as you are confident they come from unpolluted sources. Sprinkle each clam or oyster with lemon juice as you open it, and discard any that do not twitch – they are dead and could poison you.

Sea Bass with Olives
(Lavrakia me Elies)

Serves 4
Preparation time 30 minutes
Baking time 1 hour

3 lbs sea bass, bream, or red snapper
salt and pepper
2/3 cup olive oil
2 small onions, cut in rings
4 gloves garlic, slivered
3 tablespoons finely chopped parsley
2 large tomatoes, peeled and chopped
1 small green pepper, cut in julienne strips
1 cup dry white wine
10 black Kalamata olives and
10 green Greek olives, pitted and scalded

Clean and wash the fish. With a sharp knife, slice the fish into serving portions on both sides, cutting as deep as the backbone but taking care not to separate the pieces entirely. This will make serving easier. Sprinkle with salt and pepper. Heat half the oil in a frying pan and lightly sauté the onion and garlic, add the parsley, tomatoes, pepper, a pinch of salt, and pepper, and boil the sauce until it thickens. Spread half the sauce in a large baking dish and place the fish on top. Pour the remaining sauce over it, along with the rest of the oil and the wine. Scatter the olives around it. Preheat the oven to 425°F and bake for 45 minutes or until the fish flakes off the bone and the sauce is greatly reduced. Baste with the sauce 3-4 times during baking. Serve hot, accompanied by Boiled Greens.

Grilled Porgies or Sea Bream
(Tsipoures sti Skara)

Serves 4
Preparation time 15 minutes
Grilling time 20 minutes

4 porgies or other sea bream (about 1 lb each)
salt and pepper
olive oil
Oil-Lemon Dressing (page 47)
finely chopped parsley

Have your fish dealer scale and clean the fish. Wash and drain them well. Make 2-3 shallow, diagonal incisions on both sides of each fish. Rub with a little salt and pepper, and brush the fish with oil inside and out. Place on a preheated grill rack (preheating the rack will prevent the fish from sticking). Grill the fish over charcoal or under the broiler for 10-15 minutes on each side, basting occasionally with oil. Place on a platter, moisten the fish with oil-lemon dressing, and sprinkle with chopped parsley. Serve immediately, accompanied by Boiled Greens or Tomato and Onion Salad.

Sea Bream Spetses-Style
(Sinagrida Spetsiotiki)

Serves 5-6
Preparation time 1 hour and 30 minutes
Cooking time 1 hour

1 whole sea bream, porgy, red snapper (about 3 lbs) or
5-6 slices of any large fish
1/4 cup lemon juice
2/3 cup olive oil
salt, pepper, and flour
1 large onion, thinly sliced
4 garlic cloves, chopped
1½ lbs fresh tomatoes, chopped
1/2 cup dry white wine
1/2 cup finely chopped parsley

Have your fish dealer clean and scale the fish. Rinse and drain, patting dry with paper towels. With a sharp knife, score the fish along the backbone on both sides. Place in a baking pan, rub the fish with lemon juice and seasonings, and sprinkle with a little flour. Pour half the oil over the fish and let it stand for 1 hour. Heat the remaining oil in a saucepan and sauté the onion and garlic until transparent. Add the tomatoes, wine, and parsley, and simmer, covered, until the sauce is very thick. Preheat the oven to 325°F, pour the sauce over the fish, and bake for about 1 hour. Baste the fish occasionally with the pan juices. Serve with Boiled Greens, Asparagus or Broccoli.

Steamed Shrimp with Oil-Lemon Dressing
(Garides Achnistes Ladolemono)

Serves 4
Preparation time 35 minutes
Cooking time 8-10 minutes

2 lbs large shrimp
1/2 cup water
salt and white pepper
Oil-Lemon Dressing (page 47)
finely chopped parsley

Shell and devein the shrimp, leaving the heads and tail fins intact. Wash and drain well. In a large saucepan bring the water, seasoned with salt and white pepper, to a rapid boil. Put the shrimp in a steamer basket, cover, and boil rapidly for 8-10 minutes. Place the shrimp on a platter and pour the oil-lemon dressing over them. Sprinkle with finely chopped parsley and serve warm or cold, accompanied by Greek Village Salad or Boiled Greens.

Shrimp with Sauce
(Garides me Zoumi)

Serves 4-5
Preparation time 35 minutes
Cooking time 8 minutes

3 lbs large fresh shrimp
1/2 cup olive oil
1/2 cup water
1 small green chili pepper, sliced
1 small onion
1 small carrot
1 celery stalk
1 teaspoon paprika
1/2 teaspoon black pepper
1 teaspoon salt
1/2 cup lemon juice

Use fresh shrimp if you can find them. Otherwise buy frozen, raw, unshelled shrimp. Before cooking, thaw them rapidly in lots of cold water and peel as soon as possible. Devein shrimp from the head, without slitting the shrimp. If using fresh shrimp, leave head and tail fins intact. Wash and drain well in a colander. Put the oil and water in a pot, add the remaining ingredients, except for the lemon juice. Bring to a boil and cook, covered, for 5 minutes. Remove and discard the pepper, onion, carrot, and celery stalk and drop in the shrimp. Cover and boil rapidly for 7-8 minutes, shaking the pot occasionally while cooking to redistribute the shrimp. Do not overcook. Remove from the heat and pour the lemon juice over the shrimp, shaking the pot instead of stirring. Serve in soup plates or small bowls. *Note:* You may substitute 1 ½ teaspoon seafood seasoning for the chili pepper, onion, carrot, celery, and paprika.

Fried Shrimp
(Garides Tiganites)

You can fry shrimp both peeled and unpeeled. When frying unpeeled shrimp, simply remove the black vein along the top by slitting the shell with a sharp knife. Wash and drain well. Dredge them by tossing in a plastic bag with a cup or so of flour seasoned with salt and pepper. Empty them into a colander and shake to remove excess flour. Fry them in hot oil for about 4-5 minutes, but no longer or they will be dry out. For peeled shrimp, after you have removed the shell and deveined them, wash and drain. Dredge them in the same way, dip one by one in egg white beaten with 1-2 tablespoons of oil, and then roll in bread crumbs. Fry them over medium heat in a deep fryer for 2-3 minutes until they become golden. Garnish the fried shrimp with lemon rosettes, and serve with iced retsina or ouzo and Greek Village Salad.

Baked Shrimp Casserole
(Garides Yiouvetsi)

Serves 6
Preparation time 30 minutes
Cooking time 30 minutes

3 lbs shrimp
1/4 cup butter or margarine
1 large onion, sliced
1 carrot, sliced
1 long green pepper, cut in strips
2 lbs fresh tomatoes or
1 lb canned tomatoes, puréed
1/2 lb feta cheese, crumbled
1/4 cup finely chopped parsley
1/2 lb kasseri or Swiss cheese, cubed
salt and freshly ground pepper
cayenne (optional)

Shell, devein, wash, and drain the shrimp. Steam them in a small amount of water for 5 minutes and drain again, reserving the liquid. In a saucepan, melt the butter and gently sauté the onion until soft but not brown. Add carrot and pepper and sauté for 5 minutes. Pour in the tomatoes, reserved shrimp liquid, a few grindings of pepper, and boil until the sauce is thick. Remove from the heat, stir in the crumbled feta and parsley. Adjust the seasonings. Layer the shrimp over the bottom of an ovenproof baking dish and pour the sauce over them. Top with kasseri or Swiss cheese cubes, dot with butter, and sprinkle with a pinch of cayenne. Preheat oven to 425°F and bake for about 30 minutes, until the surface is lightly browned. Serve immediately.

shrimp and cook 3-5 minutes. Prepare the Rice Pilaf, top with the shrimp and sauce, and serve hot.

Shrimp Pilaf with Tomato Sauce
(Garides Pilafi me Saltsa)

Serves 4
Preparation time 45 minutes
Cooking time 30 minutes

2 lbs shrimp
Tomato Sauce (page 53)
finely chopped basil
1 teaspoon Worcestershire sauce
15 drops Tabasco
Rice Pilaf (page 129)

Shell and devein the shrimp, leaving tail fins and heads intact. Wash and steam the shrimp in a little water for 5 minutes. Drain them, reserving the liquid. Set aside. Prepare the Tomato Sauce, substituting chopped basil for the chopped parsley. Add the reserved shrimp liquid, Worcestershire sauce, Tabasco or a pinch of cayenne. Boil until the sauce is very thick. Fold in the

Lobster Salad
(Astakosalata)

Serves 6
Preparation time 45 minutes
Cooking time 20 minutes

1 Boiled Lobster (page 129)
2 tablespoons capers
1/2 cup cooked peas
1 hard-boiled egg, chopped
1/4 cup finely chopped pickles
1 carrot, boiled and diced
2 tablespoons finely chopped parsley
salt and pepper
2 tablespoons lemon juice
1 1/2 cups mayonnaise

Prepare the recipe for Boiled Lobster (page 129). Shell and cut the meat in small pieces. Place in a bowl with all the other ingredients except for the mayonnaise and mix well. Add mayonnaise and toss lightly. Cover and refrigerate until ready to serve. Garnish with lettuce hearts.

SHRIMP-STUFFED AVOCADOS, PAGE 127 • SKEWERED PRAWNS, PAGE 127

Shrimp-Stuffed Avocados
(Garidosalata se Avocados)

Serves 4
Preparation time 45 minutes
Cooking time 8 minutes

2 lbs shrimp
2 large avocados
1/4 cup lemon juice
salt
1 cup mayonnaise
2 tablespoons finely chopped parsley
watercress sprigs
freshly ground pepper

Devein the shrimp, wash, and drain well. Steam in a small amount of lightly salted water for 5-8 minutes. Drain, allow to cool, and shell the shrimp. Separate the larger shrimp from the smaller ones. Set aside. Wipe the avocados with a damp cloth and cut them in half lengthwise, removing the seed. Brush with lemon juice to prevent discoloring and sprinkle with a little salt. Put 2 small shrimps in each avocado half. Fill the cavity with 2-3 tablespoons mayonnaise and place 3 large shrimps on top. Sprinkle with parsley and arrange on a platter garnished with watercress sprigs. Cover with plastic wrap and keep refrigerated until ready to serve. Grind some black pepper on top just before serving.
Alternate: Substitute green goddess or another sauce of your preference for the mayonnaise.

Skewered Prawns
(Garides Souvlaki)

Serves 4
Preparation time 45 minutes
Cooking time 8 minutes

2¹/₂ lbs large prawns
bacon slices, cut in strips
2 green peppers, cut in small squares
Oil-Lemon Dressing (page 47)

Shell and devein the prawns, leaving the tails intact. Wash and dry thoroughly. Wrap each prawn in a strip of bacon. Thread 3 prawns onto each skewer, with a green pepper square between each. Place the skewered prawns on a platter, brush with oil-lemon dressing, and set aside for 30 minutes. Grill on a rack over charcoal, or broil, for approximately 4 minutes per side, basting frequently with the dressing. Transfer to a platter lined with tender lettuce leaves. Serve immediately, accompanied by the sauces of your choice.

Note: For skewered prawns without bacon, mix some minced garlic and parsley into the oil-lemon dressing.

Braised Salted Cod
(Bakaliaros Pastos Yiachni)

Serves 6-7
Preparation time 12 hours
Cooking time 55 minutes

3 lbs salted cod
1 cup olive oil
flour for dredging
2 lbs onions, thinly sliced
2-3 garlic cloves
2 lbs ripe fresh tomatoes, chopped
1 tablespoon vinegar
pepper

Prepare the cod according to the recipe for Fried Salted Cod (page 131). Dredge the fish with flour. In a heavy-bottomed pan add the oil and fry the fish over high heat, until light brown on both sides. Remove with a slotted spoon and set aside. Sauté the onion and garlic in the remaining oil until transparent. Stir in the tomatoes, vinegar, and pepper. Cover and simmer for approximately 45 minutes, or until the onion is soft and the sauce is thick. Place the fish in the sauce, cover, and simmer 10 minutes. Equally good hot or cold.
Alternate: Sauté 1 lb finely chopped green bell peppers along with the onion.

Broiled Langoustines
(Karavides Psites)

Serves 4
Preparation time 20 minutes
Cooking time 15 minutes

2¹/₂ lbs jumbo langoustines (scampi)

the seasoned butter
1/2 cup softened butter
salt
1 garlic clove, crushed
finely chopped dill
white pepper
2-3 drops Tabasco (optional)

the garnish
dill sprigs
lemon wedges

Wash the langoustines and drain well. Sprinkle with salt, and broil or grill over charcoal, for about 10 minutes, turning once. In the meantime, mash the butter with the garlic, dill, pepper, Tabasco, and a pinch of salt. Using a sharp knife, cut each langoustine in half lengthwise. Remove the black vein. With a small spatula spread some of the seasoned butter over the surface of each half. Broil for 5 minutes away from the flame. Serve immediately, garnished with sprigs of dill and

lemon wedges. Accompany with Marinated Vegetables and Tzatziki or Eggplant Salad.

Charcoal-Grilled Lobster
(Astakos sta Karvouna)

Serves 4
Preparation time 30 minutes
Cooking time 15 minutes

2 small lobsters (1¹/₂ lbs each)
salt and pepper
Vegetable Broth (page 49) or water
2 tablespoons lemon juice
Oil-Lemon Dressing (page 47)
assorted sauces

In a large kettle bring to the boil 4 pints of vegetable broth or water. (Fishermen boil lobsters in seawater.) Add the lemon juice and plunge the lobsters into the kettle. Simmer, covered, for 10 minutes. Drain and cut in half, lengthwise, with the aid of a sharp knife. Remove the black intestinal vein. Discard all organs in body section near the head, except the red roe (coral) if the lobster is female and the greenish tomalley. Brush with oil, season with salt and pepper, and grill over charcoal for approximately 7 minutes on each side, shell side down first. Serve immediately with oil-lemon dressing or assorted sauces, such as tartar, hollandaise, or hot barbecue sauce.

Lobster with Oil-Lemon Dressing
(Astakos Vrastos Ladolemono)

Serves 4
Preparation time 30 minutes
Cooking time 20 minutes

> *1 large lobster or two smaller ones (3 lbs)*
> *1 medium onion, peeled*
> *1 carrot, scraped*
> *1 celery stalk*
> *2 teaspoons salt*
> *10 black peppercorns*
> *1/4 cup lemon juice*
> *Oil-Lemon Dressing (page 47)*

Tie the lobster tail to the body with string. In a large pot boil enough water to cover the lobster. Add onion, carrot, celery, salt, and pepper or 1 teaspoon seafood seasoning. Boil for 10 minutes. Add lemon juice. Grasp the lobster by the back and drop it into boiling bouillon (immerse the head first to kill the lobster). Boil for 25 minutes. Remove and drain in a colander. When it is cool enough to handle, remove the string and place on a flat surface, back side up. Place a weight on its back to keep it straight and let cool completely. Turn the lobster over. Using kitchen scissors, cut each side along its entire length. Pull away the bony membrane that protects the underside. Carefully remove the flesh. Cut in slices and arrange on a platter. Cut out the meat from the head, as well as the red coral (roe) and green tomalley. Crack the claws and legs and remove the meat. Place on the platter with the rest of the meat and sprinkle with oil-lemon dressing and finely chopped parsley. Serve immediately with Boiled Asparagus or Broccoli.

Monkfish with Celery and Egg-Lemon Sauce
(Peskadritsa me Selino Avgolemono)

Serves 4
Preparation time 35 minutes
Cooking time 30 minutes

> *3 lbs monkfish tails or grouper*
> *1 lb celery, tender stalks and leaves only*
> *1/3 cup olive oil*
> *salt and 20 peppercorns*
> *2 large onions, sliced*
> *1 egg*
> *1/3 cup lemon juice*
> *freshly ground pepper*

Have the fishmonger clean the fish. Rinse and drain. Wash the celery and separate the stalks. In a large saucepan add the oil, 1 cup water, salt, and the peppercorns, and bring to the boil. Add the onions and

when they are soft, lift them out with a slotted spoon and spread them on a deep platter. Boil the celery in the same manner, drain it, and place it on the platter with the onions. Now add the fish to the pan and boil for 20 minutes or until tender. Lift out the fish and strain the broth into a clean saucepan. Remove the skin and bones and place the fish on the platter with the vegetables. In a small bowl lightly beat the egg with the lemon juice, add a little of the broth to it, and pour the mixture back into the saucepan. Stir briskly. Pour the sauce over the fish and vegetables. Serve hot in soup plates.

Seafood Pilaf (Pilafi me Thalassina)

Serves 8-10
Preparation time 45 minutes
Cooking time 40 minutes

> *1 lb mussels, clams, or oysters*
> *1/2 lb shrimp*
> *2 medium squid or cuttlefish*
> *1/2 cup olive oil*
> *1/4 cup margarine*
> *2 medium onions, thinly sliced*
> *2 garlic cloves, sliced*
> *2 green bell pepper, cut into small strips*
> *2 lbs tomatoes, skinned and chopped*
> *3 tablespoons ketchup*
> *3 tablespoons chopped parsley*
> *salt and pepper*
> *cayenne*
> *2 cups long-grain rice*
> *1/2 cup pine nuts (optional)*

Clean, steam, and shell the shellfish according to the recipe for Steamed Mussels (page 11). Reserve the liquid. Set aside. Wash, steam, and shell the shrimp. Reserve the liquid. Set aside. Trim and wash the squid or cuttlefish, until they are white and clean. Cut in small strips and leave to drain in a colander. In a large, heavy-bottomed pan heat the oil and margarine. Add the onions and garlic, and sauté over high heat until they are transparent. Add the green peppers and sauté them lightly. Add the tomatoes, ketchup, parsley, squid strips, and seasonings. Cover and simmer over medium heat, until the sauce is very thick. Measure the reserved mussel and shrimp juices and add enough water to make 4 cups. Pour into the pan and bring to a boil. Stir in the rice. Reduce the heat to low and simmer, covered, for about 20 minutes, until all the liquid is absorbed and the rice is cooked. Add the mussels and shrimp, stir gently, and simmer for another 3 minutes. Pack the pilaf into an ungreased fluted cake pan. When ready to serve, either hot or cold, invert the pilaf onto a large plate and garnish with pine nuts browned in a little butter.

Mussel Pilaf
(Midia Pilafi)

Serves 6
Preparation time 30 minutes
Cooking time 25 minutes

the pilaf
1/4 cup butter
1¹/₂ cups uncooked long-grain rice
4 cups vegetable or beef stock
salt to taste

2 lbs shelled mussels, fresh or frozen
1/2 cup olive oil
1 medium onion, thinly sliced
1 garlic clove, finely chopped
1 cup tomato purée
1 tablespoon tomato paste
2 tablespoons finely chopped parsley
2 tablespoons finely chopped celery
1 small red hot pepper
1 teaspoon Worcestershire sauce
salt and pepper
1/2 cup grated feta cheese

Prepare the pilaf: Melt the butter in a saucepan, add the rice and sauté over high heat for 5 minutes. Pour the stock over the rice, add seasonings, and simmer, covered, for approximately 20 minutes until all the liquid is absorbed. Remove from the heat, place a thick paper towel or clean dish cloth between the lid and the pan, and allow to stand for 5 minutes before serving. In the meantime, in another saucepan, heat the oil, add onion and garlic, and sauté over high heat. Add the remaining ingredients, except for the mussels and cheese. Simmer the sauce until thick, about 15-20 minutes. Add the mussels and cheese and simmer for 5 more minutes, stirring once or twice. Remove from the heat and spoon the sauce over the rice. Serve immediately, accompanied by Greek Village Salad.

Mussel Pilaf with Dill
(Midopilafo me Anitho)

Serves 4
Preparation time 50 minutes
Cooking time 25 minutes

3 lbs fresh mussels, unshelled
1/2 cup olive oil
1/2 cup grated onion
1/2 cup finely chopped spring onion
1¹/₂ cup long-grain rice
1/2 cup finely chopped dill
salt and freshly ground pepper

Scrub the mussels, under running water, with a stiff brush to remove seaweed and barnacles. Discard any open shells. Debeard with a sharp knife. Place the mussels in a large pan with a tiny amount of water and bring to a boil over high heat. Cover the pan and shake it from time to time, until all the mussels have opened. Discard any that do not. Strain and reserve the broth. In a clean pot, heat the oil and sauté the onions until well wilted. Add the rice and sauté, stirring, until it becomes opaque. Measure the mussel broth and add hot water to it until you have 3 cups of liquid. Bring to a boil and add it to the rice. Add salt to taste and simmer, covered, for about 20 minutes. Stir in the dill, mussels, and pepper. Place a clean cotton dish towel over the pot and replace the lid. Turn off the heat and let the rice stand for 10 minutes. Serve the pilaf hot or cold, sprinkled with a little lemon juice, some more pepper, and a little cayenne, if desired.

side). Fry only a few pieces at a time. Remove with a slotted spoon and drain on paper towels. Arrange on a platter, garnished with parsley sprigs and lemon slices. Serve hot with Garlic Sauce and Boiled Greens or salad.

Codfish Lefkada-Style
(Bakaliaros ala Lefkadita)

Serves 4
Preparation time 12 hours
Cooking time 1 hour and 30 minutes

2 lbs cod, salted or fresh
5-6 large potatoes (about 3 lbs), sliced
1 large onion, grated
5 garlic cloves, sliced
1 cup olive oil
1 teaspoon oregano
salt and freshly ground pepper
1/3 cup lemon juice
finely chopped parsley

If using salted cod, prepare the fish for cooking according to the previous recipe. If using fresh cod, clean it, wash it well, and cut it into serving portions. Put the fish into a large pot along with the potatoes, garlic, onion, half the oil, and water to cover. Add the oregano, pepper, and salt (if needed), cover and simmer for about 20 minutes, until the fish and potatoes are soft and a little thick broth remains. Put the remaining oil with the lemon juice in a bottle, shake until it emulsifies and pour it over the food. Shake the pot from right to left to distribute the sauce and remove it from the heat. Sprinkle with freshly ground pepper and finely chopped parsley. Serve hot, accompanied by Cabbage Salad.

Fried Salted Cod
(Bakaliaros Pastos Tiganitos)

Serves 4
Preparation time 18-20 hours
Frying time 15-20 minutes

2 lbs salted cod
oil for frying

the batter
3 eggs
salt and pepper
self-raising flour

the garnish
parsley sprigs, lemon slices

Remove the skin and cut the fish into 3-inch serving or bite-size pieces. Rinse off loose salt under the tap. Soak in cold water, refrigerated, for 18-20 hours, changing the water several times, until the fish is only lightly salted. Remove the bones and drain the fish thoroughly.
Prepare the batter: In a bowl lightly beat the eggs with 3-4 tablespoons water until fluffy. Stir in enough flour to make a medium thick batter. Adjust the seasonings and set aside. If desired use the Batter for Frying (page 51). In a large skillet, pour oil to a depth of 1/2 inch. Heat until the oil reaches the smoking point. Dip the cod pieces one by one into the batter and drop into the hot oil. Lower heat to medium and fry until lightly browned on both sides (approximately 4 minutes per

Cuttlefish in Wine
(Soupies Krassates)

Serves 4
Preparation time 30 minutes
Cooking time 1 hour and 30 minutes

> 2 lbs cuttlefish
> 1 cup olive oil
> 2 lbs onions, thinly sliced
> 6 garlic cloves
> 3 tablespoons tomato paste
> 1 cup white wine
> 2 bay leaves
> 3 allspice berries
> 10 peppercorns
> salt and pepper
> 1/2 teaspoon sugar

Wash the cuttlefish thoroughly in cold water. Detach the head from the body. Using a sharp knife, sever the tentacles from the rest of the head, cutting just above the eyes (do not sever the tentacles). Squeeze out the

beak and discard. Discard the rest of head with viscera and ink sac. Slip out the cuttlebone and discard. Wash under running water and peel off the translucent membrane. Rinse well inside and out. If the cuttlefish are very small, leave whole. If large, cut into rings. Place in a colander, drain, and pat dry with paper towels. Heat the oil in a large heavy-bottomed pan, add the onions and garlic, and sauté until transparent. Add the cuttlefish and sauté until all the liquid has evaporated. Dilute the tomato paste in the wine and pour it over the cuttlefish. Add the rest of the ingredients and stir. Cover and simmer over medium heat, until the cuttlefish are tender and the sauce is thick.
Alternate: Squid or octopus may be used instead of cuttlefish. For squid, follow the cuttlefish recipe. For octopus, prepare according to the recipe for Octopus in Vinegar (page 10). After you peel off the skin, cut it in small pieces and follow the cuttlefish recipe. Add more water if the dish seems dry and simmer until the octopus is tender and the sauce has thickened.

Cuttlefish with Olives
(Soupies me Elies)

Serves 4-5
Preparation time 1 hour
Cooking time 1 hour

> 3 lbs cuttlefish
> 2 large onions, grated
> 1 cup olive oil
> 2 garlic cloves
> salt and pepper
> 2 bay leaves
> 1/4 cup dry red wine
> 1/4 cup tomato purée
> 1/2 lb Greek green olives, pitted

Clean and wash the cuttlefish according to the previous recipe for Cuttlefish in Wine. Cut in small pieces and pat dry with paper towels. Rub the onion with a little salt in a sieve, rinse, and squeeze out the excess liquid. Heat the oil in a saucepan, add the onion and sauté quickly until transparent. Add the cuttlefish, garlic, salt, and pepper, cover, and simmer until no liquid remains and only the oil is left. Add the wine, tomato purée, and bay leaves. Simmer another 5-10 minutes. In the meantime, blanch the olives in boiling water for 5 minutes, remove from the heat, and let stand for another 5 minutes. Drain and rinse thoroughly in hot water. Drain again and add to the pan with the cuttlefish. Simmer, covered, for 10 minutes. Delicious hot or cold.

Octopus with Macaroni

(Ktapodi me Makaronaki)

Serves 4-5
Preparation time 30 minutes
Cooking time 1 hour

3 lbs small frozen octopus (2-3), defrosted
1/4 cup vinegar
1/3 cup olive oil
2 garlic cloves, mashed
1/4 cup grated onion
1 16-oz can chopped tomatoes
2 tablespoons tomato paste
2 tablespoons ketchup
1/2 cup dry white wine
6 allspice berries
2 bay leaves
1 lb macaroni (ditali, elbow, or other)
salt, pepper, cayenne

Rinse the octopus and boil them in salted water with the vinegar until soft. Drain, reserving 1 cup broth. Remove the beaks and dark membrane but leave the suckers intact. Cut the octopus in bite-sized pieces. Heat the oil in a large pot and sauté the garlic and onion until translucent. Add the reserved broth and remaining ingredients, except for the pasta and the octopus. Bring to a boil and simmer, covered, for 10 minutes. Add the octopus and simmer until it is fork tender and the sauce is reduced. Boil the pasta separately in plenty of salted water with 2 tablespoons of olive oil. Drain and mix it with the octopus. Serve immediately.

Cuttlefish with Spinach

(Soupies me Spanaki)

Serves 4
Preparation time 1 hour
Cooking time 40 minutes

2 lbs cuttlefish (fresh or frozen)
3/4 cup olive oil
1 large onion, sliced
1 tablespoon tomato paste
1/2 cup white wine
salt and pepper
2 lbs fresh or frozen spinach
1/2 cup finely chopped dill
freshly ground pepper

Wash and clean the cuttlefish as in the recipe for Cuttlefish in Wine (page 132). Cut in smallish pieces, drain, and pat dry with paper towels. Heat the oil in a large pot, add the onion, and sauté until transparent. Add the cuttlefish and sauté until all the liquid has evaporated. Dilute the tomato paste in the wine and pour it over the cuttlefish. Stir in the seasonings. Cover and simmer for about 10 minutes until the cuttlefish are almost tender. Add a little hot water, if necessary. If using fresh spinach, blanch for 5 minutes in boiling water and drain. Frozen spinach should be added directly to the pot. Add the spinach and dill to the cuttlefish, stir, cover, and simmer for about 20 minutes until the spinach is done and the sauce is thick. Sprinkle with freshly ground pepper and serve. Equally good cold.

Seafood in Scallop Shells
(Thalassina se Kohilia)

Serves 4
Preparation time 1 hour
Cooking time 20 minutes

1 lb mussels, clams, or oysters
2 cups boiled shrimp, lobster, or crab cut in small pieces
salt and pepper
butter or margarine
2 tablespoons fine bread crumbs
1 cup thick White Sauce (page 52)
1 cup heavy cream
1 cup grated kefalotiri or Romano cheese
nutmeg and cayenne
4 scallop shells

Steam the mussels, clams, or oysters in a small amount of water. Shell and combine with the remaining seafood (any seafood combination will do). Reserve 4 shrimp for garnish. Season to taste. Butter the scallop shells and sprinkle lightly with bread crumbs. Line a baking pan with a bed of coarse salt and place shells on it to prevent tipping. Fill the shells with the seafood mixture. Prepare the white sauce, stir in the cream, grated cheese, and a pinch of nutmeg, if desired. Spoon the sauce over the filled shells, sprinkle with grated cheese, and a dash of cayenne. Preheat the oven to 400°F and bake for 10 minutes. If the surface has not browned, put the shells under a hot broiler for 2-3 minutes. Garnish with a boiled shrimp and serve immediately.

Skewered Swordfish
(Xifias Souvlaki)

Serves 4
Preparation time 1 hour
Grilling time 15-20 minutes

2 lbs swordfish
1 large onion
1 large green bell pepper
1 large tomato
1 chili pepper (optional)
salt and pepper
2 tablespoons lemon juice
6 tablespoons olive oil
12 small skewers

Wash and drain the fish well, cut into 1½ inch cubes. Cut the onion, green pepper, and tomato into cubes about the same size. Thread the fish onto skewers, alternating with onion, pepper, and tomato cubes. If using chili pepper, add a small piece to each skewer, or more if desired. Brush with oil, sprinkle with seasonings, and grill over charcoal or under the broiler. Baste with oil and turn twice. Cook for about 15 minutes, or until the fish is done to your taste. Do not overcook. Place on a platter. Mix the lemon juice and olive oil, pour it over the fish, and serve immediately, accompanied by Marinated Vegetables.

Sea Bass with Mayonnaise
(Lavraki Mayoneza)

Serves 6
Preparation time 1 hour
Cooking time 30 minutes

1 whole sea bass, red snapper, grouper (about 3 lbs)
3 carrots, peeled and cut in large pieces
1 onion, peeled
1 leek, washed and cut in 3-4 pieces
2 celery stalks
5 parsley sprigs
2 teaspoons salt and a few peppercorns
1/4 cup lemon juice

the garnish
Mayonnaise, capers, and lemon slices

Half fill a large pot with water and add the carrots, onion, leek, celery, parsley, salt, lemon juice, and peppercorns. Boil covered, for about 20 minutes, then strain, reserving the broth and carrots. Put the fish in a oblong baking pan and pour the vegetable broth over it. Preheat oven to 350°F, bring to a simmer on top of the stove, and then bake for about 30 minutes. Remove from the oven. When cool, transfer the fish onto a platter. Carefully remove the head and tail, set aside. Peel off the skin and discard. Split the fish in half lengthwise and remove the backbone. Sprinkle the flesh with a little lemon juice, salt, and pepper. Carefully reassemble the fish on a decorative fish platter. Cover the entire fish, except for the head and tail fins, with mayonnaise. Garnish with the boiled carrots,

capers, and lemon slices. Serve cold with boiled potato balls, asparagus, artichoke hearts, or marinated mushrooms. An excellent dish for a special dinner.

Rolled Sole Fillets
(Glosses Rola me Garides)

Serves 4
Preparation time 1 hour
Cooking time 10 minutes

12 fillets of sole, fresh or frozen
salt and pepper
12 large shrimps
2 tablespoons lemon juice
1/2 cup olive oil
1 cup dry white wine
5-6 parsley (stems only), coarsely chopped
10 peppercorns

Wash and drain the sole fillets. Season with salt and pepper. Clean and shell the shrimp, leaving tail fins intact. Devein, wash, and drain. Roll the sole fillets. Place a shrimp on top of each roll, and fasten with wooden toothpicks. Arrange the rolls in a baking dish. Mix lemon juice, oil, and wine, and pour the liquid over the rolls. Sprinkle with the chopped parsley stems, peppercorns, and a little salt. Preheat oven to 350°F, cover with aluminum foil, and bake for 10 minutes. Serve hot or cold, accompanied by hollandaise or cocktail sauce, Boiled Greens or Asparagus.

Marinated Mackerel
(Skoumbria Marinata)

Serves 4
Preparation time 30 minutes
Cooking time 30 minutes

2 lbs mackerel, or other similar fish
2 tablespoons lemon juice
salt and pepper
flour for dredging plus 2 tablespoons
oil for frying
2 garlic cloves, crushed
3 tablespoons vinegar
1½ cups puréed fresh or canned tomatoes
1/2 teaspoon sugar
1 bay leaf
rosemary (optional)
finely chopped parsley or mint

Clean, wash, and drain the fish well. Sprinkle with lemon juice, salt, and pepper. Dredge with flour and fry in hot oil. Strain the oil, allow to settle, and reserve 1/4 cup of the clear oil. Pour it into a clean frying pan, stir in 3 tablespoons of flour, and brown lightly. Add garlic, vinegar, tomato purée, sugar, and a few rosemary leaves, if using. Simmer the sauce until thick, approximately 15 minutes. Pour the sauce over the fish and serve hot or cold, sprinkled with finely chopped parsley or mint.

Baked Red Mullet
(Barbounia sto Fourno)

Serves 4
Preparation time 30 minutes
Baking time 30 minutes

3 lbs red mullet
2 tablespoons lemon juice
2/3 cup olive oil
2 medium onions, sliced
5 garlic cloves, sliced
2 long green peppers, sliced
5-6 parsley stems, coarsely chopped
rosemary
4-5 bay leaves
5-6 allspice berries
10 peppercorns
2 cloves
1/2 cup dry white wine
salt and pepper

Clean and rinse the fish well. Drain and place in a baking pan. Sprinkle with lemon juice. Set aside. Heat the oil in a saucepan and sauté the onion and garlic, quickly, until transparent. Add the remaining ingredients, season to taste, and stir over high heat, until most of the wine has evaporated. Preheat oven to 400°F, pour the sauce over the fish, and bake for approximately 30 minutes, or until only a small amount of sauce is left. Serve immediately with Boiled Greens.

Fried Red Mullet
(Barbounia Tiganita)

Serves 4
Preparation time 30 minutes
Frying time 15 minutes

2¹/₂ lbs red mullet, scaled and gutted
salt and pepper
flour for dredging
oil for frying
tender lettuce leaves
lemon slices
radishes

Wash and drain the fish thoroughly. Season with salt and pepper. Put a few fish at a time in a plastic bag with a cup of flour and shake to coat. Place the fish in a sieve or colander and shake to remove excess flour. Fry in very hot oil, for 7-8 minutes on each side, turning once. Transfer the fish to a platter lined with lettuce leaves. Garnish with lemon slices and radishes. Serve the dish accompanied by Greek Village Salad or Cucumber and Tomato Salad.

Bonito Baked in Paper
(Palamida sto Ladoharto)

Serves 4
Preparation time 15 minutes
Baking time 45 minutes

1 bonito or small tuna (3 lbs)
1/4 cup olive oil
2 tablespoons lemon juice
2 garlic cloves, crushed
salt, pepper, and oregano

Clean, wash, and drain the fish well. Place the fish on top of 3 layers of greaseproof paper. Combine the oil, lemon juice, garlic, pepper, and oregano in a small jar with a tight lid and shake well. Rub the fish inside and out with the mixture. Wrap the fish in the paper, tying the ends with string. Place on a greased baking sheet and brush the paper with a little oil to prevent burning. Preheat the oven to 450°F and bake the fish for 10 minutes. Lower the temperature to 375°F and bake for another 35-40 minutes. Serve the fish hot with Boiled Greens or Beet Salad with Garlic Sauce.
Note: You can also wrap the fish in aluminum foil.

Marinated Red Mullet
(Barbounia Savoro)

Serves 6
Preparation time 3-4 days

3 lbs red mullet, fried
1 cup tomato juice
3 cups olive oil
1 cup vinegar
15 garlic cloves
1 tablespoon rosemary
salt
2 tablespoons flour

Fry the fish as in the preceding recipe and set aside to cool. In a saucepan add the tomato juice, oil, vinegar, garlic, rosemary, and salt and simmer for 10-15 minutes, until the garlic softens. Pour a little of the hot marinade into a clay bowl and arrange as many of the fish on top of it as will fit, side by side. Pour over some more of the marinade and arrange the fish in a second layer. Continue in the same way until you have no more fish. Pour in the remaining marinade, which should cover the fish. Refrigerate and let stand 3-4 days before eating. Fish prepared this way will keep 15 days and the taste keeps improving. This is a very old recipe which predates refrigerators by hundreds of years.

Fried Sole (Glosses Tiganites)

Serves 4
Preparation time 15 minutes
Frying time 15 minutes

4 large soles or flounders (2 lbs)
salt and pepper
flour for dredging
melted butter or oil

the garnish
finely chopped parsley
lemon slices
butter curls

Have your fish dealer skin and clean the fish. Wash well and drain. Trimming the fins will make the fish easier to eat, leaving them intact will make them more presentable. Season the fish with salt and pepper and dredge with flour. Heat the butter in a large frying pan (15 inches in diameter). Add the sole, two at a time and sauté over medium heat until lightly browned on both sides (approximately 4 minutes per side). Keep warm in a low oven while you are frying the other fish. Place all the fish on a platter, each garnished with a lemon slice and topped with a curl of butter. Sprinkle with finely chopped parsley and serve immediately, accompanied with Buttered Asparagus and green salad or Tomato and Cucumber Salad.

Stuffed Squid
(Kalamaria Yemista)

Serves 4
Preparation time 30 minutes
Cooking time 1 hour

3 lbs medium squid (10-12)
3/4 cup olive oil
1½ cups grated onion
1/2 cup finely chopped spring onions
salt and pepper
1/2 cup short-grain rice
1/2 cup finely chopped parsley
2 red pimientos, finely chopped
2 tablespoons ketchup
1/8 teaspoon cayenne
1/2 cup dry white wine
3 tablespoons lemon juice

Clean and wash the squid according to the recipe for Fried Squid (page 11). Finely chop the heads, tentacles, and fins. Heat the oil in a saucepan, add the onions and sauté lightly. Add the finely chopped squid, salt, and pepper, and stir until all the liquid has evaporated and only the oil remains. Remove from the heat, add the rice, parsley, peppers, ketchup, and cayenne. Pass the mixture through a sieve, reserving the sauce. Stuff the squid with the mixture and arrange in a baking dish just large enough to hold them. Combine the reserved sauce with the wine and lemon juice and pour it over the squid. (At this stage you may freeze the squid. When ready to bake, thaw out first.) Preheat the oven to 350°F and bake for approximately 1 hour. If the sauce seems too thin, strain it into a saucepan and reduce to the desired consistency. Pour it back over the squid. Serve hot or cold.

Grilled Stuffed Squid
(Kalamaria Yemista sti Skara)

Serves 4
Preparation time 30 minutes
Grilling time 15 minutes

2 lbs large squid (10-12)
1/4 cup olive oil
1/2 cup finely chopped spring onions
salt, pepper
1/4 cup finely chopped parsley
1 roasted red pepper, chopped
1 cup diced kefalograviera
or Romano cheese
1/8 teaspoon cayenne
2 tablespoons lemon juice
1/4 cup extra virgin olive oil

Clean and wash the squid according to the recipe for Fried Squid (page 11). Finely chop the heads, tentacles, and fins. Heat the oil in a saucepan, add the onions and sauté lightly. Add the finely chopped squid, salt, and pepper, and sauté, stirring, until all the liquid evaporates and only the oil remains. Remove from the heat, stir in the parsley, red pepper, cheese, and cayenne. Fill the squid bodies, but do not overstuff them, and place them on a hot, oiled grill. Grill them for 7 minutes per side, basting with olive oil occasionally. Prepare a sauce with the lemon juice and extra virgin olive oil. Slice the squid, pour the sauce over them, and serve. Equally delicious hot or cold.

Baked Small Fish
(Gavros Plaki)

Serves 4
Preparation time 1 hour
Baking time 1 hour

3 lbs small fish (picarel, anchovies, sardines, etc.)
1 cup olive oil
4 large onions, sliced
6 garlic cloves, sliced
2 tablespoons tomato paste
1/4 cup white wine or Fish Stock (page 46) or water
1 cup finely chopped parsley
salt and pepper to taste
2 fresh tomatoes, sliced
3 thin lemon slices, peeled

Clean the fish, removing heads and back bones, if desired. Wash and drain well. Heat the oil in a saucepan, add the onions and garlic, and sauté until transparent. Dilute the tomato paste in the wine and pour it over the onions. Add parsley and season to taste. Cover and simmer, until all the liquid has evaporated. In a "yiouvetsi" (clay) or other ovenproof dish, place half the fish combined with half the tomato and lemon slices. Cover with half the sauce, add the remaining fish, tomatoes, and lemon slices, and spread the remaining sauce on top. Preheat oven to 400°F and bake for 30-40 minutes. Equally good hot or cold.

Grilled Sardines
(Sardeles Psites)

Serves 4
Preparation time 30 minutes
Grilling time 8 minutes

2 lbs fresh sardines
salt, pepper, olive oil
oregano (optional)
2 garlic cloves, finely chopped
1/4 cup finely chopped parsley
Oil-Lemon Sauce (page 47)

Clean the sardines and pull out the backbone carefully. It should come out easily when you pull off the head and intestines. Try not to split the fish in two. Open the sardines, rinse well, drain, and line them up on a platter. Sprinkle them with a mixture of salt, pepper, oregano, chopped garlic and a little olive oil. Place them two together (bellies facing each other) and arrange on an oiled double grill. Grill them over charcoal for 4 minutes on each side. Sprinkle a little more oregano over them when finished. Transfer them to a platter, sprinkle with parsley, and serve, garnished with slices of lemon and grilled tomatoes. An excellent accompaniment to tsipouro or ouzo.

Sardines in Oil and Oregano
(Sardeles Ladorigani)

Serves 4
Preparation time 30 minutes
Cooking time 20 minutes

2 lbs fresh sardines or anchovies
3/4 cup olive oil
5-6 garlic cloves, sliced
2 tablespoons vinegar
salt, pepper, and oregano

Gut, wash, and drain the fish thoroughly; they should not have scales. Remove heads and backbones if desired. Heat the oil in a saucepan, add garlic, and sauté lightly. Add the sardines, vinegar, salt, pepper, and oregano. Boil rapidly until all the liquid has evaporated and only the oil remains. Excellent hot or cold.

Poultry and Game
(Poulerika ke Kinigi)

Chicken is such a popular food, so widespread nowadays it does not seem possible that it was a great delicacy until a few decades ago. Hens were valued for their eggs and were not killed until their laying days were over. And because one chicken would not go far in a large Greek family, it was often stewed or braised with noodles, rice, or a vegetable like okra, peas, or potatoes. As with meat, favorite sauces contain tomatoes, lemon juice, or wine, seasoned with bay leaf, garlic, and pepper. Casserole-roasted lemon chicken is one of the great dishes this country has produced. Another formidable dish is turkey, irresistibly roasted to a golden brown with a uniquely Greek stuffing. Containing ground beef and pork, rice, chestnuts, pine nuts, raisins, and brandy, this filling adds a new dimension to the Christmas feast.

With domesticated birds being scarce, Greek men regularly stalked the hills and marshes for pheasant, duck, partridge, and quail as well as rabbit, hare, venison, and wild boar. Even today, game in Greece is fairly abundant, especially in the north of the country, and is always a treat. My grandfather was an avid hunter, and nothing he shot was wasted. Not only did we cook the wild birds he brought home, we also plucked them ourselves and used the feathers to stuff our hand-made pillows and quilts. So that the soft down would not fly around and get lost, we placed the bird and our hands inside a pillow case and pulled off the feathers without being able to see what we were doing.

Because of its relative rarity and cost, game can transform an ordinary, everyday meal into an exotic feast. What could be more pleasant than a plate of hare stew or roast pheasant, a glass of red wine, and good friends to share them with?

Being so adaptable, poultry can be the basis for the easiest, simplest of meals or the star of a dinner party for important guests. Very few foods are so versatile. They are also in favor with health experts who view "white meat" as preferable to "red", because of its very low fat content.

General Instructions

The classic way of cooking poultry in Greece is in the pot on top of the stove. Perhaps the most popular favorite is chicken with tomato sauce (kokkinisto), seasoned with allspice, pepper, and bay leaves, and accompanied by rice, pasta, or a vegetable like stringbeans or okra. No matter what is to be cooked with it, the chicken, whole or cut into pieces, is always browned first in oil or *some other fat in order to seal in the juices and the flavor. Oven-roasted chick-en is even easier, requiring only occasional basting. A favorite Sunday dish is roast chicken sprinkled with lemon, oregano, or thyme, and surrounded with sliced potatoes.*

Since they are normally tender, chicken parts are ideal for grilling or deep-frying. For even better flavor, marinate them for several hours in an oil-lemon dressing with herbs and seasonings or in wine or vinegar. When frying, take care to drain the parts well and pat them dry before you roll them in flour or bread crumbs or dip them in batter. If the bird is very young and tender, serve the chicken as soon as it comes out of the frying pan. If it is larger or free-range, it may need more cooking, so roast the fried chicken parts for 35 or 40 min-utes in a moderate oven to make sure they are cooked through. When cooking poultry, special attention should be taken to prevent the meat from drying out. Most of the fat is located in and under the skin, so if you really want to cut down your intake of animal fats, remove the skin and the yellow fatty deposits before you boil or braise your chicken. Not only will this make the dish lighter, it will also make it tastier because poultry fat often has a strong smell depend-ing on what the bird has been fed. Marinating it before hand will help the chicken retain its moisture. Another trick to keep the flesh of the bird moist – chicken or even turkey – is to brine it. Fill a large bowl, a bucket, or an ice chest large enough to hold the bird with water to cover it. Pour in and dissolve the salt – 1/4 cup per quart of water – and soak the bird – a chicken for 1 hour per pound, but not more than 8 hours – in a cool place. If you intend to roast or grill, pat the skin dry with paper towels and leave the bird, uncovered, in the refrigerator for the same amount of time. In this way, you will not only have moist flesh but crispy skin. Even if you do not brine, do not remove the skin when you plan to roast or grill the chicken, since the fat under the skin melts during roasting, basting the flesh and keeping it tender.

Though rarely fried, ducks, geese, and some game birds are more or less cooked in the same manner, though being fatty they do not need brining. Likewise, chicken can be substituted for game in any of these recipes. Some birds require special preparation prior to cooking. For example, the skin of domestic ducks and geese should be pricked with a sharp fork to allow the excess fat to drain off, while in wild ducks the upper part of the tail should be removed, since the two oil glands located there have a very unpleasant smell. Most game birds larger than quail will benefit from marinating. Several hours of soaking in a marinade of wine and herbs will improve the flavor while ten-derizing the flesh and eliminating any strong odors.

Four-legged game should also be marinated before cooking, usually for sev-eral days, because the meat is apt to be tough. Here, too, the aromatic herbs in the marinade help to improve the flavor and taste of the meat. Most game meats are lean. They must be provided with extra fat to keep them from dry-ing out while cooking. Cover roasts with a thin slice of lard or strips of bacon or wrap in caul. The recipes in this chapter describe how best to cook each type of poultry and game.

Chicken Stew With Okra
(Kotopoulo me Bamies)

Serves 4-5
Preparation time 40 minutes
Cooking time 1 hour and 15 minutes

1 large chicken
1 lb okra
salt and vinegar
1/2 cup olive oil
8 small tomatoes
1/4 cup butter, clarified
salt, sugar, and freshly ground pepper

Prepare the chicken as in the recipe for Chicken Stew (page 146), but leave the chicken whole and do not add salt. In the meantime, trim the cone-shaped tops of the okra and dip them in salt. Place in a colander, sprinkle with a little vinegar, and set aside for half an hour. Rinse with lots of water and drain well. When the chicken is ready, remove it to a serving platter, and keep it warm in a low oven. Heat the oil in a heavy-bottomed shallow pan, and lightly sauté the okra. Add the stew sauce and 1/2 cup hot water to the okra. Simmer covered, for about 15 minutes, until the okra are tender but firm. Meanwhile, core the tomatoes and squeeze out the seeds and juice; drain well. In a small frying pan heat the butter and add the tomatoes. Sprinkle them with a little salt and sugar and sauté, until they are glazed all over. Arrange the okra around the chicken and garnish with the glazed tomatoes. Sprinkle with freshly ground pepper and serve immediately.

Thaw them out before cooking.) Heat the butter in a heavy-bottomed pan and lightly brown the chicken rolls on all sides over high heat. Reduce the heat to low, cover, and simmer for about 45 minutes, moistening from time to time with a few tablespoons of lemon juice mixed with wine and a little water. When cooked, remove the rolls from the pan and allow to cool slightly. Cut off the string and place the rolls on a hot serving platter. Surround with Buttered Peas and Carrots. Strain the sauce through a fine sieve and pour it over the meat. Sprinkle with freshly ground pepper and serve. Ideal for a special dinner.

Chicken Breasts Stuffed with Cheese
(Kotopoulo Rolo me Tiri)

Serves 4-5
Preparation time 1 hour
Cooking time 45 minutes

4 large chicken breasts, boned, skin attached
2 tablespoons ketchup
salt, pepper, and oregano
4 slices ham
4 sticks kasseri or other yellow cheese (5 oz)
1/2 cup butter or margarine
3 tablespoons lemon juice
1/2 cup dry red wine

the garnish
1/2 lb chicken livers, hearts, and gizzards, cut in large pieces
1 lb can mushrooms or 1½ lbs fresh mushrooms
1/4 cup heavy cream
salt and freshly ground pepper

Prepare the chicken breasts as in the previous recipe for Chicken Breasts Stuffed with Bacon. Spread ketchup instead of mustard on one side, and sprinkle with salt, pepper, and oregano. Place a slice of ham and a stick of kasseri cheese on each breast, and roll, wrap, tie, and cook the breasts, as in the previous recipe. When the rolls are cooked, remove them from the pan. Add the chicken giblets and mushrooms to the pan and cook slowly, until the juices boil down and the giblets and mushrooms begin to brown. Pour in 2 tablespoons of water and the cream. Stir and remove from the heat. Arrange the chicken rolls on a platter and garnish with the giblets and mushrooms. Serve accompanied by Cucumber and Tomato Salad.
Note: If using fresh mushrooms, blanch them first for 2-3 minutes in boiling water with a little lemon juice to prevent discoloring.

Chicken Breasts Stuffed with Bacon
(Kotopoulo Rolo me Bacon)

Serves 4-5
Preparation time 1 hour
Cooking time 45 minutes

4 large chicken breasts, boned, skin attached
freshly ground pepper
2 tablespoons prepared mustard
4 slices ham
4 strips bacon
1/3 cup butter or margarine
3 tablespoons lemon juice
1/2 cup dry white wine

Wash the chicken breasts and pat dry with paper towels. Detach the skin by sliding your fingers along the flesh, taking care not to tear the skin. Lift it off and set aside. Flatten the breasts to a thickness of about 1/4 inch, pounding lightly with a mallet or rolling pin. Cut each skin into 2 even pieces. Place each of the four flattened breasts, boned side up, on a piece of chicken skin. Sprinkle with pepper and spread a little mustard on one side. Cover each breast lengthwise with a slice of ham and a strip of bacon and roll up. Wrap each roll in a second piece of chicken skin and bind it with string. (At this stage the chicken rolls may be frozen.

Charcoal-Grilled Chicken
(Kotopoulo sta Karvouna)

Serves 4
Preparation time 24 hours
Cooking time 15-20 minutes

1 chicken, quartered (2 lbs)
Oil-Lemon Dressing (page 47)
oregano, thyme, fresh coriander
salt and pepper
1/2 cup red or white wine
1 garlic clove, finely chopped

Combine the oil-lemon dressing, herbs, wine, and garlic in a bowl. Marinate the chicken pieces in the mixture for 24 hours in the refrigerator, turning occasionally to keep them well moistened. Remove the chicken from the marinade and grill, preferably over charcoal, for 8-10 minutes on each side, basting with the marinade two or three times. Serve immediately, accompanied by buttered vegetables or fried potatoes sprinkled with kefalotiri or Romano cheese, and a Greek Village Salad.

Chicken in Red Pepper Sauce
(Kotopoulo Paprika)

Serves 4-5
Preparation time 15 minutes
Cooking time 30 minutes

1/2 cup olive oil
1 large chicken, cut into serving pieces
1½ cups Red Pepper Sauce (page 50)
salt (optional)

Heat the oil in a heavy-bottomed pan. Add the chicken pieces and sauté over high heat, until well browned on all sides. Add the pepper sauce and 1/2 cup water. Add salt, if needed. Simmer, covered, until the chicken is tender and the sauce is thick. Serve the dish with pilaf and boiled vegetables.

Chicken in Aspic (Kotopoulo Zele)

Serves 6-8
Preparation time 1 hour
Cooking time 1 hour

1 small chicken
1 small onion, peeled
2 small carrots, scrubbed
salt and pepper
3-4 sour gherkins, chopped
1 tablespoon capers
2 tablespoons unflavored gelatin
2 teaspoons prepared mustard
2 hard-boiled eggs, sliced
3-4 pimiento-stuffed olives, sliced
parsley leaves

Clean and wash the chicken. Place it in a pot with a little water; add the onion, carrots, and seasonings, and bring slowly to a boil, skimming off. Cover and simmer until the chicken is tender. Lift the chicken out onto a plate, remove, and discard the skin and bones. Dice the chicken meat, cube the carrots, and combine them in a mixing bowl with the pickles and capers. Strain and degrease the stock; you should have about 2 cups. Strain the stock once more through a fine sieve. Dissolve the gelatin in the stock. Ladle some of the liquid into a chilled rectangular mold (4x12 inches) to a depth of about 1/4 inch and refrigerate to set. To decorate, make a design with the parsley leaves, a few egg slices, and olive slices on the surface of the jelly, and lightly pack the chicken mixture on top. Finely chop the onion and mix it with the mustard and the remaining gelatin-stock mixture. Spoon it carefully over the chicken in the mold. Cover and refrigerate for 5-6 hours or, preferably, overnight. To unmold, run the tip of a knife around the rim of the mold to loosen the gelatin. Then lower the mold, almost to its rim, into a bowl of hot water for 1-2 seconds. Put a chilled serving plate, upside down, on top of the mold and invert them together. Hold the mold firmly against the plate and give it a good shake to release the vacuum. Lift the mold away. Garnish with parsley leaves and flower-shaped carrots. An exceptional dish for a buffet.

Roast Lemon Chicken
(Kotopoulo Lemonato Fournou)

Serves 4-5
Preparation time 30 minutes
Baking time 1 hour and 30 minutes

1 large chicken
1/2 cup lemon juice
salt, pepper, and oregano
1/2 cup olive oil
4 lbs potatoes, peeled and sliced
1/2 cup butter, cubed

Wash the chicken and drain well. Rub the chicken inside and out with half the lemon juice, salt, pepper, and oregano. Place the chicken, breast side up, in a roasting pan. Coat with oil and surround with potatoes. Pour the remaining lemon juice over the potatoes, season them with salt, pepper, and oregano, and dot with the butter cubes. Cover with aluminum foil, preheat the oven to 350°F, and bake for about 1 hour and 30 minutes, or until the chicken and potatoes are soft and most of the juices have been absorbed. Add a little hot water if the dish seems dry. Half an hour before the dish is completely cooked, remove the foil to brown, or place under the broiler for a few minutes before serving.

Pot-Roasted Lemon Chicken
(Kotopoulo Lemonato Katsarolas)

Serves 4-5
Preparation time 30 minutes
Cooking time 1 hour

1 cup olive oil
1 chicken, cut into serving pieces
1/2 cup lemon juice
4 lbs puréed potatoes, peeled and quartered
salt, pepper, and oregano

Heat the oil in a heavy-bottomed casserole, add the chicken pieces, and brown lightly on all sides over high heat. Pour the lemon juice over the chicken, add the potatoes, and season with salt, pepper, and oregano. Add hot water to cover the potatoes and simmer, covered, until the chicken and potatoes are tender and the sauce is reduced. Serve the dish accompanied by Cucumber and Tomato Salad.
Note: The potatoes can be fried and added to the chicken about 20 minutes before it is completely cooked. Add water as needed.

Chicken Stew
(Kotopoulo Kokkinisto)

Serves 4-5
Preparation time 15 minutes
Cooking time 1 hour

2 tablespoons butter
1/3 cup olive oil
1 large chicken, cut into serving pieces
1 small onion, grated
2 cups puréed fresh or canned tomatoes
2 tablespoons ketchup
salt and pepper

Heat the butter and oil in a large casserole, and sauté the chicken pieces, until they are golden brown on all sides. Remove them with a perforated spoon onto a platter. In the same pan sauté the onions and as they begin to brown, return the chicken pieces to the pan and pour in the tomatoes. Add the ketchup and season to taste. Cover and simmer, until the chicken is tender and the sauce is reduced and thick. Serve the dish hot with pilaf, macaroni, or potatoes.

Stewed Cockerel (Kokoras Kokkinistos)

Serves 4-5
Preparation time 30 minutes
Cooking time 1 hour and 30 minutes

1/2 cup olive oil
1 young cockerel (3 lbs), in portions
1 large onion, grated
2 lbs ripe tomatoes or
1 16-oz can, finely chopped
2 tablespoons tomato paste
1 tablespoon vinegar
1 teaspoon sugar
2 bay leaves
8 allspice berries and 10 peppercorns
salt and freshly ground pepper
1 lb medium macaroni (ziti)

Heat the oil in a stewing pot and brown the poultry pieces in it, a few at a time, on all sides. Remove to a platter while you wilt the onion in the same oil. Add the tomatoes, tomato paste diluted in a little water, the vinegar, sugar, bay leaves, and seasonings, and stir well to loosen any browned bits that have stuck to the bottom. Return the cockerel pieces to the pot, cover, and simmer until the meat is tender and the sauce has thickened. Add a little water if the dish seems dry. Meanwhile, boil the macaroni in plenty of salted water with 2 tablespoons of oil, according to package directions. Drain, place on a deep platter, and pour the sauce and meat on top. Serve immediately, accompanied by a bowl of grated cheese.

Fried Chicken (Kotopoulo Tiganito)

Serves 4
Preparation time 24 hours
Frying time 15-20 minutes

2 young chickens, cut into serving pieces (3 lbs)
Marinade No 1 (page 52)
flour for dredging
2 eggs, lightly beaten
fine bread crumbs
oil for frying

Mix the marinade ingredients in a bowl. Place the chicken pieces in the marinade, coating on all sides. Cover and marinate in the refrigerator overnight. Remove the chicken pieces from the marinade, drain, and pat dry with paper towels. Season lightly with salt and pepper. Shake the chicken pieces in a plastic bag with a cup or two of flour, until they are well coated. Dip them one by one into the beaten eggs and roll in bread crumbs. Arrange them on wax paper and refrigerate for one hour to set the coating. The chicken pieces can also be dipped in a batter instead of the egg and bread crumbs. Heat about 1/3 inch of oil in a heavy-bottomed frying pan. Slip in the chicken and fry until crisp and lightly browned on all sides. Drain the chicken, arrange on a platter, and serve garnished with lemon wedges and parsley or watercress sprigs. Accompany with buttered vegetables, mashed potatoes, and a green salad.
Note: If the fried chicken pieces seem a little tough, put them in an oven preheated to 350°F and bake them until crisp and dark brown.

Chicken Stew with Chick-peas
(Kotopoulo Kokkinisto me Revithia)

Serves 4-5
Preparation time 12 hours
Cooking time 2 hours

3/4 lb chick-peas or
1 package frozen chick-peas
2 cups vegetable broth
3 lbs chicken, in portions
1/3 cup olive oil
1 large onion, grated
1 small leek, white part only, finely chopped
2 garlic cloves, mashed
1 large carrot, diced
1/2 yellow pepper, diced
1/2 red pepper, diced
1 cup chicken broth
1 16-oz can tomatoes, passed through a sieve
1 tablespoon ketchup
1/2 teaspoon oregano
1 teaspoon hot pepper flakes
salt and freshly ground pepper
2 tablespoons finely chopped parsley

Soak the chick-peas for 12 hours in water with 1 tablespoon of salt. Frozen chick-peas need no soaking, because they are already soft and puffed-up. Drain, rinse, and put them in a pot with the vegetable broth and boil until half tender. In a separate pan lightly brown the chicken pieces in hot oil on all sides. Add the onion, leek, garlic, carrot, and peppers and sauté them, stirring, until they start to soften. Stir in the chicken broth, tomatoes, ketchup, oregano, and pepper flakes. Add the chick-peas and their broth. Sprinkle in a little salt – the chickpeas will have already absorbed enough – and plenty of freshly ground pepper. Bring to the boil and simmer, covered, for 35-40 minutes until both the chick-peas and the chicken are tender and the sauce has reduced. Scatter the chopped parsley over the dish and serve accompanied by Constantinople-Style Salad or Cabbage Salad.

Chicken with Peppers and Onions
(Kotopoulo me Piperies ke Kremmidia)

Serves 4-5
Preparation time 30 minutes
Cooking time 1 hour

1 cup olive oil
2 lbs onions, thinly sliced
1½ lbs long green peppers, cut into rings
1 long hot green pepper, cut into rings (optional)
2 garlic cloves, sliced (optional)
1 large chicken, cut into serving pieces
1 cup chopped fresh or canned tomatoes
1/2 cup red wine or 2 tablespoons vinegar
1 tablespoon tomato paste
2 tablespoons minced parsley or
1 bay leaf
salt and pepper
2 tablespoons heavy cream (optional)

Heat the oil in a heavy-bottomed frying pan and sauté the onions and garlic, followed by the peppers. Remove with a perforated spoon to a bowl. In the same pan lightly brown the chicken pieces on all sides. Return the sautéed vegetables to the frying pan, add the tomatoes, wine, tomato paste, parsley, and season to taste. Stir gently, cover, and cook slowly, until the chicken and vegetables are tender and the juices are reduced. Add the cream, stir, and remove from the heat. Serve the dish with pilaf or steamed potatoes.

Chicken Stew with Potatoes
(Kotopoulo Kokkinisto me Patates)

Serves 4
Preparation time 25 minutes
Cooking time 1 hour and 15 minutes

1 recipe, Chicken Stew (page 146)
6 allspice berries
2 lbs potatoes
salt and freshly ground pepper

Prepare the Chicken Stew according to the recipe on page 146, adding 1/4 cup more oil and the allspice. In the meantime, peel and cut the potatoes in quarters and fry them lightly in hot oil. Remove with a slotted spoon, and add to the chicken casserole when the chicken is nearly cooked. Add 1 cup warm water, adjust the seasonings, cover, and continue to simmer, until the potatoes are soft and almost all the liquid is absorbed. Remove from the heat, sprinkle with freshly ground pepper, and serve immediately with a green salad.

Chicken Stew with Peas
(Kotopoulo Kokkinisto me Araka)

Serves 4
Preparation time 30 minutes
Cooking time 1 hour and 15 minutes

1 recipe Chicken Stew (page 146)
2 lbs fresh green peas, shelled or
1 lb frozen peas
freshly ground pepper

Prepare the Chicken Stew according to the recipe on page 146, adding the peas, 1/3 cup more oil, and 1 cup hot water. Cover and simmer, until the chicken and peas are tender and the sauce is reduced. If necessary, add a little more water and adjust the seasonings. Remove from the heat. Sprinkle with a little freshly ground pepper and serve with Cucumber and Tomato Salad.

Pheasant with Almonds and Pine Nuts
(Fasianos me Amigdala ke Koukounaria)

Serves 4-5
Preparation time 45 minutes
Cooking time 45 minutes

1 pheasant, cut into portions
salt and pepper
flour for dredging
1/3 cup olive oil
1/3 cup butter, clarified
1/2 cup blanched almonds
1/3 cup pine nuts
1/2 cup dry white wine
2 tablespoons vinegar
1/2 cup orange juice
2 oranges, sliced

Season the pheasant portions lightly with salt and pepper and dredge with flour. Heat the oil and butter in a heavy-bottomed casserole, and lightly sauté the almonds and pine nuts. Remove the nuts with a slotted spoon, and in the same fat lightly brown the pheasant pieces on all sides. Add the wine and a little water, cover, and simmer until the meat is tender and the sauce is reduced. Remove the pheasant and arrange the pieces on a hot platter. Keep warm. Add the almonds, pine nuts, vinegar, and orange juice to the pan and mix with the sauce. Reduce the sauce again and check the seasonings. Pour a small amount of sauce over the pheasant and surround with the orange slices. Serve the dish with pilaf or mashed potato, topped with the remaining sauce.

Woodcock Braised in Wine
(Bekatses Krassates)

Serves 4-5
Preparation time 30 minutes
Cooking time 40 minutes

8 ready-to-cook woodcock, partridge, or quail
salt, pepper, and oregano
olive oil
1/2 cup clarified butter
1 cup dry white wine
1 tablespoon lemon juice
1 cup tomato purée (optional)

Wash and drain the birds well. Rub with salt, pepper, and oregano, and brush them with oil. Set aside for about 30 minutes. Heat the butter in a heavy-bottomed saucepan over medium heat and brown the birds on all sides, about 10 minutes, turning frequently. Pour the wine and lemon juice over them, cover, and simmer, until all the cooking juices boil down. Reduce the wine to a half cup and add the tomato purée, if desired. Cook slowly, until the sauce is thick. Arrange the birds on a platter and cover with the sauce. Serve with french fried potatoes or Buttered Vegetables and a green salad.

Venison with Onions and White Sauce
(Elafi me Kremmidia ke Aspri Saltsa)

Serve 4-5
Preparation time 1 hour
Cooking time 1 hour and 30 minutes

3 lbs leg or saddle of venison
salt
1 tablespoon lemon juice or vinegar
1 medium onion or 2 small ones, peeled
1 celery stalk
2 carrots, scrubbed
3 parsley sprigs
2 bay leaves
10 peppercorns
3 whole cloves
4 tablespoons olive oil
2 lbs shallots
1 large lamb's caul or bacon

the sauce
2 tablespoons butter
2 tablespoons flour
2 egg yolks
3 tablespoons heavy cream
1 tablespoon finely chopped parsley

Place venison in a large casserole with enough lightly salted water to cover it. Bring slowly to the boil over medium heat, skimming the scum that rises to the surface. When no more scum appears, add the lemon juice, onion, celery, carrots, parsley, bay leaves, peppercorns, and cloves. Cover and simmer for about 30 minutes. In the meantime, heat the oil in a frying pan and sauté the shallots over medium heat, until they are transparent. Transfer them to an ovenproof dish. Set aside. Remove the venison from the pan, let it cool slightly, and wrap in caul or bacon. Place the meat in the baking dish together with the onions. Add 1 cup of liquid from the pan, and season to taste. Cover with aluminum foil, preheat the oven to 350ºF, and roast for approximately 1 hour, or until the meat is completely cooked. Meanwhile, strain the remaining liquid through a sieve into a saucepan and reduce until you have about 2 cups. Heat the butter in a saucepan, add the flour, and stir briskly with a wooden spoon, until the mixture begins to bubble. Off the heat, quickly pour in the reduced liquid and stir rapidly to blend together. Return to the heat, cover, and simmer for about 30 minutes, until the sauce thickens a bit, stirring occasionally to prevent sticking. Lightly beat the egg yolks with the cream and pour the mixture slowly into the sauce, stirring constantly. Remove from the heat and adjust the seasonings. Slice the venison and arrange on a platter. Surround with the onions, pour the sauce over the meat, and sprinkle with parsley. Serve immediately.

wine and a half cup water. Add the bay leaves and season to taste. Cover and simmer until the meat is tender and the sauce is reduced to about 1 cup. Add more hot water during the cooking time, if needed. Remove from the heat, lift out the meat, and place on a hot platter. Keep warm in a low oven while you make the sauce. Discard the bay leaves and garlic. Strain the sauce and vegetables through a sieve, pressing the solids firmly to extract all the juices. Slowly bring the sauce back to a boil, skimming off the fat, until the sauce is reduced by about 1/3. For extra smoothness, pass the sauce once more through a fine sieve, adjust the seasonings, and stir in the cream or butter as desired. Pour the sauce over the meat and serve immediately accompanied by pilaf, french fried potatoes, potato purée, or pasta.

Note: You can cook other game (hare, pheasant, or wild duck) in the same way.

Stewed Thrush with Rice
(Tsichles Kokkinistes me Rizi)

Serves 4
Preparation time 12 hours
Cooking time 1 hour

1/2 cup orange juice
1/4 cup lemon juice
1 teaspoon prepared mustard
12 thrush (or quail), plucked and cleaned
1/4 cup olive oil
1/4 cup brandy
1/4 cup dry red wine

Salmis of Wild Boar
(Agriogourouno Salmi)

Serves 5-6
Preparation time 24 hours
Cooking time 2 hours

3 lbs wild boar, cut into portions
Marinade No 2 (page 52)
1/2 cup olive oil or margarine
1 cup dry red wine
1 large carrot, sliced
1 small onion, sliced
1 small celery root, diced
2 garlic cloves
2 bay leaves
salt and pepper
3 tablespoons butter, cubed or
1/4 cup heavy cream

Prepare the marinade, add the meat portions, and marinate for 24 hours in the refrigerator, turning occasionally. Lift the meat out of the marinade and allow to drain in a colander. Discard the marinade. Heat the oil in a heavy-bottomed casserole and brown the meat lightly, on all sides. Remove it with a slotted spoon and in the same fat gently sauté the onions, carrots, celery, and garlic. Return the meat to the pan, pour in the

1 16-oz can finely chopped tomatoes
1 tablespoon ketchup
1 teaspoon tomato paste
6 allspice berries
1 teaspoon spice for game
salt and freshly ground pepper
1½ cups long-grain rice

Stir the juices and mustard together and rub the birds with the mixture. Refrigerate, covered, and let marinate for 12 hours. Drain well. Heat the oil in a heavy-bottomed saucepan and brown the birds on all sides. Pour in the brandy and scrape the bottom and sides of the pan with a wooden spoon. Add the wine, tomatoes, ketchup, tomato paste, and seasonings. Bring to a boil and simmer for 40 minutes or until the birds are tender. Place the birds on a platter and keep warm in a low oven. Add the rice to the sauce along with 1 cup of hot water, stir, cover, and simmer until done, about 20 minutes. Transfer the rice to a platter, place the birds on top, and serve, accompanied by Greek Village Salad.

Stuffed Turkey Greek-Style (Galopoula Yemisti)

Serves about 10
Preparation time, about 1 hour and 30 minutes
Cooking time depends on the weight of bird

1 turkey (8-10 lbs)
1/4 cup lemon juice
1/2 cup orange juice
1/2 cup butter, clarified
salt and pepper

the stuffing
6 tablespoons butter
turkey giblets (liver, heart, gizzard)
1/2 lb ground beef
1/2 lb ground pork
1 small onion, finely chopped
1/4 cup short-grain rice
1/2 lb chestnuts, boiled, shelled, and chopped
1/4 cup pine nuts
1/4 cup currants (optional)

2 tablespoons brandy (optional)
2 cups Chicken or Meat Stock (page 44)

the garnish
1 lb chestnuts, blanched and shelled
1 lb dried prunes, pitted
1 lb dried apricots
3 large quinces or cooking apples
4 cups Meat Stock (page 44)
1 cup butter, clarified
sugar, salt and pepper

Remove the innards. Wash the turkey and pat dry. Melt the butter, blend with the lemon and orange juices, and rub the turkey with the mixture inside and out. Reserve the remaining liquid. Sprinkle the turkey cavities and skin with salt and pepper. Set aside.

Prepare the stuffing: Wash the giblets and cut them into small pieces. Heat the butter in a saucepan, and sauté the onion until transparent. Add the chopped giblets and ground meat and brown them lightly. Add half the meat stock and all the other stuffing ingredients and mix well. Remove from the heat, adjust the seasonings, and allow to cool. You may cook the stuffing separately, if you wish, as follows. After the chopped giblets and ground meat are browned, add the beef stock, cover, and simmer for 10 minutes. Add the rice and continue simmering, for about 20 minutes, until the rice is soft. Add the remaining ingredients and stir well. Remove from the heat, place a thick piece of paper towel or a clean dish cloth between the lid and the pan, and let rest for 5 minutes before serving.

To stuff the turkey: Place the turkey, breast side down, on a cutting board. Spoon in enough of the uncooked stuffing to loosely fill the neck cavity. Fold the neck skin over the back, close the neck opening, and truss with a piece of string. Fold the wing tips back and under the bird's backbone. Turn the turkey over, breast side up, on the board. Fill the body cavity with the rest of the stuffing and sew up the vent with a trussing needle. Do not overfill the bird as the stuffing will expand while cooking. With a long piece of string tie and secure the legs to the tail and the wings to the body. Place the turkey, breast side up, in a large, shallow pan. Add water to cover the bottom of the pan. Cover the breast and drumsticks with aluminum foil, leaving the sides open. Preheat oven to 325⁰F and roast for half an hour per pound. Add water frequently during roasting. Baste the turkey with the reserved butter and juices mixture from time to time. When the bird is almost cooked, remove the foil to brown. Transfer the turkey to a platter. Pour the remaining stock into the roasting pan, mix with the pan juices, and stir well to scrape up any bits of meat stuck to the bottom. Pour the mixture into a saucepan, skim off most of the fat, and reduce the sauce over medium heat.

To prepare the garnish: Cook the chestnuts, prunes, and apricots separately, each in 1 cup meat stock, with 3 table-spoons butter and 2 tablespoons olive oil. Boil until all the liquid evaporates and the fruits are glazed with the butter. Wash and rub the quinces until the skin shines. Cut into eighths and remove the seeds. Boil the quinces in 1 cup meat stock with 1/3 cup butter, and seasonings until all the liquid evaporates. Season to taste with a little nutmeg, allspice, and sprinkle with 2-3 tablespoons sugar. Shake the pan gently, to distribute the seasonings, and stir until the sugar melts and the quinces are caramel-glazed. Place the turkey on a large platter, and surround with the buttered chestnuts, prunes, apricots, and quinces. Serve the gravy separately.

Roast Duckling with Apples
(Papakia Psita me Mila)

Serves 4
Preparation time 24 hours
Roasting time 40 minutes

2 small duckling or wild ducks
salt and pepper
Marinade No 2 (page 52)
2 tablespoons butter or margarine
2 tablespoons flour
3 tablespoons heavy cream (optional)
2 lbs tart apples, pared, cored, and sliced
clarified butter for frying

Wash the duckling well, especially the cavities, and trim off excess fat at the base of the tail and inside. Rub inside and out with salt and pepper. Prick the skin in several places with the tip of a knife to allow the fat to drain. Tie the legs together. Prepare the marinade according to the recipe on page 52 and pour it over the duckling. Cover and refrigerate for about 24 hours. Turn occasionally to keep ducks well moistened. Remove them from the marinade and place them on a rack in a roasting pan. Add 1 cup water to the pan, preheat oven to 350⁰F, and roast the duckling for about 40 minutes, until the skin is golden brown. Remove from the oven, cut each duckling in half, and place on a hot platter. Keep warm. Strain the pan juices though a fine sieve into a bowl. Skim off and discard the fat. You should have about 1½ cups of liquid. Heat the butter or margarine in a saucepan, add the flour, and stir briskly with a wooden spoon, until the mixture begins to bubble. Slowly pour in the duckling juices and stir rapidly to blend together. Simmer for about 15 minutes until the sauce is reduced, stirring occasionally. Stir in the cream after about 10 minutes. Remove from the heat, adjust the seasonings, and keep covered. In a large frying pan heat a small amount of margarine and fry the apples, a few at a time, until lightly browned on both sides. Drain and arrange the apples around the duckling. Pass the sauce in a heated gravy boat.

Note: The duckling can be served with apple sauce instead of fried apples.

Rinse the birds well and with a pair of scissors split them along the backbone from the neck to the tail. Open the birds and remove the innards, taking care not to puncture the gall bladder, which would make the flesh bitter. Rinse well again and place them, breast up, on a flat surface. Press down with the palm of your hand and break the breast bone. With a knife make a slit in the skin in the lower part of the breast cavity between the legs. Fold the legs carefully and slip them under the slit. Rub the birds with oil and sprinkle with salt, pepper, and oregano. Let stand, covered, for 1-2 hours. In a deep, heavy-bottomed frying pan heat the oil and butter. When they have ceased to bubble, add the birds, a few at a time, and fry about 8 minutes on each side. Remove them with a slotted spoon to a platter and keep them warm in a low oven while you fry the rest. When you have fried them all, add the onions to the fat remaining in the pan and sauté them lightly. Add the mushrooms and sauté them quickly over high heat, until they reabsorb their liquid. Add the parsley, lemon juice and wine, stir well, and boil for 1 minute. Slide the mushrooms and sauce into the middle of a warmed platter and arrange the birds around them, garnished with a few watercress sprigs. Serve immediately.

Hare with Garlic Sauce
(Lagos Skordatos)

Serves 5-6
Preparation time 24 hours
Baking time 2 hours and 15 minutes

> 1 hare or rabbit (4-5 lbs), cut in portions
> vinegar
> water
> flour for dredging
> 1/2 cup olive oil
> 1/2 cup dry white wine
> salt, pepper, and allspice
> Garlic Sauce with Walnuts (page 50)

Wash the hare and place the pieces in a large bowl. Add equal parts vinegar and water to cover the meat, and refrigerate for 24 hours. Drain the meat well, pat dry with paper towels, and coat with flour. Heat the oil in a frying pan, add the hare, and brown lightly on all sides. Transfer to an ovenproof dish. Pour the wine and 1/2 cup of hot water into the frying pan and stir with a wooden spoon to dislodge any meat glaze. Pour the liquid over the hare and season with salt, pepper, and a pinch of allspice. Cover tightly, preheat the oven to 350°F, and bake for about 2 hours, until the meat is tender and the sauce reduced. In the meantime, prepare the garlic sauce, spread it over the hare, and bake the dish, uncovered, for another 15 minutes, until the

Fried Quail
(Ortikia Tiganita)

Serves 4
Preparation time 1 hour
Cooking time 30 minutes

> 8 quail, thrush, or other small
> game birds, cleaned
> salt, pepper, oregano
> 1/3 cup olive oil
> 2-3 tablespoons clarified butter
> 4 spring onions, finely chopped
> 2 lbs canned mushrooms or
> 1 lb fresh mushrooms, sliced
> 1 teaspoon lemon juice
> 2 tablespoons finely chopped parsley
> 2 tablespoons dry white wine

surface is lightly browned. Serve the hare accompanied by Buttered Vegetables and Beet Salad.

Hare and Onion Stew
(Lagos Stifado)

Serves 6
Preparation time 24-48 hours
Cooking time 2 hours

Prepare the dish according to the recipe for Veal and Onion Stew (page 113). Wash hare pieces with water and vinegar. Prepare the marinade, add the hare, cover, and refrigerate for 2-4 days. Turn and baste the meat 4-6 times. Rabbit or other game or poultry is also excellent prepared this way.

Quail Wrapped in Vine Leaves
(Ortikia se Klimatofylla)

Serves 4-5
Preparation time 30 minutes
Cooking time 30 minutes

8 quail, plucked and cleaned
salt and pepper
softened butter
8 large vine leaves
8 thin slices lard or bacon

Season the birds well with salt and pepper. Cover the whole breast of each with a thin coating of butter and place a vine leaf on top. Place a slice of lard or bacon on top of the vine leaf and secure with some cotton thread. Do the same with the remaining birds. Preheat the oven to 425°F, place the birds in a baking dish, and bake for 15 minutes. Remove the birds, discard the lard and the vine leaves, and replace them in the oven for another 10 minutes, to brown. Serve with fried potatoes and toasted garlic bread, a green salad, and radishes.

Skewered Woodcock with Bacon
(Bekatses Souvlistes me Beikon)

Serves 4-5
Preparation time 30 minutes
Cooking time 20 minutes

8 woodcock, quail, or other small game
birds, cleaned
salt, pepper, oregano
olive oil
8 strips bacon
1 lb large fresh mushrooms
3 large onions
3 green peppers
olive oil

Rub the birds with salt, pepper, oregano, and olive oil. Let stand 30 minutes. Wrap each bird in a strip of bacon and slip them, sideways, onto 2 or 3 long skewers, separated by a large mushroom. Put the rest of the mushrooms on 1 or 2 separate skewers, brush with oil, and sprinkle with salt, pepper, and oregano. Grill the mushrooms and birds over charcoal, basting frequently with oil and oregano, and turning them so they cook on all sides. Cut the onions and peppers into thin slices, sprinkle with a little salt, and sauté them quickly in a little olive oil stirring all the time until they are wilted and slightly browned. Slide the vegetables onto a platter, slip the birds and mushrooms off the skewers on top of them, and serve immediately.

Mini-Dictionary of Culinary Terms

bake: the process of preparing food by cooking it in the oven to make it tender and to add flavor.

baste: to moisten foods with pan juices, drippings or special sauce during baking or grilling, using a spoon, bulb baster, or brush.

blanch: to immerse food quickly in boiling water.

boil: to cook food in water or other liquid until tender.

blend: to combine two or more ingredients with a spoon or an electric blender, until the ingredients are indistinguishable.

braise: to brown meat in hot fat, searing all sides, then adding a small amount of liquid, covering, and simmering for a long period of time.

breading or flouring: to coat foods by dipping into flour, beaten egg, or bread crumbs before frying. Breading or flouring seals the juices in and prevents foods from drying while frying.

broil: to expose food to direct heat, by cooking under or over a flame or heating element.

brown: searing the outer surface of food to seal in the juices.

choke: the hairy part in the center of the artichoke.

chop: to cut food into bits or tiny pieces.

colander: a perforated metal or plastic basket for draining liquids.

deep fat: hot fat or oil which is deep enough to cover food during frying.

deep fry: to cook food immersed in large amount of hot shortening or fat or oil.

drain: to separate solid foods from liquids. When solids are finely chopped, draining is done with a sieve, when solids are coarsely chopped, the liquid is drained through a colander.

dredge: to coat food with flour or crumbs, until surface is completely covered.

escalope: meat cut in thin slices which is beaten flat.

fishermen's soup: the stock obtained from boiling a variety of small and large fish. It is the fishermen's favorite soup.

fold: to mix food from the bottom of the bowl to the top in an under-over motion that distributes ingredients without destroy air bubbles.

flake: to break food into flat pieces, usually done with a fork.

giouvetsi: a fire-proof clay dish used for cooking food in the oven.

glaze: to apply a transparent mixture to food before or after cooking, such as: dissolved gelatin, syrup, beaten egg, milk or butter. Glazing adds flavor as well as a glossy appearance to food.

grill: to cook by broiling on a rack, over or under an open heat.

ground meat: minced meat.

knead: to fold, press, and stretch dough, until it becomes smooth and elastic.

lard: the fat of a pig.

marinade: blend of oil, wine, or vinegar, herbs, and spices. Used to tenderize and flavor meat, game, or fish.

mince: to chop food very fine.

offal: all meats that are found inside the carcass of an animal, such as liver, heart, lungs, spleen, kidneys, sweet-breads (entrails) and also the extremities, head, feet, ears, and tail.

pane: breaded or floured food.

panfry: to cook in a shallow pan over high heat with a small amount of shortening or fat. Foods have to be turned to fry on both sides.

parboil: to cook food partially in boiling water.

pare: to cut off the peel of fruits and vegetables.

phyllo dough: very thin pastry sheets for pies and desserts. Sometimes called strudel leaves, phyllo can be found in grocery stores.

pickle: to preserve in brine or vinegar solution.

poach: to cook food in simmering liquid, under a lid.

purée: to blend or force food through a strainer or blender until it is a smooth sauce.

roast: to cook meat in an oven or on a spit, over or under an open flame.

salted: meat, fish, or other foods cured in vinegar, salt, or pickling brine.

salmi: a stew especially of game cooked in wine and aromatic herbs, celery, carrot, and bay leaf.

sauté: to fry lightly and quickly, stirring frequently, in a small amount of hot fat over high heat. This forms an outside crust which seals in the juices and prevents foods from drying out.

scald: to dip foods quickly in boiling water or to heat a liquid to just below boiling.

score: to make cuts across the surface of food before roasting or baking.

sear: to brown quickly, sealing in the juices either over high heat or in a hot oven.

sieve: an open vessel with meshed or perforated bottom for sifting dry ingredients such as flour, confectioners' sugar, etc.

sifter: a sieve with very fine metal mesh.

simmer: to cook slowly over low heat.

soak: to let food steep in liquid (usually water) for a certain period of time to become soft and moist.

spring onions: fresh green onions or scallions.

skewer: to pierce food on long metal or wooden sticks before cooking.

skim: to remove floating fatty substances from liquid, usually with a spoon.

sprinkle or dust: to coat with confectioners' sugar, flour, or other fine substance.

steam: to cook food in the steam rising from boiling water. There are special pots equipped with wire baskets for this purpose (steamers).

strain: see-drain.

strainer: a fine metal mesh for draining foods.

stir: to mix ingredients with a slow circular motion.

stew: to cook food in liquid, over low heat, for a long time.

stir-fry: see sauté.

tenderize: to marinate certain cuts of meat, especially game, (under refrigeration) for a certain length of time until tender.

thicken: to add cornstarch (corn flour), flour, egg, or fresh cream to thicken sauces, stock, or other liquids.

toast: dry, hard bread. Acquired through slow baking in the oven, under the grill or in a toaster.

whip: to beat rapidly, inflating the volume of the ingredients.

Helpful Information for the Accurate Measuring of Ingredients and Right Baking Temperatures

Apart from experience and the use of high quality ingredients, there are two factors that have to be taken into consideration in order for a recipe to turn out successfully: the accurate and correct measuring of ingredients and correct baking and cooking temperatures. The measuring systems used in cooking vary from country to country. The basic systems used in the world are the following:

1. Imperial: According to this system, dry ingredients are measured in ounces (oz.) and liquids are measured in fluid ounces (fl. oz). Used mainly in England and Australia.

2. Metric: According to this system dry ingredients are measured in grams (g), and liquids in cubic centimeters (ml). Used in France, Greece, Germany and other European countries.

3. American: According to this system all ingredients whether dry or liquid are measured in the standard measuring cup, which is equal to 240 ml. The measuring cup measures volume and all ingredients are measured according to volume. The weight of one cup of different types of ingredients varies.

For example:

1 cup flour weighs . . . . .125 g
1 cup sugar weighs . . . . .225 g

1 cup confectioners' sugar weighs . . . . .160 g
1 cup grated almonds weighs . . . . .150 g
1 cup grated walnuts weighs . . . . .125 g
1 cup bread crumbs weighs . . . . .105 g
1 cup dry cocoa weighs . . . . .100 g
1 cup milk weighs . . . . .240 g
1 cup whipped cream weighs . . . . .125 g
1 cup oil weighs . . . . .220 g
1 cup water weighs . . . . .240 g
1 cup fresh cream weighs . . . . .225 g
1 cup butter weighs . . . . .225 g
1 cup rice weighs . . . . .225 g
1 cup grated cheese weighs . . . . .110 g
1 cup honey weighs . . . . .350 g
1 cup semolina weighs . . . . .170 g

The standard measuring cup is divided into thirds and fourths. For quantities less than 1/4 cup the standard measuring spoon is used. 1/4 cup is equal to 4 level tablespoons, consequently 1 cup is equal to 16 level tablespoons. 1 level tablespoon is equal to 3 level teaspoons. The equivalent of 1 level tablespoon is 15 ml. in the metric system. For measuring liquid ingredients there are glass measuring cups that hold 1 to 2 individual cups each with its own subdivisions. For measuring dry ingredients there are measuring cups that hold 1 individual cup, 3/4 cup, 2/3 cup, 1/2 cup etc. Flour and other such ingredients have to be poured lightly into the measuring cup and not packed firmly. Fill to the rim and level off. The same applies for tablespoons and teaspoons. They are always measured as level tablespoons or teaspoons unless stated otherwise. Do not measure ingredients in a regular cup or glass, since it may not hold the same volume as a standard measuring cup. There are big and small cups as well as glasses. All ingredients for the recipes in the book

are carefully measured in the standard measuring cup and the standard measuring spoons. Listed below are some approximate equivalences of grated or finely chopped ingredients used daily:

1 bunch of parsley or dill finely chopped equals. 1/2 cup
1 large onion, grated, equals. . . . . .1 cup
1 medium onion, grated, equals . . . . .1/2 cup
1 small onion, grated, equals. . . . . .1/4 cup
1 bunch fresh spring onion, (8), finely chopped, equals1 cup
250 g butter, minus a thin slice, equals. . . . . .1 cup

Measuring Equivalents

measures	symbol	metric system	symbol
1 teaspoon	tsp	5 cu. centimeters	ml
1 tablespoon	tbsp	15 cu. centimeters	ml
1 fluid ounce	fl. oz.	30 cu. centimeters	ml
1 cup	c	0,24 liters	l
1 pint	pt.	0,47 liters	l
1 quart	qt.	0,95 liters	l
1 ounce	oz.	28 grams	g
1 pound	lb	0,45 kilogram	kg

Food should be cooked over low heat, covered well, simmered slowly, allowing only a small amount of steam to escape. Care and patience are needed in cooking a good, tasty meal. The same can be said of baking or roasting in the oven. The oven is always preheated to the temperature in the recipe, unless specified otherwise. The oven temperature is calculated depending on the recipe. In this cookbook the temperatures are in Fahrenheit (^{0}F) degrees. The chart below shows how to change or calculate temperatures in degrees Celsius (^{0}C), or how to regulate temperatures in a gas range whether slow, moderate, or hot. When baking or roasting, the food is placed low in the oven so that the surface reaches the middle part of the oven. It is placed higher only when the surface has to brown quickly and even higher to grill or broil.

Oven Temperature Chart

	Electric		gas range
	^{0}F	^{0}C	regulator
very slow oven	225	110	1/4
	250	120	1/2
slow	275	140	1
	300	150	2
moderate	325	160	3
	350	180	4
moderately hot	375	190	5
	400	200	6
hot	425	220	7
	450	230	8
very hot	475	250	9